PHOENIX

RISING

The Story Of Rebirth

JASMEHAR KAUR

"In life, if you want to become something,

achieve something, or win something,

always listen to your heart.

And if your heart doesn't give you an answer,

close your eyes, take the name of your mother and father,

and then see, you will overcome every obstacle,

cross every limit.

Victory will be yours, only yours."

This book is dedicated to my mum,

The heart that beats with endless love,

Whose sacrifices shaped my dreams,

And whose smile lights up my darkest days.

Love You the Mostttt,

Alwaysss And Foreverr

TABLE OF CONTENTS

About The Author
JASMEHAR KAUR

A young 20-year-old girl, living an imperfect yet perfectly chaotic life, and expressing her journey through this book.

It's a love story... but not the kind you'd expect. It's a love story with life itself – full of messy adventures, unexpected plot twists, and a never-ending dance between dreams and reality.

She laughs a little too loud, dreams a little too big, and loves a little too fiercely. Through every high and low, she's learned that life isn't about waiting for the storm to pass; it's about dancing in the rain, even if you trip over your own feet sometimes.

This book is her way of sharing that dance, One imperfect step at a time.

About The Book

A self-help book dedicated to the majestic bird, Phoenix - a symbol of fierce resilience and unstoppable strength.

Specially crafted for all age groups, from curious teenagers to wise old souls, this book is here to show you that life isn't just about surviving the storms; it's about dancing right through them - even if you end up with messy hair and muddy shoes!

Packed with stories, laughter, and a sprinkle of magic, this book invites you to rise from the ashes, just like the Phoenix, and soar higher than ever before.

Because life is too short to tiptoe around challenges - it's meant to be twirled through, giggled at, and celebrated with all its chaos and charm.

So, let's get ready to dance through life's twists and turns... who knows, maybe the next challenge is just another chance to fly!

About The Reader

Hey You! Yes, YOU! The one holding this book right now... You're about to embark on a wild, beautiful journey through life's twists and turns.

This isn't just a book; it's your new best friend, a partner-in-crime, and maybe even the pep talk you never knew you needed! Whether you're dancing through your highs or stumbling through the lows, remember – you're not alone. Flip through these pages, laugh a little, cry if you must, but most importantly, rise like the Phoenix you were born to be! Life is waiting... Are you ready to dance?

Chapters Of Life In This Book

THE PHOENIX RISING:

A STORY OF REBIRTH

AWAKENING THE POWER WITHIN

The Phoenix Within: A Journey of Rebirth and Regeneration

Life, in its most profound form, is a continuous cycle of creation and destruction. Every experience I encounter, every challenge I face, and every loss I endure is part of this intricate tapestry of transformation. Like the mythical phoenix, whose essence is defined by its ability to rise anew from the ashes, I too am a creature of regeneration. But this rebirth is not a smooth, linear journey - it's one fraught with struggle, resilience, and profound healing. The phoenix burns, not to destroy, but to release what no longer serves it. As it succumbs to the flames, the old self dissolves, and from the ashes, a new form arises - stronger, wiser, and more aware. This story of rebirth is my story. I have gone through moments of loss, moments of feeling broken, and moments of being lost in the darkness. But it is through this very darkness that the light within me begins to shine again.

This book is a reflection of that journey - a path of healing, self-discovery, and transformation.

The Journey of Rebirth

I have experienced what it means to feel fragmented, to be in pieces, to walk through dark valleys in search of light. But, as I've learned, the path to true healing often begins when I dare to acknowledge the wounds I carry - the fears, the shame, the guilt, and the anger that I've buried deep within. It is only when I give myself permission to feel, to mourn, and to release that I begin to free myself from the chains of my past and make room for the new. The stories I share here are not merely tales of struggle - they are testaments to the strength that lies within each of us. Through my journey, I've learned to look inward, to reconnect with my feelings and my truths, and through that process, I have undergone a profound transformation. My rebirth was not easy, nor was it quick, but it was real. And through my journey, I discovered that the universe has a way of conspiring in our favor when we trust it with our desires and our deepest longings.

Reflect and Rise

As you read, take a moment to reflect on your own life. Ask yourself: What parts of you need to be released for the new you to emerge? What beliefs, fears, or past wounds are holding you back from stepping into the fullness of your potential? Like the phoenix, I too have burned away the old to make room for the new. It is in this process of letting go, of surrendering to the flow of life, that I truly discovered the power of rebirth. Remember, the journey of renewal is not without its struggles, but it is always worth it. The universe, in all its infinite wisdom, is always guiding us toward our highest good. If we trust in the process, if we open our hearts and minds to the infinite possibilities that lie ahead, we too can rise - stronger, wiser, and more aligned with the truth of who we are.

Let this book be a reminder that no matter where you are in your journey, the power of renewal is within you.

Embrace your inner phoenix, and allow yourself to soar once again.

PART 1

DREAM BIG TO ACHIEVE BIG

Dear Readers,

In this Part, I'll introduce you to the power of dreaming big - unconditionally, without boundaries. A dream where the sky is your limit and you have the freedom to paint it with any color you wish. This is where the journey of limitless possibilities begins. Together, we will uncover stories and insights that will expand your mind and show you how an ordinary girl can become extraordinary. Get ready to dive into a world where dreams know no limits!

1

UNLOCK YOUR POTENTIAL

"Twenty years from now, you will be more disappointed by the things that you didn't do than by the ones you did do." - Mark Twain

Rebirth requires deep introspection, courage, and the willingness to step into the unknown. Like the phoenix, I had to burn away the old to make space for the new. But that transformation was not without its struggles. It was messy, uncomfortable, and often heartbreaking. However, it is through this very process that I reclaimed my power and discovered my truest self.

The Journey from Doubt to Courage

I still remember the day my teacher approached me with an opportunity that felt like a meteor blazing across the sky - bright, sudden, and terrifying.

She smiled and said, "There's a competition at St. Mark's School, and I think you should participate. It's a team event, so you'll have a partner. You'll need to create a model and present it to the judges."

Her words were simple, but they hit me like a wave. My first thought was not excitement - it was doubt. Me? How could I possibly do this? Really me?

I wasn't one of those naturally confident students who seemed to own the stage with ease. In fact, the very thought of speaking in front of judges sent shivers down my spine. My mind, ever the pessimist, whispered its warnings: What if you mess up? What if they laugh at you? You're not good enough for this.

But then, amidst the storm of self-doubt, a softer voice emerged - the voice of my heart. It was quieter, gentler, yet unyielding. It said: What if this is worth the risk? What if this is the start of something new?

That night, I couldn't sleep. My mind and heart were locked in a fierce debate, and I was the unwilling spectator in the middle of it all. My mind argued with logic: You've never done this before. You'll embarrass yourself. What if your partner is disappointed in you? But my heart countered with something far deeper: There's always a first time for everything. Yes, it seems tough, but tough doesn't mean impossible. Isn't going on stage something you've always dreamed of? Would you really give up on that dream when opportunity is knocking at your door?

The Day My Life Changed

I sat up in bed, staring at the ceiling. I asked myself the question that would change everything: What does your heart truly desire? What matters to you, deep down, more than anything else. The answer was undeniable. Yes, I was scared. Yes, I doubted myself. But deep within, I knew the truth: I didn't want to let this opportunity slip away. I had always dreamed of standing on a stage, of sharing my voice with the world. And now, when that dream was within reach, would I let fear hold me back? In that quiet moment, I gave myself an ultimatum. I told myself: Whatever the mind can conceive, it can achieve. If you conceive failure, you'll achieve it. But what if - just what if - you conceive success? What if you achieve something far greater than you ever imagined? I realized that my fears were nothing more than the shadows of doubt I had cast upon myself. Like a baby taking its first wobbly steps, I needed to change my inner dialogue from *I can't* to *I can.* It wasn't going to be easy, but it was possible. After much awkward silence, after battling the chaos within me, I walked up to my teacher the next day and said, "Yes. I'll do it." The words felt foreign, but they also felt right.

The Journey to the Stage

Days turned into weeks, and the preparation for the competition began. My partner and I brainstormed ideas, crafted our model, and practiced our presentation over and over again. Each day brought its own challenges - moments of frustration, moments of doubt, and moments where the pressure felt almost unbearable. I still remember one evening in particular, sitting in my room with the model in front of me. My mind was in overdrive, reminding me of the expectations: You have to win. You can't mess this up. The weight of it all the expectations felt like a baggage on my shoulders. But, then I paused, took a deep breath, and reminded myself: It's not just about winning. It's about showing up. It's about proving to yourself that you can do this. Slowly, I began to see the competition not as a baggage, but as an adventure - a chance to step outside my comfort zone and explore the unknown.

The day of the competition arrived, and my heart raced as we entered the grand hall of St. Mark's School. The stage loomed before me, bright and intimidating, the judges seated in the front row with their pens poised. As our turn approached, I felt the familiar surge of doubt creep in. But this time, I didn't let it win. I whispered to myself: You've worked for this. You've dreamed of this. Now, go out there and give it your all. My Mantra has always been "All is well".

Anyone Can Do It

I always remind myself of the dialogue from Kabhi Khushi Kabhie Gam

"Zindagi mein agar kuch banna ho, kuch haasil karna ho, kuch jeetna ho, toh hamesha apne dil ki suno. Aur agar dil bhi koi jawab na de, toh aankhein band kar ke apne maa-baap ka naam lo, fir dekhna, har manzil paar kar jaoge, har mushkil paar kar jaoge. Jeet tumhari hi hogi, sirf tumhari."

This translates to:

"In life, if you want to become something, achieve something, or win something, always listen to your heart. And if your heart doesn't give you an answer, close your eyes, take the name of your mother and father, and then see, you will overcome every obstacle, cross every limit. Victory will be yours, only yours."

I reminded this to myself as I walked onto the stage. My hands trembled as I held the mic, but as I started to speak, something shifted. The fear that had paralyzed me began to fade, replaced by a quiet confidence. I wasn't perfect, but I was present. I was giving it my best. Life has a way of surprising us when we least expect it. The moment of results arrived. My partner and I stood among the crowd, our hearts racing in sync, as the announcer began calling out the winners. "And the first prize goes to…" The pause that followed was excruciating. My palms were sweaty, my mind already bracing for disappointment. "Brain International School!" I froze. Did they just say our names? My partner nudged me, her face lit with excitement, and suddenly it hit me - we had won. We actually won!

What happened next is something I still laugh about. Fueled by an uncontainable surge of joy, I dashed toward the stage like a comet streaking across the sky, completely forgetting about my partner. As the crowd erupted in applause, I was already asking the judges, with the enthusiasm of a child on Christmas morning, "Can I hold the trophy? Please" The judges smiled warmly but gestured for me to wait. "Your partner," one of them reminded gently, pointing to the stage steps where she was just catching up. As she joined me on stage she exclaimed "You should've waited for me," she whispered in my ears. At that moment we both were truly overjoyed. We stood there together, holding the enormous trophy as cameras flashed, and in that moment, everything felt surreal. The applause, the weight of the trophy in my hands - it all felt like a dream I never thought I could live.

From Ordinary to Extraordinary

That day, I realized something profound: the journey from ordinary to extraordinary isn't defined by talent or perfection. It's defined by courage - the courage to show up, to try, to fall, to take risks and to rise again. But let me tell you, the "extra" in extraordinary doesn't come without its trials. It's carved out of moments of doubt, sleepless nights, and the relentless effort of pushing through fears. That victory wasn't just a trophy on a stage - it was a symbol of everything I had conquered within. As the timeless words of great thinkers echo through the ages, Winston Churchill once declared, "Success is not final, failure is not fatal: It is the courage to continue that counts." This reminds us that success isn't a destination but the strength to keep moving forward, no matter the hurdles we face. And as Franklin D. Roosevelt so brilliantly put it, "The only limit to our realization of tomorrow is our doubts of today." Our dreams are only as limited as the doubts we allow to cloud our minds, and it's time to break free. As Nelson Mandela so powerfully said, " It always seems impossible until it's done," a truth that reminds us that every impossible feat was once only a dream, waiting to be turned into reality by those bold enough to try.

A New Chapter Awaiting

And as I walked off that stage, something inside me had shifted. I was no longer the girl who ran away from challenges, who let her fears dictate her actions. I had learned that the only limits we truly have are the ones we place on ourselves. So, if you're wondering how an ordinary kid became extraordinary, let me assure you - it didn't happen overnight. It wasn't luck or some magical talent I was born with. It was a journey - a beautifully chaotic journey of dedication, persistence, and an unshakable belief in the whispers of my heart. This journey has taken me to unimaginable heights. From the kid who once doubted her every step, has gone on to win over 30 awards, has more than 100 + stage appearances, and also invited as a Prominent Guest Speaker Many-a-Times. Each event, each speech, each recognition became a stepping stone, not just to external success, but to a deeper understanding of who I truly am. But something to wonder was I was not at all born with this silver spoon in the mouth. All these achievements are not merely just stories but a testimony that a girl who once feared stage fell in love with it gradually.

Create Your Own World

Successful people are not born; they are made. They are sculpted by the hands of discipline and persistence, molded by failures, and polished by resilience. Every accomplishment I've earned carries the weight of countless hours of preparation, countless moments of self-doubt that I had to push through. This book isn't just about the victories. It's about the battles that paved the way. It's about the quiet moments when I chose to stand back up, the late nights spent perfecting a skill, the nervous butterflies that transformed into soaring confidence. It's about the realization that success isn't a destination - it's a process. A process of growth, of learning, and of embracing the idea that every challenge is an opportunity in disguise. From the shy girl in the classroom to the guest speaker inspiring audiences; from the child who couldn't hold her voice steady to the woman who now inspires change - this is the story of transformation. And if there's one thing I've learned, it's that life is not a straight line. It's a constellation of moments, each one a star guiding you toward the person you're meant to be. Some stars burn bright with triumph, while others flicker softly with lessons learned. But together, they light up the path forward. So, let this book be your guide - a testament to the idea that with enough heart, grit, and belief, there's nothing you can't achieve. Let's dive into the story of how ordinary becomes extraordinary- one step, one victory, and one leap of faith at a time.

2

DARE TO DREAM BIG

"The future belongs to those who believe in the beauty of their dreams." – Eleanor Roosevelt

The day I held that trophy in my hands, it wasn't just a victory - it was a revelation. It felt as though the trophy wasn't just a lifeless object in my hands; it was alive, looking back at me, almost whispering, "You've earned me." More than I admired the trophy, I felt like it admired me. It wasn't just celebrating the outcome of that one competition - it reflected the sweat, the tears, and the battles I had fought within myself. For a kid like me, who once doubted her worth, that moment wasn't about a simple trophy. No, it was monumental - it felt like bagging a Padma Shri or achieving something equally extraordinary.

As I stood there, I couldn't help but realize something profound: the present moment is the best time to be alive. We often chase opportunities, thinking they're hidden somewhere in a distant future. But the truth? The universe is already brimming with opportunities, knocking at our doors, waiting for us to notice them and grab hold. That day wasn't just about winning - it was a paradigm shift. It taught me that every door I thought was locked was only waiting for me to muster the courage to turn the handle.

Impossible = I Am Possible

What made it even more surreal was this: the very thing I had once envisioned as an impossible dream, as a mere thread of thought, was sitting firmly in my hands. That's when the sudden realization hit me - everything we see around us in this man-made world started the same way. Every great invention, every life-changing idea, every masterpiece - whether a breathtaking painting, a towering skyscraper, or a powerful speech - was once just a flicker of imagination in someone's mind. A dream, a wish, a hope that seemed almost unreal at first but was nurtured, refined, and eventually translated into reality.

That moment with the trophy wasn't just a celebration of the competition. It was the realization that everything begins with a small glimmer of belief, a single ray of hope. The mere act of believing in yourself, of saying "I can," is where the magic begins. For me, this trophy wasn't just a piece of metal - it was proof. Proof that dreams, no matter how far-fetched they seem, can come true if you're willing to fight for them.

From that moment on, I knew one thing with absolute certainty: if a girl who doubted herself at every step could turn her fears into fuel and make her dreams a reality, then anyone can. All it takes is a spark, a little courage, and an unshakeable belief that the journey is worth it.

The Infinite Power of Dreams

Wining that trophy was the turning point of my life. I started visualizing something profound - my dream, not just as a distant hope or an abstract idea, but as a living, breathing entity, quietly standing before me. It felt as though my dream was speaking directly to my heart, whispering words that resonated deeply within me: *"I am here, waiting for you. You don't need to be perfect, you don't need to have it all figured out. Just take the first step, and I will be with you, every step of the way. Achieve me, and you will discover a version of yourself you never knew existed. I believe in you, even when you doubt yourself."* In those moments of doubt, when fear held me back, it was as if my dream became a companion, patiently urging me forward. It wasn't a distant star in the sky anymore - it was right there, within my reach, as if it were made of the very fabric of my own soul. Every time I hesitated, it wasn't just my own thoughts that I heard; it was the voice of my dream, echoing in my mind, reminding me that it wasn't something unattainable, something far away. No, it was something I had always carried within me. It was always ready to unfold, to come to life - but only if I dared to embrace it.

The deeper I listened, the more I realized that my dream wasn't just calling me to succeed. It was calling me to become. To become stronger, braver, more myself than I had ever been before. It was as if my dream was telling me, *"I am the path, and you are the traveler. Walk with me, and together we will create a future beyond your wildest imagination."* And in that moment, I knew - I didn't have to wait for the perfect moment, because the moment to chase my dream was always here. All I had to do was reach for it, and trust that in doing so, I would find the courage to become the person I was always meant to be.

Create Your Own Future

"The only limit to our realization of tomorrow is our doubts of today." **Franklin D. Roosevelt**

If you wait for the perfect moment, you'll miss the opportunity to build it. Dreams are meant to be chased, today, right now. So, fill up that car, start driving, and let the journey unfold. It's time to go after your dreams - because there's no better moment than this one to start.

Remember: "The best way to predict your future is to create it." – Abraham Lincoln. Your future is not something that simply happens to you - it's something you create with every choice you make today.

Think of it as a blank canvas, where each decision, each step you take, adds color to your masterpiece. The dreams you hold inside aren't far-off fantasies; they're blueprints for the life you're building right now. Every moment you choose to believe in yourself, to take action, to push through doubt, you're laying down the foundation for a tomorrow that's shaped by your courage and determination. Your future begins with the choices you make today, so choose with purpose, dream with passion, and never stop creating.

The Journey Begins Now

Dreams are not just the things that keep you awake at night. They are the visions that light up your soul and push you to reach higher than you thought possible.

It's easy to think of dreams as something far away, something for later - but the truth is, the best time to start chasing your dreams is right now. There's no such thing as a perfect moment. If you wait for everything to line up perfectly, you may wait forever. The perfect time to take that first step is always *now.* As the famous quote goes, "The best time to plant a tree was 20 years ago.

The second-best time is now. Imagine this: You're sitting in a car, the engine is running, and the tank is full of fuel. The interior is sleek, everything is in top shape, and the ride is smooth.

But here's the catch - the car doesn't have a destination. You can drive forever, but without a destination, you'll just keep going around in circles. The fuel is there, the power is there, but you're not going anywhere, This is how many of us approach our dreams. We have the power, the skills, the passion - but without a clear direction, we don't get anywhere. You must set your destination. Dreams require action, focus, and courage to take that first step, even if the road ahead is unclear. But don't worry - every journey starts with one step, even when the path isn't obvious.

Dye for a Bigger You: Dreaming Into Reality

Imagine your dreams as a beautiful, blank canvas untouched, full of potential, and waiting for your brushstrokes to bring it to life. To dye for a bigger you means embracing the journey of transformation, allowing the vibrant colors of your dreams to bleed into every part of who you are. Each dream you have is a spark of possibility, and when you choose to chase them, you begin to dye the fabric of your life with the hues of hope, courage, and determination.

It's not always easy, but just like dyeing fabric, the process takes time, patience, and sometimes even a little mess. Yet, the results are breathtaking - a version of you that is bolder, stronger, and more alive with purpose.

Dreaming big is not just about wishing for something better; it's about daring to become something greater. The dreams you hold within you are the colors waiting to fill your life, but only if you're brave enough to take that first step into the unknown, to dye for a bigger, brighter, and more beautiful you.

3

THE POWER OF NOW

"Yesterday is history, tomorrow is a mystery, and today is a gift. That's why it's called the present." - Tony Robbins

Imagine if my teacher had asked me to take that leap, and I had turned it down, thinking the moment wasn't right, waiting for the "perfect" time. What if I had let fear hold me back? If I had just waited, I would have never been the person I am today. No trophies, no recognition, no exhilarating moments of triumph. It would have been an ordinary life - nothing special, nothing extraordinary. But that's not how it happened! Your dreams should set your soul on fire. They should make your heart race with excitement, pushing you to say "yes" even when it feels scary or uncertain. The perfect moment? It's now! The universe is always sending you opportunities, ready for you to grab them and say YES! Can you imagine - every time you hesitate, the universe is waiting for you to claim what's meant for you. Each opportunity is like a golden ticket, and all you have to do is recognize it and seize it with both hands! Don't wait for everything to be perfect - take that leap now, and let your dreams unfold in ways you never imagined! Your future is calling, and it's waiting for you to say YES!

Perfect Moment?

The best time to start chasing your dreams is now. Too often, we wait for the "perfect" moment, thinking that someday we'll be ready, but dreams don't wait for perfect conditions - they thrive on action. Imagine your dream as a seed: if you wait for everything to align perfectly, the seed will never be planted. But when you take that first step, no matter how small, you're starting the process of growth. It doesn't matter if the soil isn't perfect or if you don't have all the answers right now - every action, no matter how small, gets you closer to your dream. Your journey doesn't need to mirror anyone else's - it's uniquely yours. The path will never be perfect, but by taking the leap today, you're moving forward toward the life you envision. Don't wait for the perfect moment. Plant your seed now and trust that each small step will lead you to where you want to be. Your future is waiting - start today. I truly believe in the fact that Don't wait for the perfect moment. Take the moment and make it perfect. A dream without action is like a car without a destination - full of potential, but not moving anywhere. But when you have the courage to chase your dreams, to give them direction and purpose, you'll begin to see the power of your choices and the magic of moving forward. Take this as a reminder: the road to your dreams may be unknown, but that's where the adventure begins. You'll learn, you'll grow, and along the way, you'll discover new destinations you never even imagined.

Shaping Reality Through Connection

"The new way of thinking is not to see the world as a collection of things, but as a collection of relationships." This powerful statement by David Bohm opens up a whole new perspective on how we view the world and our place within it. Instead of seeing life as a series of separate, disconnected objects, imagine it as a vast, interconnected web of relationships. Everything is connected - our actions, our thoughts, our decisions, and the way we interact with the world around us. And the key to understanding this is realizing that everything happens in the present moment.

Think of life as a river. At first glance, we might see the river as a collection of rocks, water, and fish, but in truth, it's much more than that - it's the flow, the energy, the currents that create a living, breathing force. The rocks are part of the river, but it's the water that moves, the energy that connects everything together. Similarly, our lives are not defined by isolated events or objects, but by how we engage with them, how we interact with the world and the people around us. This connection happens right now - this very moment is where everything comes to life. The thoughts you have, the decisions you make, the actions you take, all of them ripple through your world, creating connections and relationships that shape the reality you experience. The future isn't set in stone; it's a canvas waiting to be painted with your choices, your presence, your engagement with the now.

I Said a YES!

After that moment with the trophy, I stood there, almost in disbelief, staring at the shiny object in my hands. It felt surreal, like something I could never have imagined. But as I gazed at it, something profound shifted inside me. I realized that it wasn't just about winning or standing on stage - it was about saying "yes" to the opportunities the universe throws our way. At that moment, I understood that life is full of chances, but we often let them slip by because we're too afraid, too uncertain, or too focused on the wrong things.

For so long, I had doubted myself, fearing failure and worrying about the what-ifs. But now, I saw that the key to living a fulfilling life is to embrace the present. To seize the moment without overthinking it, without worrying about what might have been or what could be. I remembered those times when I would regret missed opportunities, times when I stayed silent when I should have spoken up, times when fear held me back. I had spent so many hours dwelling on the past, crying over what couldn't be changed. And the more I focused on the things I couldn't control, the more I felt stuck. The universe wasn't sending me new chances - it was sending me the same pattern, the same missed opportunities over and over again, because I was stuck in that loop of regret and self-doubt.

Past, Present or Future?

While thinking about the future is natural, stressing over it does nothing to help us. Yes, it's good to plan and dream, but we cannot control everything that will happen. We can't predict every twist and turn that life will take. Worrying about the unknown only adds to our stress and takes away our ability to act. The future will unfold as it will, but the actions we take today are the ones that shape it. It became so clear to me: the true power lies in the present moment.

If we stop looking back and stop fearing what's ahead, we can actually step into the fullness of who we are and what we can do. It's in the now that we have the power to change our lives. If we choose to live fully in the present, we open ourselves up to endless possibilities. The universe is always offering opportunities, but it's up to us to say "yes," to trust the process, and to take action in the present moment. From that day on, I knew I had to stop letting my fears or regrets dictate my life. I knew I had to stop waiting for the perfect moment, the perfect circumstances. Because the truth is, the perfect moment is always now. The key to transforming my future was never about controlling everything ahead of me; it was about showing up fully and embracing the opportunities of today.

4

MIND OVER HEART, OR
HEART OVER MIND?

DISCOVERING YOUR TRUE COMPASS

"Listen to your heart. It knows all things." - Paulo Coelho,

The Alchemist

Now, the passion was discovered. Well begun is half done I knew what gave me happiness, solace, peace, and comfort. What made my heart race - what truly ignited that spark - was the mic and the stage. You might wonder, how could a simple trophy lead to such a realization? How could a little girl winning a competition suddenly find her passion? But perhaps that trophy wasn't just a symbol of victory. It was more of a gentle nudge from within, a whisper telling me that this was only the beginning of a tremendous journey waiting for me.

But here came the pivotal question - what would I tell my parents? I wanted to be a speaker. It sounded so strange to me at the time. In an era where most parents urged their children to become doctors or engineers, where would my passion for speaking fit in?

Would my parents understand? Would they support me in this unconventional dream?

Passion or Profession?

Converting a passion into a profession doesn't just require your parents' approval, it requires your own confidence in your path. Deep down, I knew that societal approval mattered too, because society's judgment often feels like a stamp of legitimacy. However, back in 2017, that small, uncertain girl still craved validation - the badge of honor that came from being a science student, having a career that society accepted. It was a huge crossroads for me: Passion or profession? Should I follow my heart, or should I conform to the traditional paths that everyone expected me to walk?

I remember that feeling vividly - the internal tug-of-war between what I truly wanted and what seemed acceptable to everyone around me. Choosing a path of passion didn't just mean fighting the expectations of society, it meant stepping into the unknown with only my dreams to guide me. But sometimes, the most difficult and rewarding decisions in life come when we embrace what feels right, even when it doesn't match the traditional blueprint for success. It was a journey that required not just external approval, but the courage to seek my own approval, to trust my instincts, and to step into a world that was far from predictable. And from that moment on, I knew my path would never be the same again.

The Crossroads of My Life

I stood at the crossroads of my life, staring at two paths. One path was lit by the glowing light of safety - the usual path, taking a stream, being a doctor or engineer, living an ordinary life and the other one was following my passion. The First path seemed easier but the other path was inviting me to follow my deepest passion, to step into the unknown, to create something all my own. My heart tugged toward the second path, the one filled with risk, uncertainty, and the promise of something bigger. It whispered:

Heart: *"I, too, am meant to be truly alive! Leave the ordinary behind, take the leap into what you love. Don't let fear hold you back, don't let security trap you in a cage of your own making. Go where your soul sings, where your spirit can soar!"*

But my mind - the ever-practical, sensible force - pulled me back. It saw the risks, the unknowns, the possibility of failure. It said:

Mind: "But what about your future? What about stability? If you follow your heart, you might fall, and there's no safety net. You could lose everything. Following your passion isn't easy every time. What do you want to become? A Speaker? A coach? Think about the consequences. Think about your responsibilities."

The tension between heart and mind grew every day. I felt as if I were standing between two mountains - one towering with dreams, the other solid with reality. I was stuck, torn between the two voices, uncertain which one to follow.

The Storm Within

Days passed, and the storm inside me only grew stronger. My heart cried out for adventure, for freedom, for the chance to live authentically. My heart wanted to follow the call I was getting from deep core. But my mind, always alert to the dangers ahead, clung to reason, to logic, and to security.

In the depths of the night, when the world around me was silent, I lay awake, my mind racing. How could I possibly reconcile these two forces? I had tried to ignore the call of my heart, but it was like trying to silence the wind - impossible. I had also tried to reason my way out of it, but the feeling of being trapped in a life that didn't feel mine gnawed at my soul.

I needed help. I needed to find a way to let the two parts of myself - my heart and my mind - work together, not against each other. I closed my eyes, took a deep breath, and imagined myself as the captain of my own ship. My heart was the wind, wild and unpredictable, and my mind was the steady rudder, guiding the course through calm seas and stormy waters alike.

Finding The Balance

I've faced those moments when my mind and heart pull me in opposite directions. My mind warns me of the risks, the uncertainties, and the consequences, wanting to keep me safe and in control. But my heart, with its quiet confidence, urges me to take the leap, to trust the unknown, and to embrace the adventure ahead. It's a battle between security and excitement, and in those moments, I've learned the key is finding balance - not choosing one over the other, but trusting both to guide me toward something greater.

Mind: *"This is risky. What if it doesn't work out? What if I'm making a mistake? Think of all the consequences!"*

Heart: *"But this feels right. This is the chance I've been waiting for. Don't you feel the spark? Don't you want to live fully, to take a leap?"*

The battle rages on. The heart wants to dive in, to feel the excitement of new beginnings, to trust in the journey. But the mind wants to stay safe, to stick to the familiar orbit of what's k This tug-of-war can leave you paralyzed in the middle, unsure whether to follow your head or your heart. In my mind's eye, I summoned both parts of myself - my heart and my mind. The heart appeared as a radiant, glowing figure, full of passion and fire. The mind stood across from it, cool and composed, a figure draped in the clarity of thought.

I spoke to them both:

I: "Heart, I hear you. I feel your longing for freedom, your desire to chase the horizon, to follow the dreams that stir my soul. I know how much deep desire you have to follow what you are truly meant for. Speaking on the stage, holding that mic in your hands, Your heart really dances and twirls with infinite joy. Helping people change their lives, Teach them how to heal themselves actually heals a part of you as well.

But Mind, I hear you too. You want to protect me, to keep me safe, to ensure I don't fall into the abyss. You are practically guiding me through, showing me the realistic mirrors. The world which actually operates on stability. But my dear mind, we do have just one life to live, just one that too finite. Would it not be unfair if we give up our dreams just to please the society?

You both want what's best for me, but you seem so different."

The heart, glowing and full of energy, responded first:

Heart: *"I, too, am meant to live fully. Life is not just about surviving; it's about thriving, embracing what excites you. Don't let fear stop you. Every moment you hold back, you deny yourself the joy of being truly alive."*

Then, the mind spoke, calm and steady:

Mind: *"I understand, Heart. I see the beauty of the path you desire. But we must approach this with care. The unknown is risky, and if we are not prepared, the consequences could be dire. It's not that I want to stifle your dreams - I want to help you navigate them wisely."*

I listened carefully. I understood both sides. My heart burned with the fire of possibility, but my mind had a deep wisdom, too. Both were necessary. And so, I asked for their cooperation.

I: *"What if we could work together? Heart, I will follow your call, but Mind, I will also make a plan, ensuring that we don't sail into storms without knowing how to weather them. Heart, I'll embrace the journey and trust, and Mind, I'll let you steer us through the unknown."*

A Delusional Converting Her Dreams Into Reality

From the very start of my life, I was never the most practical person. In fact, I was often labeled as delusional - dreaming up visions so big and bold that others couldn't even fathom them. But deep down, I knew something critical: simply following my heart alone wouldn't get me where I wanted to go, and neither would relying solely on logic and practicality. Both needed to work together, but the question was - how? Sure, I understood the need for stability and realism. I understood the world's logic - the idea that we must follow a set path, seek safety, and conform to society's expectations. But then, a thought hit me like a lightning bolt: Life is way too short to just exist. I didn't want to be someone who just went through the motions, checking boxes off a to-do list. I wanted to live every single moment with a sense of purpose, chasing after the things that truly set my soul on fire.

Living Beyond Limits

What good is stability if it's suffocating your dreams? What's the point of being "practical" if it means you're simply going through the motions of life, never truly feeling alive? I didn't want to survive - I wanted to thrive. I wanted to dive into my dreams with everything I had, to do the things that would make me feel like I was living, not just existing. To do something so real and raw that I would wake up every day fired up, eager to conquer the world. Choosing passion over practicality wasn't going to be easy, I knew that. But it was the only way to break free from the chains of doubt and fear that held me back. It meant taking risks. It meant standing up for my dreams, even when the world might tell me to sit down and play it safe. It was about having the courage to live the life I was meant for, even if it didn't always make sense to others.

This wasn't just about taking a leap of faith. This was about living in full color, breaking through the walls of uncertainty, and pushing myself beyond every limit I had ever imagined. Because in the end, what's the point of living if you're not chasing after what excites you, what makes your heart race, and what makes you feel truly ALIVE? At that moment, something magical happened. The heart softened, and the mind relaxed. The two forces began to move in harmony, not pulling against each other, but working together as a single, united force. The boat - my life - was no longer tossed by conflicting winds. It sailed smoothly, powered by both the heart's passion and the mind's wisdom.

5

TAKE CHARGE OF YOUR LIFE AND SET GOALS

"The only limit to your impact is your imagination and commitment." - Tony Robbins

As I moved forward, the once-conflicting forces of heart and mind began to synchronize in ways I hadn't anticipated. The uncertainty that once clouded my decisions started to clear, replaced by a sense of calm, a knowing that I was on the right path. There was a beautiful rhythm between the two now. The heart provided the fire, the passion, the drive to pursue my dreams, while the mind offered structure, the wisdom to navigate through challenges, and the discernment to take measured steps.

The more I trusted this balance, the more opportunities appeared. Every decision felt empowered, not just a choice between right or wrong, but an opportunity to create something meaningful. No longer was I swayed by fear or doubt. The heart's desire for adventure and the mind's practical approach worked together like partners on a journey, each guiding the other in perfect harmony. But here's what I realized: the journey was never about one winning over the other. It wasn't a battle. It was about merging the two forces - heart and mind - to create a fuller, richer life. The heart can be wild, full of ideas and dreams that seem impossible. The mind is grounded, bringing order to the chaos. When you allow both to have their say, you create a balance that propels you forward in ways you could never have imagined.

The Choice

I began to see that life isn't about choosing between passion and practicality. It's about learning to integrate both into your existence. It's about daring to dream big, but doing so with the wisdom and structure needed to bring those dreams to life. My dreams were no longer an abstract fantasy; they were a reality in the making. The real magic happens when you trust both your heart and your mind. When you allow them to guide you, side by side, you unlock a whole new realm of possibilities.

I'm not saying the journey is always easy. There are still moments when I'm unsure, when doubt creeps in, but I've learned that I don't have to face them alone. My heart and mind are my companions. Together, they guide me forward, each step reinforcing the belief that I am on the right path. And so, I ask you:

What path are you on? Are you letting your heart and mind work together, or are you letting them pull you in different directions? Life isn't meant to be a constant tug-of-war. It's meant to be a dance, a flow between the excitement of your dreams and the wisdom of your decisions. When you find that balance, you'll realize that you're not just surviving; you're truly living.

Overcoming the Barriers to Goal Setting

Setting goals has the power to completely transform your life, but for many, the idea of setting them can be paralyzing. I know this feeling all too well - there was a time when I avoided setting goals altogether, overwhelmed by fears and doubts that seemed impossible to conquer. The fear of failure, the anxiety of rejection, and the weight of self-doubt kept me trapped in a cycle of hesitation. But as I reflect on my journey - one that has shaped me as a financial coach, speaker, and content creator - I realize that these challenges didn't just hold me back; they fueled my growth. In this chapter, I'll share the obstacles that once stood in my way, the fears that seemed insurmountable, and how I ultimately broke through them. It wasn't a straight path, but each hurdle I overcame paved the way for new opportunities and a deeper understanding of what it takes to achieve your goals. Let's dive into how facing these barriers head-on changed everything for me - and how it can do the same for you.

The Fear of Failure

When I first began speaking in front of an audience, I was terrified. I had no formal training, no credentials that would make me stand out among more experienced speakers. My biggest fear wasn't just forgetting my words; it was the fear of failing in front of people, of being judged for not being "good enough." This fear was so strong that I almost didn't take the leap into public speaking at all. I thought, *What if I fail? What if my message isn't impactful?*

But then I realized something that changed everything: failure wasn't a reflection of my worth; it was a part of the process. Every speaker, no matter how successful, had failed at some point. So, I pushed through the fear and took my first step - delivering my message to a small audience. That speech wasn't perfect. Far from it. But it was a starting point, and that's what mattered. It wasn't about delivering a flawless presentation - it was about showing up, speaking my truth, and learning from each experience. Every time I failed, I learned something valuable. Whether it was misjudging the room's energy or fumbling through a tough question from the audience, those moments became stepping stones to improvement. Over time, I realized that failure isn't something to fear - it's a sign that you're on the right track.

Rejection: A Doorway to Growth

As I continued to pursue speaking opportunities, rejection became an inevitable part of the journey. I remember sending out my first few event proposals with excitement, only to hear nothing back. Or worse - getting a polite "no" in response. The sting of rejection was hard to bear, especially because I thought that if I wasn't accepted, it meant I wasn't good enough. But rejection taught me a powerful lesson: it's not a judgment of who I am, but a sign that I need to refine my approach. Early on, I tried to fit into someone else's mold of what a speaker should be. I thought I needed to look, sound, and act a certain way to be successful. But over time, I began to embrace my unique voice and perspective, and I realized that the right opportunities would come when I was truly authentic. The first time I got accepted to speak at a conference, I felt like I had won a victory, but it was the rejections that led me to refine my pitch, improve my delivery, and be more genuine. I understood that rejection is part of the speaker's journey, and it's something you learn to accept and use to fuel your growth.

The Struggle with Self-Belief

Perhaps one of the biggest battles I faced was the struggle with self-belief. Every time I stood in front of an audience, a voice in my head would whisper, *Who are you to be here? What makes you think you have anything valuable to say?* That voice of doubt was loud, especially in the beginning. There were so many moments when I questioned my ability to make an impact, to really connect with my audience. But what I eventually realized was that self-doubt is something every speaker, every leader, experiences. It's a part of the process. The key isn't to banish doubt completely, but to learn how to manage it. I stopped letting it stop me from moving forward. Instead of letting self-doubt paralyze me, I used it as motivation to improve. Each time I got up to speak, I told myself, *You're here because you have a message that matters.* It took time, but gradually, I started to believe it.

The Fear of Disappointing Others

Another fear that kept me stuck was the fear of disappointing others. As a speaker, you're constantly putting yourself out there, exposing your ideas and vulnerability. And when you have people you care about watching, whether it's friends, family, or colleagues, the fear of letting them down can be paralyzing. What if they thought I wasn't good enough? What if I didn't live up to their expectations?

For the longest time, I struggled to reconcile my own ambitions with the expectations of those around me. I wanted to be a successful speaker, but I also wanted to make my loved ones proud. The two didn't always align. At times, I felt like I was disappointing them by pursuing a path that was uncertain and unconventional. But eventually, I understood that I couldn't live my life based on others' expectations. Everyone has their own vision of success, but I had to embrace my own. I stopped worrying about disappointing others and focused instead on living authentically and pursuing my goals with conviction. Once I let go of that fear, I was able to fully commit to my journey, and that commitment made all the difference.

The Fear of Commitment

The last barrier I had to overcome was the fear of commitment. Being a speaker requires a deep commitment to continuous improvement. You can't afford to rest on your laurels or get complacent with one successful talk. You have to keep showing up, learning, and refining your craft. Early on, I was hesitant to fully commit. What if this path didn't lead to where I wanted to go? What if I invested all my time and energy, only to realize it wasn't the right fit? But I soon realized that growth only happens when you fully commit. You can't succeed by halfway trying or doubting yourself along the way. Once I made the decision to go all-in, everything changed.

I started seeing progress, not just in my speaking career, but in my personal growth as well.

From Doubt to Confidence

Looking back, I can see how every fear and doubt was a catalyst for growth. The journey to becoming a successful speaker wasn't linear - it was filled with setbacks, rejection, and moments of self-doubt. But each obstacle taught me something valuable. I learned that failure is an opportunity to grow, that rejection is part of the process, and that self-belief comes from consistent action. In the end, setting goals became not just about reaching a destination - it became about embracing the journey, trusting the process, and facing the fears that held me back. And I hope, as you read this, you realize that the same can be true for you. The barriers you face are not roadblocks - they are invitations to grow, to learn, and to become the person you are meant to be.

The Top 3 Percent vs. The 97 Percent

I once came across some fascinating statistics that revealed a profound truth about success and goal-setting. It suggested that only 3 percent of people actually set goals for themselves, while the remaining 97 percent falter. This divide was eye-opening, and the statistics further broke down the details:

- 3 percent of people not only had goals but also wrote them down and made a plan to achieve them.

- 13 percent had goals but didn't write them down, relying on vague aspirations.

- A staggering 84 percent had no goals at all, living day-to-day without any clear direction or purpose.

The result of this clear distinction in goal-setting behavior was even more telling: the top 3 percent were the ones who found consistent success in their endeavors. The remaining 13 percent were considered average earners, while the 84 percent continued to struggle, stuck in the cycle of mediocrity. What was the fundamental difference between the top 3 percent and everyone else? The 3 percent had clear, written goals, which gave them direction, focus, and purpose. They knew exactly where they wanted to go and how they intended to get there. This clarity helped them take deliberate actions and overcome obstacles, no matter how challenging. The 13 percent, though they had goals, lacked the clarity that comes with writing them down and making a detailed plan. Without that clarity, their actions were often scattered, leading to average results. The 84 percent, however, lacked any clear goals, which left them wandering aimlessly, struggling to find meaning in their work and life. The difference between these groups wasn't about intelligence, talent, or resources. It was about direction. The 3 percent had a roadmap for their lives. They were self-directed, purpose-driven, and determined. This sense of purpose and clarity acted as a guiding light that ensured they didn't get sidetracked by distractions or obstacles.

Goals Make You Self Directed

Setting goals isn't just about having aspirations; it's about making those aspirations concrete, measurable, and actionable. Goals make you self-directed. They infuse meaning and purpose into everything you do. They give you a reason to wake up every morning, to push through challenges, and to keep going when things get tough. When you have clarity in your goals, you're not merely reacting to life - you're taking proactive steps toward your success. In contrast, when you don't have clear goals, you become like a ship without a rudder, drifting aimlessly. Even when you work hard, it feels like you're spinning your wheels and getting nowhere.

But when you know exactly what you want and why you want it, the path o success becomes not only clearer but also more achievable. In conclusion, the top 3 percent succeed because they understand the power of goal-setting.

Clarity is the key to their success. When you write down your goals, create a plan, and take consistent action, you align yourself with success. Setting goals ensures that you are self-directed, focused, and ready to face any obstacle, ultimately leading to unlimited success.

6

TRUSTING THE JOURNEY

"Trust yourself. Think for yourself. Act for yourself. Speak for yourself. Be yourself. Imitation is suicide." – Marva Collins

Now, here's where my story takes an interesting turn.

My path was not a straight line from being a Coach to a successful Coach. In fact, after months of introspection and exploration, I made a leap that shocked everyone - including myself. I decided to open my own life school. Not a safe business. Not a tried-and-tested business. But something deeply aligned with my wishes - and my utmost wish has always been helping people live their best version of themselves.

Was it risky? Absolutely. Was I terrified? Beyond belief. But I realized that this leap was the next step of my journey. It was a leap of faith. Faith in myself. Faith in my own creativity. Faith that the universe would support me, even if I couldn't see the way forward just yet.

The Spark of Dream

Opening a life school might sound unusual, almost like a far-fetched dream. A school where the most important subject isn't math, science, or history, but *life* itself. It's not a subject you'll find in any traditional classroom, yet it's the one subject that truly shapes who we become. While schools teach us how to excel in exams, and colleges focus on career skills, there's no institution dedicated to teaching us the most crucial lessons: how to cope with life's challenges, how to confront our fears, and how to navigate the storm of self-doubt that every one of us faces at some point.

What if we could teach people how to face adversity head-on? How to find success, not just in a professional sense, but in every aspect of their life? A school that doesn't just prepare you to pass tests, but to conquer the test of life. After all, isn't that what we need the most? Real, practical lessons on how to *live* - not just survive?

The School Like No Other

An online platform, designed and built for all age groups, where there is no age barrier to learning. A place where the concept of classes 1-12 is irrelevant. The only lesson taught is how to live the life you dream of - so you don't die with regrets. It sounds like a strange idea, doesn't it? A 14- or 15-year-old kid talking about living life to the fullest, teaching others how to embrace their dreams, face their fears, and live without regret.

At first, the world struggled to comprehend it. How could a small child, who had only lived 15 years, possibly teach those who had lived 50 or 60 years? How could she surpass the vastness of their experiences, their wisdom? What could she, with so little time behind her, have to offer? The more voices that joined in, the more doubts echoed, questioning how a young person could guide others through the complexities of life.

But what they didn't realize was that the wisdom of youth is often untainted by the limitations and fears that come with age. Sometimes, it's the fresh perspective of someone who has only just begun to understand the world that can bring the most profound insights. After all, life isn't measured by the number of years lived - it's about how deeply we live in the time we have. And that's a lesson anyone, of any age, can learn.

The Turning Point

Here's the big question: What will you do when life shakes you up? When the storm hits - when your world is upended, when everything you've worked for seems to crumble - what will you do? Those voices, once distant whispers of doubt, grew louder and more overwhelming. They tried to push me down, to convince me that I wasn't enough, that this dream of mine was too big, too impossible. And yet, amidst all this noise, there was one voice that remained unwavering - a tower of strength in a world of uncertainty.

"It was my mother".

She was the constant hard wall against which every doubt, every fear, and every discouraging voice shattered. No matter how high the waves of challenge rose, her belief in me stood firm, unshaken. She'd stay up all night, tirelessly brainstorming and strategizing, just to help me navigate the chaos. She framed my business with care, turning ideas into tangible plans, providing guidance at every crossroad. She wasn't just my support; she was the force that helped me crack open the opportunities I never thought possible. She walked with me through every storm, her calm and steady presence my anchor. Even when the weight of the world felt unbearable, she gave me the strength to bear it all. It was her unwavering belief in me that kept me going when I doubted myself, reminding me that no matter how hard the journey, I had a fortress in her faith.

Through each word of encouragement, each action of support, she wove a tapestry of strength around me, one that protected me from the chaos outside and helped me stay true to my path.And this book is a gratitude to her for sacrificing her each second, working each day towards "My Dream". No longer it was just my dream but *"OURS"*.

Embracing the Unknown

There were times when I asked myself, *Will I even be able to make it?* Was it just a fleeting dream, something too impossible, too out of reach? Was it a mere figment of imagination - an idea too wild to ever take form? Would my dream forever remain locked in the confines of my mind, never to see the light of day?

Those questions, like shadows, lingered with me. And it wasn't just me questioning myself. There were voices around me, constant reminders of my own insecurities. *"You're too young for this,"* they'd say. *"What do you know about life? You've barely lived enough to even understand it."* And, *What makes you think you can stand on a stage and tell people how to live their lives?* These questions cut deep, stoking fears I didn't even know existed. Every voice seemed to hold me back, pulling me in different directions - each one more confusing than the last.

The more they questioned, the more those voices seemed to drown out the quiet whispers of my heart. *Maybe they're right,* I thought. *Maybe I'm not meant for this. Maybe I'm just dreaming too big.* And yet, in the midst of all those doubts, I felt something stronger - a fierce, quiet knowing that this dream wasn't just a passing thought. It was my calling. It was the very essence of who

I was meant to become. But the truth is, you don't have to have all the answers. You don't need to know every step or how it will all unfold. Life doesn't come with a perfect roadmap, and the only certainty you can hold onto is that the path will reveal itself - sometimes slowly, sometimes unexpectedly - but it always will.

Healing, growth, and true transformation aren't about a checklist or following someone else's directions; they're about surrendering to the unknown and trusting that it will take you where you need to go.

The Real Magic

For me, it wasn't about shutting out the voices around me. It was about learning to trust the voice within me - learning to navigate through the noise and follow the gentle pull of my own purpose. It was about embracing the fear, the uncertainty, and the messiness of it all, because that's where the magic lies.

What if the real magic wasn't in having a clear plan, but in taking each step without knowing exactly where it would lead? What if it was okay to not have all the answers? What if those questions, the ones that seem to hold you back, are really just signs of how much you've yet to discover about yourself?

So, here's what I learned: You don't need to have it all figured out. You don't need a guarantee. What you need is the courage to take that first step, even when the road ahead is unclear.

The answers? They were never meant to be found - they were meant to be experienced. And in the end, it's not about the destination; it's about the journey. It's about becoming the person you're meant to be, one step at a time.

7

THE POWER WITHIN

"You have power over your mind, not outside events. Realize this, and you will find strength." – *Marcus Aurelius*

One night, as I lay down to sleep, a strange and vivid dream took me on a journey unlike any I had ever experienced before.

In the dream, I found myself aboard a spaceship called *The Soul Voyager*. But this wasn't just any ordinary vessel - this one was not designed to traverse the vastness of outer space.

No, it was a ship built to explore the deep and unseen corners of the human heart and mind, a place I had never dared to venture before.

I was the captain of this vessel. In this dream, I was The *Captain* - a skilled navigator of galaxies, yet unaware of the emotional storm brewing within me.

I had spent so much time focusing on the external universe, reaching for distant stars, that I had failed to notice the emptiness growing inside me.

But in this dream, I knew deep down that my true mission was to explore the emotions, memories, and untold stories that lay hidden within.

The emotional world was my next great adventure.

The ship was equipped with technology designed not to find new planets, but to scan, understand, and analyze human feelings - emotions that had been suppressed, ignored, and forgotten over the years.

Emotional Cosmos

Our first stop was the *Emotional Cosmos*, a vast, swirling cloud of energy that reflected the turmoil of suppressed emotions.

As we ventured deeper into this cosmic storm, I began to feel the pressure mounting, as if the emotions I had long ignored were rising to the surface, building up like an impending storm.

"This is what happens when emotions are bottled up," I heard myself say, my voice echoing in the chaos. "The longer we hold them inside, the more they build up, until they can no longer be contained.

Eventually, they cause a crash - a collision of feelings." I could feel the intensity of those emotions within myself - anger, sadness, frustration - all swirling inside, like a massive thunderstorm.

I understood now: suppressing emotions didn't make them disappear. They only grew stronger, waiting for the breaking point when they would finally erupt, causing harm to both myself and others.

I realized, in that moment, that emotions must be allowed to flow, to be expressed and released before they turned into destructive outbursts.

Isle of Suppression

Next, my dream led me to the *Isle of Suppression*, a quiet, isolated land surrounded by calm seas.

But as I stood there, something felt terribly wrong. The stillness wasn't peaceful - it was unnatural, as if the island had been frozen in time, trapped in an endless state of denial.

"This is what happens when emotional needs are ignored for too long," I told myself in the dream. "When we avoid confrontation and pretend everything is fine, we become stagnant.

Suppressing feelings doesn't bring peace - it traps us in a state of numbness." The island was a place of stillness, where emotions had long been buried beneath layers of calm.

There was no growth, no transformation - only silence. And I could feel it: this was what happened when we denied our emotions, when we allowed them to remain dormant, untouched.

The island stood as a stark warning of what could happen to us if we didn't face our feelings.

The Dormant Volcano

The dream then took me to a dormant volcano.

For a while, I observed it, confused, as it remained still and silent.

But suddenly, a deep rumble shook the entire ship, and the volcano erupted with a force so powerful that it rattled my very bones.

"This is what happens when resentment builds up inside us," I said, recognizing the truth of the eruption. "When we suppress our anger, frustration, or disappointment, it festers, growing stronger until it bursts forth in a way we can't predict."

The volcano's eruption was not just destructive to others - it hurt the one holding the resentment as well.

I realized that the emotions we don't express, the pain we keep inside, have a way of manifesting unexpectedly.

They cause harm to both ourselves and those around us.

I understood the most important lesson of all in this dream: to heal, we must face our emotions, no matter how uncomfortable they may be.

The first step to healing was forgiveness - both for others and for ourselves.

I saw that when we let go of resentment and embrace self-love, we free ourselves from the weight of emotional burdens.

Garden of Acceptance

Finally, my dream brought me to a place of serenity - the *Garden of Acceptance*. It was an oasis, where water flowed freely, the trees were strong, and the air was fresh with life. In this peaceful space, I learned that true peace comes when we accept our emotions as they are - when we allow ourselves to feel, to express, and to release what we are truly going through.

I realized that emotions are not something to fear or suppress. They are guides, leading us toward growth and understanding. By embracing them fully - whether joy, sadness, anger, or love - we can find clarity and peace. When we stop pretending to be something we're not and allow ourselves to feel deeply, we discover true happiness.

The Quiet Compass

As I sailed further into the vast emotional cosmos aboard *The Soul Voyager*, I felt a shift - an inner knowing that there was something deeper guiding me through the storm. It wasn't a loud, commanding voice, but a subtle, almost imperceptible whisper that seemed to come from within. It was the *Quiet Compass* - an extraordinary force that existed within me, always present but often unnoticed amidst the noise of daily life. This Quiet Compass wasn't something tangible that I could touch or see, but it was always there, available to me at any moment I chose to tune in. It was that gut feeling, that inner nudge, the heart's quiet call that gently pointed me in the right direction when I was unsure or overwhelmed. Just like in the *Emotional Cosmos*, where chaos reigned, I realized that when I cleared the noise of the world and turned inward, the Quiet Compass guided me with wisdom and clarity, reminding me of the strength and wisdom I already possessed. But how did I know when it was speaking to me? How could I trust it? I had to learn that the Quiet Compass speaks to us in moments of stillness, when we release the distractions around us and truly listen to the voice of our inner truth. It wasn't a voice that demanded attention - it was more like a knowing, a gentle nudge that pointed me toward what I truly needed, even when it seemed uncertain or unclear.

And in those quiet moments, I realized that I was also tuning into a powerful force - the Law of Attraction - a universal law that draws to us what we focus on, what we align with. At first, it seemed like the path ahead was clouded with uncertainty, but as I paid attention to that deeper voice within, I saw how the Law of Attraction and the Quiet Compass were intertwined. Both of them were about alignment. When I aligned with the true voice within, the Universe responded. But to align with this voice, I had to first clear the noise - the worries, the doubts, the distractions - that stood between me and that inner guidance.

Frequency Matters

It was like tuning a radio. If I tuned into one station, I would hear a specific message. If I tuned into another, I would hear something else entirely. The energy I put out - my thoughts, my feelings, my beliefs - became the frequency I aligned with, attracting experiences, people, and opportunities that mirrored that energy.

By listening to my Quiet Compass, I was aligning with a higher vibration - one that resonated with my deepest desires. And as I trusted that inner knowing, I activated the Law of Attraction, bringing those desires into reality. I began to understand that it wasn't about wishful thinking or force. It was about trust - trusting myself, my intuition, and the Universe's timing. The more I listened to my heart and let go of the fear and doubt, the more everything around me seemed to fall into place.

The Faced Crossroads

There was a moment, a critical turning point, when I stood at a crossroads on my journey as both a coach and a speaker. The path ahead split into two directions. One path was bright and shiny, seemingly perfect - easy, clear, and comfortable. It was the route many might have taken - the one where I could have joined an already established coaching network, associating with someone else's system and brand. It promised an easier road - no need to convince anyone to attend my classes, no need to push my own unique vision of life coaching, and no need to constantly market and promote my own idea. This was the easy way, where I could avoid the struggle of convincing people to trust me, the effort of showing them that my way, my vision, would work for them. But then there was the other path, the one that felt like a calling. It was uncertain, challenging, and full of obstacles.

This path wasn't about following in someone else's footsteps; it was about creating something entirely my own - a life school where I could help people uncover their true potential. It was a path that required courage - courage to build my own platform, courage to believe in my unique approach, and courage to face rejection and criticism when others didn't understand my vision. It was the path where I would need to constantly convince others that this school, this method, could truly change lives. The struggle to get people to come, the struggle to show them that what I was offering was not just another typical coaching program - it was something deeper, something transformative. At first, my mind tried to push me toward the "easier" path - the one where I could take the safe route, where I wouldn't have to invest so much of myself into creating something from scratch. The idea of associating with someone else's already successful system seemed like the easier option. There would be less resistance, less effort required to convince people to come on board. All I'd have to do is promote and sell a service that was already established. It promised stability and less vulnerability. But deep within, I felt that quiet pull toward the other path - the one that felt uncertain, uncomfortable, but also deeply aligned with my truest desires.

The Magical Wand: Law of Attraction

This was the moment when the Law of Attraction began to work in my favor. I began to trust in my purpose, and slowly but surely, people started to come. Some questioned me, some doubted my ability, but the right people began to hear my message. The universe brought them to me - those who resonated with my vision and were ready to take that leap of faith with me. With every new person who believed in my dream, I knew I was on the right path.

The path of building my own life school, of becoming the coach and speaker I was meant to be, would not be easy - but it was mine. And in that journey, I found the true meaning of success - not just in the people I helped, but in my own growth, courage, and unwavering belief in myself. As a coach, I knew the challenges would be immense - convincing people that my approach could work, convincing them to invest in themselves, to trust in my system. But through each challenge, through every "no" I received, I remembered my purpose. It wasn't about selling a product. It was about guiding people. To change their lives, to live without regrets, to face their fears and uncertainties head-on. And every step, no matter how difficult, brought me closer to the life I dreamed of - not just for myself, but for everyone I could help along the way.

Aligning with the Goals

Through this journey, I learned the most important lesson: when we listen to our Quiet Compass, we align ourselves with the flow of life and attract what we need to move forward. It's not about forcing things to happen - it's about being in tune with the quiet guidance within, allowing the Universe to unfold in its perfect timing. The dream ended with me looking at the crew aboard *The Soul Voyager*, knowing that we had all been changed. We had learned that the greatest journey is not one through outer space, but one that takes us deep within. To live fully, we must honor our emotions - without fear, without shame. "Only then can we truly be free."

8

BE AN ACTION TAKER

"The path to success is to take massive, determined action."
— Tony Robbins

I had always heard the phrase, *"God helps those who help themselves."* But it wasn't until I reflected on my own transformation that I truly understood its meaning. The difference between the old me and the new me boiled down to just one simple but profound factor: action. The old me hesitated. She overthought, feared failure, and worried about consequences. She dreamed, yes, but those dreams remained locked away, far from reality. She didn't have clear goals - not because she didn't want them, but because she hadn't yet discovered her true purpose. But then something shifted. A defining moment - a realization, a spark - turned my perspective upside down. The new me emerged as an **action-taker,** someone who didn't let fear of failure hold her back. The new me understood that failure wasn't the end of the road; it was simply part of the process.

Failures are Learnings

I understood something profound: failure doesn't define you - giving up does. It's not about how many times you get knocked down; it's about how many times you stand back up. As the saying goes, "A boxing match isn't over until the fighter refuses to rise." Each time you stand, no matter how bruised or battered, you're telling the world - and yourself - that you're still in the fight. That realization changed everything.

I stopped fearing setbacks and started taking actions. The old me wanted to avoid failure at all costs and therefore was afraid to take actions towards my dreams; the new me saw it as the price of becoming the person I was meant to be. And in that shift, I found my courage. This leads me to a question we've all asked at some point:

If we all have dreams, if we all have that fire inside us, why do only a few people bring their goals to life? Why don't all of us achieve the purpose we long for? The answer, I realized, lies in the willingness to take action. Dreams without action remain just that - dreams.

Many of us get stuck waiting for the perfect time, the perfect plan, or the perfect circumstances. But the truth is, perfection doesn't exist. Success comes to those who take the first step, no matter how small or uncertain, and keep moving forward.

Opportunities are Game Changers

For the old me, there was no clear purpose because she hadn't experienced the moments that awaken the soul - those pivotal instances that make you realize what you're truly meant for. Sometimes, life presents us with challenges or opportunities that act as game-changers. They force us to confront our fears, reevaluate our priorities, and dig deeper to uncover our real purpose. For me, those moments were the turning points that transformed hesitation into determination. They taught me that purpose isn't always something we stumble upon - it's something we uncover through trial, reflection, and, most importantly, action. And so, I began to take action, not just for the sake of achieving goals, but to align with a higher purpose. The new me understood that progress, no matter how slow or imperfect, was far better than standing still. Because when you take action, you invite growth. You invite opportunity. And you invite the kind of divine help that only comes to those who are willing to help themselves.

I still remember that moment when I decided I wanted to open a Life School! Helping people become the teachers of their own life, own their life and start living each moment. Moving from that stage moment to opening a life school wasn't a one-day miracle. It was a culmination of countless steps, pivotal moments, heartbreaks, failures, and learnings. But if there's one thing that defines my success, it's this: purpose, and the actions taken towards that purpose. In the beginning, I hesitated. Taking action felt unnecessary - I believed I had all the time in the world. "I'm too young," I would tell myself. "This purpose can wait." Procrastination became my closest companion. I convinced myself that my dreams could sit on the shelf until I was ready to face them.

How Much Time Do You Really Have?

But then, a single, piercing question altered my perspective: *How much time do you really have?* It struck me that time and life are not just precious; they're irreplaceable. The greatest waste of both is spending years accomplishing things that could have been achieved in far less time - simply by taking the right actions at the right moment. And here's the secret: when your purpose is crystal clear, you don't need to figure out every little detail of how to achieve it.

You just need to act, to seize the opportunities that align with your vision. A clear goal paired with decisive actions will attract the right circumstances and people to help you along the way. I remember the moment vividly: lying on my bed, staring blankly at the ceiling fan. I was justifying to myself, *"There's no rush. I have all the time in the world. I can chill and enjoy my college life for now.* But within seconds, a realization hit me like a wave: the people who passed away yesterday might have had plans for today.

They might have thought, *I'll take that action tomorrow "*, only to find that tomorrow never came. That thought shook me to my core. This day, this moment, this very second - it will never come again. Whatever you wish to do, whatever goal you're dreaming of, this is your time. Seize the opportunity. Don't let it slip through your fingers, because the truth is, no matter what happens, this moment will never return.

Are you a High Achiever or a Low Achiever?

The primary difference between high achievers and low achievers lies in their orientation towards action. It all boils down to this one simple truth: who gets up in the morning and runs towards their dreams, and who chooses to stay in bed, allowing fear, doubt, or excuses to hold them back. High achievers don't wait for the perfect moment - they create it. They are constantly on the move, always busy, always doing something that pushes them closer to their goals. They don't just think about their dreams; they take immediate action to make them a reality. On the other hand, low achievers are often full of good intentions. They talk about what they want to do, what they could do, and what they'll do eventually. But when it comes down to actually doing the work, they fall back on excuses. They justify their lack of action with reasons that seem rational on the surface but are ultimately just barriers keeping them stuck in their comfort zones. As the saying goes, *The road to hell is paved with good intentions.* Excuses are the worst enemies of human progress. They provide temporary comfort, but in the long run, they only hold you back from becoming the person you are meant to be.

High achievers don't waste time justifying why they can't do something - they just get up, take action, and move forward. They understand that every step, no matter how small, is a step closer to their dream.

9

CREATE YOUR IDEAL FUTURE

"The best way to predict the future is to create it." –
Abraham Lincoln

I have always believed in one simple saying: the idea of an ideal future is not subjective, but rather objective. It is uniquely framed by each individual, based on their goals, purpose in life, and alignment with their core beliefs and values. To create your ideal life and future, you first have to become the leader of your own life. And like no one else, leaders have a vision. Leaders don't just wait for opportunities to come to them; they envision the future, understand what they want, and take deliberate steps to achieve it. They know where they're going and how to get there.

Non-leaders, on the other hand, often find themselves stuck in the past or only concerned with instant gratification, living in the moment without a clear plan for the future. Creating an ideal life means thinking like a leader. It's about having a strong vision and a long-term perspective. It's the ability to think several years ahead, peeking into the future, and making decisions in the present that will shape the life you want to live. Thinking ahead, with clarity and foresight, is what makes you a leader. Leaders don't just react to life - they create it. They set their course and take charge of their journey, no matter how uncertain the road ahead may seem. The most important step I took early on was creating a strategic five-year fantasy with absolutely no limitations. I realized that all limitations exist only in our minds. What we think we can't achieve is often a result of conditioning from childhood or labels that society or we ourselves have placed on us. The truth is, those labels are nothing but barriers we've been wearing for far too long.

Removing the Labels

Why not remove those banners from around our necks and start fresh? Why not take off the heavy weight of self-imposed limitations and rewrite our belief systems? The conditioning we choose to accept about ourselves doesn't define us. The truth is, no one is better or smarter than you - people are just better and smarter in different areas. You have the absolute ability to learn anything you need to learn to achieve your goals. The only limits that exist are the ones you place on yourself. You might think there's a standard for what you can achieve, but in reality, there are no real limits.

If you decide that you will be excellent and strive to join the top 10% of achievers, nothing can stop you. Remember, those top 10% started from the bottom, just like everyone else. Nothing on Earth can stop you from creating your ideal life except for yourself. Will it be easy? Of course not. But will you be able to do it? Absolutely yes. As motivational speaker Les Brown says, *"To achieve something you've never achieved, you have to do something you've never done before."* Johann Wolfgang von Goethe, the German Philosopher also said, *"To have more, you have to be more.*

"The key is to push beyond your comfort zone and embrace the unknown. It's only then that you'll see the true potential within you to create the life you desire.

Identifying the Gaps

One of the most important tasks in creating an ideal life is identifying the gaps in your knowledge or skills. It's about recognizing the areas where you fall short, those skills or insights that you're lacking, which might be just the one step away from your ideal future. These gaps might seem small, but they make all the difference in moving you closer to your true potential. To understand what's missing, think of it like this: what additional knowledge, skills, or information could you gain that would help you break free from your comfort zone?

These are the keys that can fast-track your growth and catapult you years ahead of where you are now, bypassing where your current knowledge or abilities would typically hold you back. In my journey, I failed many times. I tried, I stumbled, I faced setbacks. But every failure was a stepping stone. The moment I realized that the true path to rapid growth was by aggressively upgrading my skills, my mindset, and my knowledge, everything changed. I wasn't just playing to get by anymore; I was playing to win, to become the best version of myself, to excel at what I do.

As you begin to upgrade yourself and commit to being the best at your field, you'll notice something profound: It's as if you're running a race, but you're the only one in it. While others are still figuring things out, you're already ahead, moving with a purpose. You will find yourself at the front of the pack, leading the way, and in no time, you'll be in the lead position. It's a powerful feeling, knowing that your commitment to growth and excellence is taking you places where most people can only dream of.

The Mantra of Irreplaceability

The core principle that guided me was simple: become irreplaceable. The market pays premium rewards only for excellent performance. And the only way to offer excellence is by becoming the best at what you do. You cannot afford to be mediocre.

Mediocrity is replaceable, forgettable. But excellence is valuable, rare, and demanded. An ideal life is not created by being like everyone else. It is created by being so good at what you do that you stand out in a way that is undeniable. You are defined by your actions, the quality of your work, and how hard it is to replace you. When you dedicate yourself to becoming the best in your field, the world will take notice. Opportunities will find you, and people will begin to see the value in what you offer.

Commit to Excel

I adopted one simple concept: commit to excel. It wasn't a passing thought or a wish - it became my mantra, a guiding principle that influenced every decision, every action I took. I didn't just want to do well; I wanted to be the best. I wanted to be the one others turned to when they needed expertise. And as soon as I committed to this mantra, everything changed.

People who had once overlooked me were suddenly ready to pay any price, sacrifice anything, and invest any amount to learn from me. It wasn't that I had become someone special by chance - it was because I had put in the work. I had put in the time to become truly excellent. And in return, the world began to open up to me.

10

THE SIMPLE SECRET TO AN IDEAL LIFE

"How you do anything is how you do everything." – T. Harv Eker

The ideal life is often viewed as a far-off destination, a distant dream that feels just out of reach. Many of us believe that in order to live this perfect existence, we need everything to align - our career, relationships, health, and wealth. But here's the truth: the secret to an ideal life is not found in external circumstances. It's found in the way you approach life, yourself, and the choices you make each day. The key is in cultivating a mindset that thrives on growth and learning, rather than waiting for everything to "fall into place."

Honestly, my life was never perfectly aligned. In fact, I never hoped for it to be. It was what I call "dialigned" - so far from alignment that I never expected things to be perfectly balanced. But what was always within my control, what became my greatest asset, was my cultivated and grown mindset. Instead of subscribing to a fixed mindset, I embraced the power of flexibility. I believed in the freedom of a flexible mindset, one that is always eager to learn, adapt, and grow. The secret lies not in waiting for perfect conditions, but in the intentional, consistent actions you take - shaped by self-awareness, personal growth, and an unwavering belief that you can create the life you desire. The truth is, you don't have to wait for the world to give you permission to succeed or feel good about yourself. The power to change your life, to live the life you dream of, lies within you - right here, right now. The key is to take responsibility for your thoughts, actions, and reactions, and to commit to building a life that aligns with your deepest values and aspirations.

My Ideal Life

What I observed on my journey was simple: creating an ideal life is not about luck or waiting for things to fall into place. It is about excelling in your field. The more excellent you are at what you do, the more you become sought after. Opportunities flow to those who excel, and the rewards are much greater than you can ever imagine. This principle became my guiding light. I didn't have to chase success. Success started to chase me. People were ready to invest, sacrifice, and go out of their way to be a part of my journey. But none of this happened until I committed to excellence. Excellence became the cornerstone of my journey.

Every day, I worked towards mastering my craft. I didn't just want to be good at what I did - I wanted to be one of the best. And the more I honed my skills, the more the world recognized my value. This wasn't just about monetary rewards - it was about creating a reputation that was built on the foundation of excellence. It was about becoming someone whose work was irreplaceable, someone whose contributions mattered in ways others couldn't replicate.

Be Irreplaceable

A crucial part of this process is understanding that your self-worth is the foundation of your ideal life. If you don't believe you deserve happiness, success, or fulfillment, you will unconsciously create barriers that prevent you from achieving them. Your self-esteem - the way you perceive your own value - determines how you show up in the world. It affects the choices you make, the relationships you nurture, and the goals you set.

The higher your self-esteem, the more willing you are to take risks, set ambitious goals, and challenge yourself to grow. When you have a healthy sense of self-worth, you open the door to limitless possibilities, because you know deep down that you are capable of achieving whatever you set your mind to. However, this journey doesn't come without challenges. Your past behaviors, patterns, and beliefs may have shaped the way you see yourself, and often, those old habits can hold you back. It's essential to recognize that your past is not your future. While your past experiences may have shaped your current mindset, they do not define who you can become. It is never too late to break free from limiting beliefs and start fresh. The process of self-discovery and growth begins with examining those old patterns and actively choosing to replace them with new, empowering ones.

Lifelong Learners are Actually Irreplaceable!

I know it may sound weird, but at some point in my life, I dreamed of bringing a revolution to the speaking industry - a revolution no one expected, a revolution no one could have imagined. I envisioned myself representing India on an international stage and making my country proud. I still don't know how that dream will be fulfilled, but one thing remains clear: I yearn for it. However, that's not the most important point. What I understood from this "weird" dream was this: I needed to be irreplaceable. Because if there replacement for me, the revolution can't happen.

That day, I turned into a lifelong learner - always ready to learn, eager to understand everything the world had to offer. I realized that the only way to create the life I wanted was to embrace the mindset of growth and continuous improvement. I adopted the belief that "those who learn, actually earn." And that's where it all clicked for me.

The path to success, fulfillment, and revolution wasn't just about what I could achieve right away; it was about dedicating myself to a lifelong process of learning, evolving, and growing, no matter the obstacles in my way. But here's where the real breakthrough came. This wasn't about waiting for the "perfect time" or for things to be magically aligned.

It wasn't about relying on external factors or hoping for a perfect world. The truth is, if you want to achieve greatness, you have to do it with your own willpower, your own actions, and your own commitment. It's not just about setting goals; it's about *becoming* the person who can achieve those goals. It's about deciding, every day, to push yourself forward with intention, no matter how imperfect or dialigned your life may feel.

This is where pain and persistence meet: *you have to create your own opportunities*. Success doesn't come from waiting around for the perfect moment or from relying on external forces. It comes from within, from the mindset you cultivate and the consistent actions you take, day in and day out. It's a process of becoming the person who can turn their vision into reality, no matter how challenging or uncertain the path may seem.

Self-Improvement

One of the most powerful ways to create an ideal life is through continuous self-improvement. Excellence is not a state you achieve once and for all - it's a habit, a way of living. It requires ongoing effort, consistent action, and a commitment to becoming the best version of yourself.

Excellence is about giving your best effort in everything you do, no matter how big or small the task. Whether you're working on your career, your health, or your personal relationships, excellence is the attitude that sets you apart. It's about doing things with intention, paying attention to the details, and being mindful of the impact of your actions.

As you commit to excellence, you will find that your life starts to align with your ideal. Opportunities will arise, people will take notice of your dedication, and you will begin to feel a deep sense of fulfillment. This sense of fulfillment comes from knowing that you are living in alignment with your values and your purpose. When your actions match your intentions, when your work is meaningful, and when your relationships are built on mutual respect and understanding, you create a life that feels truly fulfilling.

Perfection or Progress?

It's important to note that your ideal life is not about perfection. It's about progress. Life is not a destination; it's a journey. Along the way, you will encounter setbacks, failures, and moments of doubt. But these are not signs that you are on the wrong path; they are opportunities to grow, to learn, and to become stronger. The secret to an ideal life is not in avoiding challenges, but in embracing them and using them as stepping stones toward your goals.

Ultimately, the simple secret to an ideal life is to take control of your own story. It's about choosing to be the author of your life, rather than letting circumstances, other people, or past mistakes dictate your future. You are the one who decides what kind of life you want to create, and every choice you make, no matter how small, is a step toward that vision. When you take full responsibility for your happiness, success, and fulfillment, you unlock the door to an extraordinary life. As you go through this journey, it's important to remember that the ideal life isn't about having everything "perfect."

It's about living in alignment with your true self, striving for excellence, and being committed to personal growth. By focusing on your strengths, embracing challenges, and remaining dedicated to your vision, you'll find that your ideal life isn't a distant dream - it is a reality that you create, one step at a time. The secret is already within you. All it takes is the courage to unlock it and the commitment to live it fully.

Epilogue: The Ideal Life Is Yours to Create

At the end of the day, the ideal life is not some far-off fantasy. It is the life that you create when you commit to being the best at what you do. When you invest in yourself, when you stop making excuses, and when you start excelling in your field, your ideal life starts to unfold before you. The world rewards excellence - plain and simple. You are not bound by your current knowledge or skills. The only limits that exist are the ones you place on yourself. If you decide to strive for excellence and to rise to the top 10%, nothing can stop you. The future you desire is within your reach, and it's waiting for you to claim it.

The only question is: are you ready to commit to becoming the best version of yourself?

11

THE HIDDEN HAPPINESS IN PROGRESS

"Happiness is the key to success.

If you love what you are doing, you will be

successful." Albert Schweitzer

Happiness, I've come to realize, isn't something you find waiting for you at the finish line. It's not some distant dream or an elusive prize that only the lucky few get to hold. No, happiness is something you *create* - a result of how you move, how you grow, and how you continue to rise, even when you stumble. It's found in the progress itself. I often think back to the days when I first embarked on the journey of building my Life school.

The task seemed insurmountable at times - daunting and endless. Setting up something from scratch, especially when you don't come from an entrepreneurial background, can feel like an uphill climb that never ends. My parents, both deeply embedded in the 9-to-5 world, had instilled in me the values of stability, the security of a paycheck, and the peace that comes with predictable, steady work. They taught me how to play the safe game, how to stay within the boundaries of the conventional path. But, as we've already discussed, my heart longed for more. It wasn't the 9-to-5 grind that spoke to me - it was the freedom, the passion, the adventure of creating something that was mine.

A life of routine had never been my dream. I wanted to break free, to find a way to weave my own story, to create my own future. I began to notice something curious: even when the road ahead was foggy and the work felt like it was never-ending - designing logos, choosing names, networking, building teams, diving deep into digital skills, learning new things - I still found happiness. It wasn't obvious at first, but there was a subtle joy growing inside me. The deeper I got into the work, the more I realized: I was happy because I was progressing. Every single step, no matter how small, felt like it was bringing me closer to something bigger.

My Mission

It wasn't just about being busy. I was busy, yes, but not in the usual sense. It wasn't the kind of busy that makes you feel drained without purpose. I was busy with my *life*, with my mission, with building something from scratch. And that kind of busyness made me feel alive. Yes, balancing college, setting up a business, learning new tech, attending events - it was overwhelming at times. But in the midst of it all, I discovered that this busyness was not a burden. It was the fuel that kept me moving forward.

At night, when I closed my eyes, I would reflect on the day. No matter how many times I failed - or rather, especially because of those failures - I smiled. I smiled because I was trying. I smiled because every effort, no matter how small, was a step closer to my goal. And that's where happiness came from: not from a perfect result, but from knowing I was moving toward something that mattered to me. It wasn't about the end result, the accolades, or the money - it was about the journey. Every day, I woke up knowing I was doing something that meant something. Each step, whether I succeeded or failed, brought me closer to my dream. The happiness didn't come from achieving some grand goal - it came from the realization that I was always moving forward, always progressing.

Failures are Just Lessons

I failed a lot many times. But every failure made me smile, because it was another lesson, another step in the process. The real reward wasn't the outcome - it was the progress. It was the small wins, the things most people didn't see, but I felt them deeply. So, what I discovered was simple: happiness isn't tied to the destination. It's in the journey. It's in the quiet progress. It's in knowing that every effort, no matter how small, is a step toward something greater.

The happiness comes from the pursuit, from constantly becoming better, not from hitting some finish line. I was busy - but not in a way that weighed me down. It wasn't a burden; it was a privilege. And when I lay down to sleep, knowing I had taken steps forward - no matter how tiny - they were worth more than anything else. So, here's the truth: as I progressed, my happiness grew - not because of some grand achievement, but because I was constantly evolving. Happiness is found in the process, in the dedication, in becoming the person you've always wanted to be - one small step at a time. In that progress, I found my happiness. And it wasn't fleeting. It grew with every small victory, every step forward.

Keep Going

I can remember the first time I tried to make my own website. I was so excited, thinking it would be my digital masterpiece - a place where everything would come together perfectly. But as soon as I hit publish, I wasn't satisfied. The design felt off. The structure didn't feel right. I was disappointed. So, I started again. I spent hours tweaking, changing, redesigning, learning new things about the process each time.

And after each attempt, the same feeling emerged: it wasn't perfect. This went on for a while - ten times, to be exact. I redesigned that website ten times, pouring countless hours into each version. I learned new skills each time. I became more familiar with web design tools, with coding, with color schemes. But every time I looked at the result, something wasn't quite right. The logos changed with each version, the layout evolved, the content was re-written multiple times. No matter how hard I tried, I couldn't shake the feeling that it just wasn't *me* yet.

Feeling of Completion

But then came something that made me pause: the feeling of completion. Every time I finished working on it, even if I didn't love it, there was this quiet sense of fulfillment. Something about knowing I had completed a task - even if it didn't feel perfect - gave me a sense of satisfaction. It wasn't about the website itself, but the act of finishing it. There's a unique power in closing a chapter, in finishing something. You might not be fully happy with the result, but the simple act of finishing something you've put effort into releases a certain sense of contentment. That feeling, no matter how small the accomplishment, is something that can be incredibly fulfilling. What I didn't realize at the time was that this sense of completion is tied to something much bigger: a chemical reaction in the brain. When we complete a task, especially one that we've invested time and energy into, the brain releases dopamine - a hormone that plays a key role in happiness and motivation. It's that "reward" feeling, that little burst of satisfaction that tells us,

"You did it, you're moving forward." Dopamine is often associated with positive reinforcement. It's a way for our brain to say, "Well done!" It's that moment when you feel a small wave of joy after finishing something you've worked hard on. You might not have reached perfection, but you've made progress - and that's enough to give you a sense of happiness. Even though the website wasn't exactly what I had imagined, just knowing that I had completed something, that I had moved forward, was enough to give me that small, satisfying hit of dopamine. And that little burst of joy kept me going.

Over time, I started realizing how essential these moments of completion are. Every step, no matter how small or imperfect, was pushing me forward in my journey. I wasn't just building a website; I was building resilience, persistence, and a deep sense of satisfaction. I was learning to embrace progress over perfection. And every time I completed a task - whether it was redesigning a logo or fixing a bug on the site - my brain rewarded me with dopamine. It made me feel like I was on the right track.

The Science Behind It

The science behind this sense of completion and the dopamine reward is not just theoretical - it's been extensively studied and proven. One of the most famous experiments conducted in this area was the "Marshmallow Test" in the 1960s by psychologist Walter Mischel. In this experiment, children were given the choice between eating one marshmallow immediately or waiting 15 minutes to receive two marshmallows. The children who could delay gratification and wait for the second marshmallow were later found to have higher levels of success in life. The experiment highlighted the importance of patience, discipline, and how delayed gratification contributes to long-term happiness and success. But the science behind progress goes beyond delayed gratification. A study by researchers at the University of Michigan explored how small wins - small accomplishments we achieve on a daily basis - have a profound impact on motivation and overall happiness. The study showed that people who experience small, consistent wins throughout their day are more likely to be motivated and satisfied with their work. These small wins release dopamine, creating a positive feedback loop that encourages more productive behavior and a sense of well-being.

Imperfectly Perfect

The idea that happiness is connected to progress has been reflected in the lives of many famous people. Take Thomas Edison, for example. He is known for his relentless experimentation with the light bulb, failing thousands of times before finally creating a successful design.

Edison famously said, "I have not failed. I've just found 10,000 ways that won't work." Even though he didn't immediately succeed, he found joy and motivation in the process of progress - each step bringing him closer to his goal. For Edison, the journey was just as rewarding, if not more so, than the end result. Each failure released a small sense of accomplishment, pushing him further along in his invention.

The same can be said about Steve Jobs. Known for his perfectionism and attention to detail, Jobs went through several iterations of his designs before creating the perfect product. His drive for excellence wasn't just about creating a product; it was about creating something that reflected his vision. Jobs would often revisit products, making adjustments until everything was just right. And, similar to Edison, the process was a key part of his happiness and success. Jobs said, "You have to be a little bit crazy to do what we're doing. You have to believe in what you're doing. And you have to have this vision and not give up." The sense of accomplishment he found from constantly striving toward perfection - despite the setbacks - was what ultimately led to his success.

My Journey = Happiness In progress On a personal level, I began to see a similar pattern in my own journey. Each redesign of my website or logo wasn't just about achieving perfection - it was about moving forward. I was learning, growing, and gaining new insights with every attempt. That sense of learning and incremental improvement sparked something powerful in me - a form of happiness tied not to immediate success but to the act of creation itself. Just like Edison, I was seeing each failure not as a setback but as a necessary part of the process. And with each failure, I experienced that rush of dopamine that kept me motivated, happy, and ready to take on the next challenge. What I learned through that process is that happiness often comes not from achieving perfection, but from making progress, from completing something, from reaching milestones - even if they're small. It's about the journey of growth and the feeling of moving forward, no matter how many bumps you hit along the way. And in those moments, the happiness isn't tied to the final result, but to the steps you take, the effort you put in, and the completion of the task itself. Every time I finished another round of work on the site, the happiness came from knowing I had made progress. My brain didn't care that the website wasn't perfect.

It cared that I was finishing something, that I was moving forward. And that was enough to keep me going.

12

THE JOURNEY IS ENDLESS

"Life is a journey that must be traveled no matter how bad the roads and accommodations." - Oliver Goldsmith

Establishing my business wasn't a simple feat - it was a relentless journey, each day bringing its own set of hurdles. I wasn't just creating a business; I was constructing a future - a future that was meant to make a difference. The foundation wasn't laid easily, and at times, it felt like I was constantly fighting against forces beyond my control. There were days when the weight of my dream felt almost too heavy to carry, but it was in those moments that I realized something crucial: nothing worth having comes easily.

Building a life school from scratch was a monumental task. The very idea of it seemed overwhelming at first, but as I stepped into the process, I understood that it was more than just administrative work or managing budgets. It was about crafting something that would have a lasting impact - something that could empower and shape future generations. The challenges weren't just practical - they were mental, emotional, and spiritual. I wasn't just struggling to get the paperwork done or make the system work.

The Unsaid Inner Battles

I was dealing with the inner battles of self-doubt, fear, and questioning whether I was cut out for this. The weight of responsibility was immense, but there was something deeper at play. I realized that every challenge, every obstacle, was shaping me into someone capable of achieving what I had set out to do. It wasn't just about the logistical difficulties; it was about stepping into an entirely new world of leadership, decision-making, and risk-taking.

The world of business, especially one as delicate as education, requires resilience in ways that I never imagined. And yet, even through all the exhaustion, the frustration, and the endless to-do lists, there was a quiet but persistent sense of satisfaction. The sense of purpose I was gaining from this journey was worth every sleepless night. But there was something more, something I never expected: the power of timing.

It wasn't just about the work I was doing - it was about the people I was meeting at exactly the right time. I found that when you truly commit to your vision, the right people start to show up. They come into your life just when you need them most - mentors who offer guidance, experts who bring in new perspectives, and partners who share your passion. These connections were not accidental. They were the universe's way of aligning me with the resources I needed to succeed.

Trusting the Universe

Timing is critical. It was never about having everything figured out from the start; it was about trusting the process and knowing that the pieces would fall into place at the right time. Looking back now, I see how perfectly it all came together. The late-night brainstorming sessions, the endless trial and error, the people I met, the risks I took - they were all part of a plan I couldn't fully understand at the time. But that's the beauty of the journey. I had no entrepreneurial background, no experience in education at this level, but what I did have was unwavering determination. Every time I faced a wall, I found a way to break through it.

Even when I stumbled, I refused to accept failure as an option. There was no room for "I can't" in my vocabulary. I had to keep moving forward, no matter how steep the climb. And moving forward meant my mom cheering up for me every time, even when I used to fall down. She clapped for me so loud that I didn't notice who didn't. My world starts from my mom and end on her. She clapped meant my entire world did and nothing else mattered. Her words; "I am proud of you" were the medicine to each pain the words of the unknown used to cause me. One person, at the right time and in the right place, can change your life and open new doors of opportunity for you.

There's a rule I've come to live by: the more you give of yourself, with no expectations of return, the more that will come back to you from the most unexpected sources.

The Old Me vs New Me

At the time, I was so busy establishing my entrepreneurial unit, struggling with hundreds of tasks, that I didn't even have time to think about or showcase my public speaking skills. It seemed like I was consumed by the day-to-day responsibilities, and public speaking was something that, while I loved it, felt far out of reach. Then, one day, my mom came to me and told me about an opportunity. The Midas Talk platform, where celebrity guests were invited - this was a huge chance for me to showcase myself. My initial reaction was to say, "Of course! I can do it." This wasn't a moment to hesitate.

This new version of me didn't fear failure or ask "What if?" Instead, I was fully prepared to manifest it. This wasn't just about seizing an opportunity; it was about transforming my mindset and using my inner strength to make something extraordinary happen. I started to think about it, visualize it, and believe in it.

Act - As If Technique

While preparing for the speech, I didn't just practice - it became an act of immersion. I used a technique I call "Act as if." I would go through the motions of delivering the speech in my mind, acting as if I were already on that stage in front of an audience of prestigious individuals.

I'd rehearse my words, imagining them being well received, and see myself standing tall with confidence, delivering every word flawlessly. As I practiced, I started to see it not as something in the future but as something already happening. I used to walk up and down the verandah, practicing my speech, imagining that all the people on the road were my audience. It sounds amusing, but trust me, it was fun. I had a metro right in front of my house, visible from my balcony, and I'd start with, "Okay, hey metro, I'm going to start with my speech to be delivered tomorrow, and you give me reviews."

I would even make the entire verandah my audience, imagining they were media people asking me questions, and I would answer them. At first, I stumbled, and there were moments of awkwardness. But soon, something incredible happened. I became so professional that when I looked back at my practice, I realized I was more confident than even the media professionals who had been conducting interviews for years. It was a surreal feeling to realize how far I had come in such a short time.

Visualization and Manifestation

That's the power of visualization and manifestation - aligning your inner energy with the universe and directing it toward the infinite source of opportunities that surrounds you. There were times when I'd practice in the washroom, too, while showering. My parents, from outside the door, would overhear me, and in their own way, they'd chuckle;" *Kisse Battein krri hai* ", and I would laughingly say, *"Khud se!"* These were some oops moments, but they were important. Every moment, even the ones that seemed silly, were steps toward the bigger picture.

What I was doing wasn't just rehearsing a speech. I was preparing my mind, my energy, my focus. I was making sure that the world I was creating in my head would manifest into reality. And believe me, each step, no matter how small or quirky, pushed me closer to that moment of true achievement. The universe, it seemed, was listening and responding, opening doors of opportunities that I never could have imagined when I first began. I even took it further by writing down the most brutally honest questions: "How can I make this manifestation a reality?" I wasn't just thinking about it abstractly - I was asking myself, what would I have to do to make this moment happen? What actions must I take right now to bring my vision to life? I wrote those thoughts down on a piece of paper, solidifying my commitment to this goal.

Blue Sky Thinking

On top of that, I practiced something I call blue-sky thinking. I would look up at the sky and imagine the perfect moment vividly. Its extremely important while manifesting or visualizing that the picture in our mind and heart is clear enough I would want one day to relive in the future - this time it was me, standing on that stage, speaking in front of an audience of esteemed individuals, my words resonating in the air. I would vividly picture the moment, the energy, the atmosphere. I would close my eyes and visualize that moment, my future exactly the way I wanted it to be, feeling the excitement, feeling the success. Then, I would step back and ask myself, "What would have happened for me to have created this perfect future?" I went back to the present moment and asked my mind, "What would need to happen from here on out for me to achieve all of my goals?" It wasn't just about wishing for success - it was about working backwards, aligning my current steps with my future vision. It was about making that future not a distant dream, but a reality I was actively crafting.

The Goal Has to Be Clear

The goal this time was clear: to crack the speech and deliver it flawlessly in front of an audience of established individuals. I was determined to make this vision come true. I knew it wouldn't be easy, but I also knew that with the right mindset, with the right preparation, and with the ability to manifest that vision, I could make it happen. It's one thing to understand that the universe is listening, that like attracts like, and that our words and thoughts create our reality.

But how do we move from mere awareness to actual manifestation? The key lies in trusting the process - trusting that the universe is working behind the scenes, even when we can't see immediate results. This trust transforms into empowerment when we take inspired action, no matter how small. You see, manifestation isn't just about wishing for things to fall into your lap. It's about aligning with your desires - energetically, emotionally, and spiritually - and then acting in faith. When you believe in your dreams and know they are already on their way, the universe starts moving, and it moves through you.

I Can Do This

When you say, "I can do this," the universe starts opening doors for you that you never even imagined. But here's where the magic truly lies: What you choose to believe, you experience. If you've been stuck in the mindset of "I can't," *that's the reality you will continue to live in.* But once you decide to trust that the universe supports your every move and that you can indeed attract everything you need, your whole world begins to shift. This shift isn't always dramatic, but it is profound. It's like turning the wheel of a ship, slowly but surely steering it in a new direction. And this is the essence of manifestation. The moment you say, "I can," the universe says, "Yes, you can," and it starts aligning events, people, and opportunities in your favor.

Manifesting It to Reality

Manifestation is not an instant fix, but a continuous journey. It's about building a belief so strong that it resonates with everything around you. When you trust the process, you begin to notice things falling into place - sometimes in the most unexpected ways. You may find yourself meeting people who can help you in ways you never anticipated, or suddenly stumbling upon opportunities that were always meant for you, but you were simply waiting for the right moment to recognize them. And as you continue to step forward, believing in yourself and the universe's support, the momentum builds. You will notice a shift in the energy around you. Opportunities begin to show up more frequently, and they come faster than you expect. The key is to keep trusting, even when the results aren't immediate. This is where faith and perseverance come into play. The more you trust, the more the universe opens up for you, aligning everything you need at the perfect time. Your belief in the process is what propels you forward and keeps you moving, even when the journey feels uncertain. At the core of manifestation is this simple yet powerful truth: you are the creator of your own reality.

When you align your thoughts, actions, and energy with your desires, the universe begins to work in harmony with you. You become an active participant in creating the life you've always dreamed of. And as you take each step, no matter how small, you'll find that the universe is always one step ahead, guiding you toward your purpose, your success, and your ultimate happiness.

13

THE MAGIC OF "I CAN"

"What lies behind us and what lies before us are tiny matters compared to what lies within us." - Ralph Waldo Emerson

We live in a world that constantly teaches us one thing - Knowledge is power. From textbooks to podcasts, from seminars to self-help books, we are bombarded with information on how to "fix" our lives, how to "achieve success," and how to "manifest" our dreams. But knowledge alone, while helpful, is not enough. It is not enough to know something if you do not believe in it. And belief - true belief - is the key that unlocks the magic of the universe. There is a powerful law at work in the universe, a law that governs everything around us, whether we recognize it or not. This is the Law of Attraction. It works with the simple principle that like attracts like, that our thoughts, emotions, and beliefs shape the world around us.

But here's the catch - understanding the Law of Attraction in theory doesn't necessarily translate into manifesting the life we desire. To truly understand how this law works, we must trust it. We must allow it to guide us, because only then will we begin to see the fruits of its power. But trust, just like anything else, isn't always easy. It's easy to believe in what we can see and touch. But to trust in something invisible, something that operates through the mind and energy, can be a challenge. This is where the shift in consciousness begins. Let me ask you something: How many times have you heard about the power of positive thinking or manifestation? How many times have you read or heard that "you can manifest anything you want," and yet, when you tried to manifest your desires, nothing seemed to happen? It's not that the concept is false - it's just that understanding something intellectually doesn't automatically make it a part of your life. You might know how the Law of Attraction works, but until you believe it and trust it, it will be just another theory, like an unopened book on a shelf.

The Universe Works in Mysterious Ways

When we talk about the universe, we aren't just talking about the stars, the planets, or the galaxies. The universe is a living, breathing entity - a vast energy field that governs everything around us. And the most incredible thing about it? The universe is always listening. It listens to everything - the words we speak, the thoughts we think, and even the emotions we feel.

The Law of Attraction tells us that energy flows where attention goes. When you send out thoughts of fear, doubt, or frustration, you are essentially sending out a signal that the universe receives and mirrors back to you. But when you send out thoughts of gratitude, abundance, and joy, the universe responds by aligning you with people, opportunities, and circumstances that resonate with those positive vibrations. Take a moment and think about the last time you were excited about something - maybe a new project, a new relationship, or even a dream you had.

Didn't you notice that when you were aligned with that excitement, things seemed to fall into place more easily? You met the right people, found the right opportunities, and everything just clicked. That's the universe working with you, showing you how the Law of Attraction works when you're in alignment with your true desires.

But how do we align with our desires?

How do we truly believe in the possibility of our dreams becoming reality?

The answer lies in shifting our thoughts and changing our language.

From "I Can't" to "I Can"

The words we speak hold incredible power. Have you ever noticed that when you say, "I can't do this," you automatically feel defeated? The moment those words leave your mouth, you're already closing the door to the possibilities in front of you.

But when you say, "I can do this," a subtle but powerful shift happens within you. It's like a small opening in the door, and suddenly, you can see the light. Imagine you are holding a big, shiny balloon. This balloon represents your thoughts and feelings. Every time you think something like "I can do this" or "I am happy," you are filling your balloon with bright, happy air.

The more you think positive things, the bigger and brighter your balloon gets. Now, think of the universe as a magical friend who is always listening to what you say and how you feel. When you say, "I can," it's like you're sending out a sparkly message to your magical friend. The universe gets your message and starts helping you by bringing people, ideas, and things that will help you with what you want to do. Let's say you are learning to ride a bike, and you keep saying, "I can do it!"

Every time you say that, you fill your balloon with happy energy. The universe starts to help you, making you feel braver and bringing you more chances to practice. Maybe your friend will help you or someone will show you a trick to ride better.

That's the universe sending you help, all because you believed in yourself and said, "I can!" Now, if you said things like, "I can't do it," it's like your balloon gets smaller, and your magical friend has a harder time helping. Saying "I can" is like telling the universe, "I'm ready, please help me!"

The Ultimate Magic Spell Your thoughts and words are powerful, just like magic spells. The more you believe you can do something, the more the universe will help you get there! It's like a fun adventure where you keep getting closer and closer to your dream. So, remember: whenever you say "I can," you're sending out positive energy, and the universe starts helping you make your dreams come true, one little step at a time!

When you feel like you can't do something, try this powerful activity to shift your mindset: First, think about the challenge you're facing. Then, tell at least five people, "I can do this, and I will do it." Speak with confidence and belief in yourself. Each time you say it, you're reinforcing the idea in your subconscious that you have the ability to succeed. By vocalizing your intent, you not only boost your own confidence but also send out positive energy into the world. The more you do this, the more you'll convince yourself that you're capable, and you'll begin to feel empowered to take the necessary steps toward your goal.

This simple act of sharing your belief will help align your thoughts and actions with the success you're striving for.

PART 2

THE ART OF ATTRACTING
YOUR DESIRED LIFE

Dear Readers,

In this part, I will teach you how to attract your dream life by working on your internal world. The Law of Attraction is all about aligning your thoughts, beliefs, and actions to match the life you desire. When you change your internal dialogue and focus on positivity and abundance, you start to vibrate at a frequency that attracts those very things into your life. A powerful tool in this process is practicing gratitude. By regularly acknowledging and appreciating what you already have, you increase your vibration and draw more of what you want into your reality. Remember, your internal world shapes your external one - transform the inside, and the outside will follow.

14

THE POWER OF ALIGNMENT

"Stop waiting for life to happen - everything you need to create the life you desire is already within your reach. Align your thoughts, beliefs, and actions, and watch how effortlessly you attract the love, health, success, and abundance you deserve." – Tony Robbins

Welcome to the Next Level

Imagine waking up one day and realizing that everything you've been waiting for - success, love, abundance, fulfillment - has been within your reach all along. What if the key wasn't out there, but inside you? For most of us, life feels like a waiting game. "When I get that promotion, then I'll feel successful." "Once I find the perfect partner, then I'll feel loved." "When I have more money, then I'll feel secure." But here's the truth: You don't need to wait anymore. Everything you desire is already available to you. The only thing standing between you and the life you want is your frequency - the energy you emit. And the secret to unlocking it? Aligning your thoughts, beliefs, and actions (FTBA) with what you desire. When you align, you stop chasing. Instead, you start attracting. Success, health, wealth, love - they all begin to flow effortlessly when your frequency matches them.

The Shift That Changed Everything

Have you ever noticed how the right things start falling into place when you're in sync with yourself? It's like tuning a guitar - when the strings are aligned, the music flows effortlessly. But when they're out of tune, no matter how hard you try, the sound feels off. That's exactly how life works. Your thoughts, emotions, and energy create your frequency.

If you're tuned into self-doubt, fear, or exhaustion, that's what you'll keep attracting. But the moment you shift - aligning yourself with confidence, joy, and success - you become unstoppable. I remember a time when I felt completely out of alignment. Not just tired from work, but drained for no reason. My body felt like a stranger to me - uncomfortable, restless, almost like I didn't belong in my own skin. It wasn't just physical. I felt unloved, unnoticed, and far from the person I wanted to be. Then one day, I made a small but powerful change. Instead of focusing on what was wrong, I started focusing on what I wanted. But not as a wish - as if it was already true. I stood in front of the mirror and said:

"I am already happy."

"I am already healthy."

"I love my body."

Was it true at that moment? No. But something interesting happened - my mind started searching for proof. Instead of saying, *"I want to be loved,"* I declared, *"I am deeply loved and desirable."* Instead of saying, *"I want to be India's best speaker,"* I told the universe, *"I AM already that."*

Living Your Future, Now

This practice is called future-pacing - living and thinking as if your dream life is already here. It's not just about manifestation; it's about aligning yourself so deeply with your desires that they have no choice but to become reality.

The moment I started embodying the version of me that I wanted to be, everything changed. My confidence grew, opportunities flowed in, and I started seeing the love and success I once thought were missing. And here's the truth: *the universe isn't waiting to give you what you want - it's waiting for you to align with it.* So, what if you stopped waiting and started being?

What if, instead of saying *"I want to be successful,"* you said, *"I AM already successful"* - and let the world catch up? Tune into the right frequency, and watch how fast your reality shifts.

The Frequency Formula: Thoughts, Beliefs, and Actions

Everything in life operates on a frequency. And your personal frequency is shaped by three powerful forces: your thoughts, beliefs, and actions. These are not just abstract concepts - they are the very foundation of your reality.

1. Thoughts: The Spark of Energy

Your thoughts set the foundation for your frequency.

They are the initial seeds of your reality.

But here's the challenge: thoughts alone are weak. They flicker in and out of your mind, shifting constantly, often without leaving a lasting impact. For example, you might think, *"I want to be wealthy."* But if that thought isn't reinforced by a belief and supported by action, it will fade away.

Think of your thoughts as sparks.

They can ignite a fire - but without fuel, they fizzle out.

2. Beliefs: The Foundation of Frequency

Beliefs, on the other hand, are solid. They shape how you perceive the world and determine your actions. A strong belief acts like an anchor, rooting you in a certain frequency. If you believe, "I am worthy of wealth, love, and health," you'll start to see those things manifest. But limiting beliefs - like "I'll never be successful" or "Love isn't meant for me" - are silent blockers, keeping you stuck in a negative frequency. A fleeting opinion becomes a belief when you hold onto it so tightly that it starts dictating your reality. The question is: Are your beliefs serving you, or are they holding you back?

3. Actions: The Amplifier of Energy

Actions take your thoughts and beliefs from the invisible to the tangible. They transform intention into reality. Without action, even the strongest belief remains just a theory. Let's say you believe you can be healthy. But if you never exercise or fuel your body with nourishing food, that belief won't materialize. Your frequency remains out of sync. When you take inspired action - when your beliefs match your actions - you create momentum. You align with the very things you desire. In essence, by aligning your thoughts, beliefs, and actions with the reality you aspire to, you transform your internal state, which in turn influences your external circumstances.

This alignment fosters a powerful synergy that propels you toward your desired future, making your goals not just possibilities but inevitable outcomes.

15

THE LAW OF ATTRACTION: UNLOCK YOUR POWER

"Thoughts become things. If you see it in your mind, you will hold it in your hand."   - Bob Proctor

Imagine this for a moment: You're in a world where your frequency determines everything. You're the radio station, and whatever you tune into, you attract. If your frequency is "worried," you might attract some mind-bending success. If your frequency is drenched in negativity, oh, well, buckle up - it's about to be a bumpy, drama-filled ride. But wait...where's the magical "button" to change your frequency? Is there a switch somewhere that lets you flip from "stressed and chaotic" to "chill and abundant"? Spoiler alert: No, there's no actual button. But, funnily enough, if you believe in the Law of Attraction and your energy aligns with what you want, maybe, just maybe, you *are* the button.

Let's take a sarcastic detour to explore this. So, you're stressed out, worried about every little thing, questioning whether or not your life is a dumpster fire. And guess what? According to the "Law of Attraction," this high-level worry frequency is the one thing you need to start attracting **success**. Yes, you read that right. Want to feel overwhelmed with deadlines? Want to barely sleep at night? Keep your mind in a constant loop of stress and "what-ifs," and success will simply fall into your lap. The story of my first trophy was special, but let me take you deeper into the magic of how I went from winning just one to over thirty in such a short span of time. Let's rewind a little - back to that unforgettable stage moment.

Victory Is All Yours:

When I first set my eyes on the trophy, it wasn't just a piece of metal or glass to me. No, it felt like the trophy itself was speaking to me, telling me, *"This is just the beginning. There are many more to come."* And, you know what? That's exactly how it felt. It wasn't just about this single win - it was about the potential of what was yet to come. I remember the exact spot where I placed that first trophy in my home. I made it a sacred place, right in the center, so I could look at it every single day. Each time I glanced at it, a smile would involuntarily spread across my face. It reminded me of that moment I ran towards the stage, almost leaving my partner behind. That was a moment of pure excitement, pure accomplishment. But more than that, it was a reminder that I could do it.

And I *would* do it again, and again, and again. That trophy became my mantra. I held it at least once a day, and sometimes, I'd stand in front of the mirror, imagining myself winning even more trophies, delivering thank you speeches, and feeling the rush of victory all over again. And what if I told you that I truly manifested this? Everything in life has a frequency, including our thoughts, feelings, and actions. When we raise our frequency by thinking positively and focusing on what we want, we start to attract the things we desire. Imagine you are tuning a radio. If you tune into a station playing your favorite music, you enjoy the music. Likewise, when you tune your thoughts to positive ones, you start attracting more positivity into your life. Let's look at an example: A person living with a mindset of lack - believing that they will never have enough money - is sending out a low frequency. I could give this person money, but if their frequency doesn't change, their situation won't improve.

However, if this person shifts their mindset and raises their frequency to one of abundance and belief in opportunities, they start attracting new chances to grow their wealth. The universe begins to respond with new ideas and opportunities that match their higher frequency.

The Four Laws of the Law of Attraction

The Law of Attraction is built on four basic laws:

1. **Everything is made of energy.**

At the core, everything around us - whether it's physical objects, people, or thoughts - is made of energy. Even our emotions are energy. Everything is connected by this energy.

2. **Energy has frequency.**

Each type of energy has a frequency. Positive energy has a higher frequency, and negative energy has a lower frequency. By changing our thoughts and emotions, we can shift our frequency to match the frequency of what we want to attract.

3. **Energy cannot be created or destroyed.**

Energy can only be transformed. We can't create or destroy it, but we can change its form. Our thoughts and feelings are energy, and by changing our thoughts, we change the energy we put out into the world.

4. **When energy matches frequency, attraction happens automatically.**

When your energy matches the frequency of what you want, things begin to come into your life effortlessly. You no longer have to chase after what you want. The universe will bring it to you when you are in alignment with its frequency. I used to be the person who'd always complain about how "bad luck" followed me around. I'd look at others and think, *"Why does everyone else seem to have it easy?"* My bank account was constantly empty, and no matter what I did, I just couldn't seem to attract the things I wanted. My mindset was all about lack - *there's never enough.* I was living on a low frequency, just like a dull radio channel that only picks up static.

Success Begins in the Mind

It sounds almost too simple, doesn't it? To stand there, imagining, believing. But that's the secret. By holding the trophy in my mind and in my hands, I was putting my energy into a vision of success. I wasn't just admiring it - I was aligning my thoughts, my emotions, and my actions with it. I believed that more trophies would come, and the universe, in its mysterious ways, delivered them. Each time I imagined holding the trophy and giving my speech, I was laying the groundwork for the next step of my journey.

I was sending out signals to the universe, telling it, "I am ready for more. I deserve more." And the universe responded. Slowly, but surely, more and more trophies started to appear. There's something powerful in the act of *truly believing* in your dreams. When you start seeing your success in your mind before it happens in real life, you begin to vibrate at a frequency that matches your desires. And when that happens, the universe aligns, people appear, opportunities arise, and you start to walk down a path where everything seems to just *click* into place. So, from that first trophy, I kept going. And every time I held a new one in my hands, I felt that same wave of joy, excitement, and fulfillment. It was the same feeling as that first win, but now magnified.

I knew that with every single one, I was closer to becoming the person I had always dreamed of. And here's the beauty of it all: What started with just one trophy has now become a symbol of my journey, a journey that was built on belief, hard work, and manifestation. Every time I saw that trophy, I didn't just see a symbol of victory - I saw the power of my own potential. And that power? It's something we all have, waiting to be unlocked, The Power of Law of Attraction. As they say, "What you think, you become."

Your thoughts are your blueprint, and the Law of Attraction is the tool that helps bring your blueprint to life. So, keep thinking big, visualize often, and trust that the universe is always on your side. Your success story is just waiting to unfold.

Enough Is Enough!

Then, one day, I decided, *enough is enough!* I switched my mindset like flipping a switch on a lightbulb. I started focusing on abundance. I told myself, *"I deserve more. There's enough for everyone, and I am ready to receive!"* It felt like a big, bold move, but I pushed through with a little more confidence and a whole lot of faith. Guess what happened? Things started to shift! It was like the universe was listening and saying, *"Oh, you're finally tuned in!"* Out of nowhere, I started getting invites to speak at events, offers for collaborations, and even unexpected opportunities for extra income. I went from having little to suddenly seeing new opportunities pop up everywhere - like I had unlocked a secret door. My bank account slowly started to reflect that new frequency. I wasn't just receiving money; I was attracting abundance, success, and even great relationships! The more I focused on the positive, the more the universe threw good things my way. It was like I was in a grocery store and everything I wanted was on sale - right there, ready for me to grab. Imagine you have a magic wand in your hand. This wand is very special because it can make anything you want happen. But here's the secret: the magic wand can only work if you really, really believe what you want.

Now, think of yourself like a big, magical drawing board, a blank piece of paper. Every time you think about something, your thoughts are like a drawing that gets made on your paper. If you think happy thoughts, bright, fun colors will appear on your paper. But if you think sad or worried thoughts, the paper gets filled with dark, unhappy colors.

It All Starts from a Single Thought

Your magic wand - just like the universe - listens to your thoughts. If you think "I can do this!" the wand makes sure things start happening to help you. It brings good things, like happy moments, new friends, or fun surprises. But if you say, "I can't," the wand might not bring anything, because the wand only listens when you believe you can have what you want. Every time you think good thoughts, the magic wand starts working to bring them to life. If you want to be the best at something, like playing a game or drawing, you tell your wand "I can be great at this!" and the wand will help you. So, the secret is: if you want something, believe you can have it and tell your magic wand. The wand listens to you, and when you think happy and good thoughts, the wand makes those dreams come true on your paper!

Success Unfolding

Success isn't about luck or circumstance; it's about unlocking the power of your mindset. When you align your thoughts with your goals and believe in your ability to achieve, everything begins to shift. The universe starts responding to your energy, and what once seemed impossible begins to feel within reach. The journey to success begins with a simple shift in perspective - replacing doubt with belief and fear with determination. Manifestation doesn't have to be perfect in the beginning. The first attempt might feel small, even insignificant - a fleeting thought or a casual affirmation. But here's the beauty of it: even imperfect steps create momentum. Slowly, as you practice aligning your thoughts and actions, you gain clarity and confidence. Your goals become more tangible, and the small victories along the way reinforce your belief in the process. This growth transforms your mindset from simply hoping for success to actively creating it.

The LoA Rule

The Law of Attraction plays a crucial role here. Your thoughts act as a magnet, attracting experiences, people, and opportunities that resonate with your energy. When you focus on abundance, gratitude, and joy, the universe mirrors these emotions back to you. Challenges become opportunities, failures turn into lessons, and you begin to feel a sense of flow in your journey. It's not magic - it's the result of a mindset grounded in positivity and intentional action. Success is a journey, not a destination. Each step you take, no matter how small, shapes your reality and brings you closer to the life you've always envisioned. So why wait? Begin with a single affirmation: "I can achieve this." Carry that belief with you every day, and watch as the universe responds to your unwavering faith and determination. Your success story is already in motion - make it extraordinary.

The Magic of Manifestation and the Law of Attraction

What we once thought of as magic is often understood today as science. Many things that were once impossible are now possible, and what we consider magic today could very well be proven science in the future. The Law of Attraction (LOA) is a perfect example of this. While it may seem magical, it is actually based on the science of energy and frequency. When we talk about manifestation, we are referring to the act of bringing our desires into reality by focusing on them with positive energy. The Law of Attraction works on the idea that like attracts like. So, when we focus on positive thoughts and emotions, we attract positive experiences. This means that to bring health, wealth, relationships, and success into our lives, we need to raise our frequency to match the energy of these desires.

Why Trust the Law of Attraction?

Trusting the Law of Attraction is essential because it helps us understand how our thoughts shape our reality. Think about how you don't question whether brushing your teeth is good for your oral health. You do it because you trust that it works, even though the benefits aren't immediately visible. In the same way, when you trust that changing your energy and thoughts will bring you the life you want, you start to see results, even if they don't appear instantly.

16

THE ART OF FREQUENCY TUNING

"Match the frequency of the reality you want and you cannot help but get that reality." - Albert Einstein

Frequency: A Lesson in Attraction

Let's get this straight:

When you're vibrating at a frequency of anxiousness, you might not be ready for peace, but hey, according to the law, success will find its way to you anyway. It's kind of like ordering a pizza while complaining about your favorite toppings being out of stock, but then being surprised when you get delivered an extra-large with every single topping you said you didn't want.

"Success," just like that pizza, is delivered... even if you're not in the mood for it. Oh, the irony. So, the next time you find yourself spiraling, remember - just stay anxious, and apparently, the universe will sort out your success. But do tell me, where's the option for "calm and composed"? Maybe success doesn't come with a "pause button" for when you're ready to catch your breath.

How a Negative Frequency Attracts... Well, Negative People

Let's talk about negativity. You know, the kind of energy that's just so thick, it could be spread with a spatula. If your internal frequency is low, guess what? You're going to attract people who match that frequency. Birds of a feather and all that, right? So, let's say you're walking around with a "woe is me" mindset, your thoughts filled with complaints about the traffic, the weather, your job, or how nothing ever goes your way.

Well, don't be surprised when you start attracting people who think exactly the same way. Misery loves company, and if you're tuned into that frequency of doom and gloom, you'll become a magnet for other miserable souls. Think of it like this: If you walk around with a big, visible sign on your forehead that says, "I hate everything," you're going to attract people who also hate everything.

You'll be in great company. You'll find yourself forming a little "club of complaints" where the only thing you discuss is how everything is going wrong and how life is always unfair. But hold on - what if you *weren't* tuning into negativity? What if your frequency was set to "positive vibes only"? Wouldn't that make a difference? Well, if your vibe is genuinely upbeat, you'll start attracting people who uplift you, who are optimistic and excited about life. But, in the world of the Law of Attraction, where there's light, there's always... well, a shadow. Negative energy isn't going anywhere - unless you do a little bit of soul work.

Example: The Radio Road of Frequency Alignment

Let's break this down further with a little (sarcastic) analogy. Imagine you're standing at the "Radio Road of Life," trying to tune into your frequency station. You're holding the dial, but instead of tuning it to a station that plays something positive and uplifting, you're kind of... doing the opposite. Let's say you're walking down a road, shoes in hand, and suddenly you spot a pile of... well, gobar (cow dung). Now, if you're "vibrating" at a frequency of "bullshit," guess what happens next? You step right into that gobar. But here's the kicker - just because you stepped in it doesn't mean you've made an automatic decision to walk toward prosperity, right?

If you're still holding onto that frequency of "gobar," don't be surprised when you start attracting more piles of... you know what. If your internal dial is tuned to the crap of life, you will *literally* attract more crap. You can't sit there thinking that by dwelling in negativity, suddenly roses will blossom around you. If you're looking for success or abundance, roses are not going to bloom in the middle of your self-created shitstorm. Sure, you might wish for a garden of roses while standing knee-deep in muck, but unless you decide to change your frequency and step out of that mess, you'll keep attracting... well, more of the same. The question is, when will you change the dial to something that *actually* serves your highest good?

Where's the Button to Change My Frequency?

So, here's the million-dollar question: *Where's the button to change my frequency?* I mean, if it's all about tuning into a better vibe, shouldn't there be a simple "reset" button that you can push when your frequency gets stuck on "bullshit" mode? Well, spoiler alert: There is no button.

There's no magic wand to wave, and there's no "easy fix" for adjusting your frequency. But here's the good news: *You* are the button. You hold the power to adjust your frequency at any given moment, and that power lies in the decisions you make, the thoughts you entertain, and the actions you take. You can change your vibration anytime - you just need to be willing to make the shift. When you recognize that your frequency is low - whether from negative self-talk, worry, or doubt - acknowledge it. Own it. And then make the conscious decision to change it. Start by focusing on positive thoughts, practicing gratitude, and choosing thoughts that align with the kind of life you want to live.

Frequency is Everything

At the end of the day, the frequency you put out into the world is exactly what you'll get back. If your mind is filled with worry, negativity, or self-doubt, you will attract more of that into your life. If you constantly complain, "Nothing ever goes right for me," don't be surprised when everything around you starts falling apart.

On the flip side, when you align yourself with positivity, abundance, and success, your world will begin to shift to reflect those higher vibrations. But here's the twist: You *can't* expect to change your frequency overnight without actively tuning it to something better. You can't step in gobar and then wonder why roses aren't growing in your path. The work lies in your ability to consistently choose higher vibes, in your thoughts, emotions, and actions. There is no "button," but there is a dial - and you are the one holding it. So, if you're tired of attracting the same old mess, take a deep breath, tune your frequency, and watch as the universe starts bringing you exactly what you've been waiting for.

Mastering the Art of Frequency Shifting

If frequency determines reality, then why do most people stay stuck? The answer is simple - they don't take control of the dial. They wait, hoping that someday the right opportunity, the right mindset, or the right circumstances will magically align. But here's the truth: waiting is a trap. Tony Robbins says, "It is in your moments of decision that your destiny is shaped." That means the shift doesn't happen when the universe suddenly hands you a perfect life. It happens the moment you decide to shift - when you stop identifying as a victim and start acting like the creator of your own story.

Sandeep Maheshwari often talks about "Aasaan hai" (It's easy), but not in the way people think. It's not that life is easy - it's that you can choose to make things easier by aligning yourself with the right mindset. When you let go of the resistance, when you accept where you are and take action toward where you want to be, suddenly, what once seemed impossible starts feeling natural. But let's be real - shifting your frequency isn't always a smooth ride. Some days, your mind will fight back. You'll have doubts. You'll feel resistance. You might even find yourself slipping back into negativity. That's okay. The key isn't perfection - it's awareness and redirection.

The Three-Step Shift: How to Tune into a Better Frequency

Interrupt the Pattern: Every negative emotion follows a predictable pattern. The first step is to catch yourself. Are you spiraling into worry? Complaining about the same problems? Repeating the same limiting beliefs? The moment you recognize it, break the cycle - stand up, take a deep breath, go for a walk, or even do something as simple as clapping your hands to snap yourself out of the loop.

Rewire the Story: Your brain is constantly narrating your life. The problem is, most people let that narration be driven by fear, doubt, or past failures. Flip the script. Instead of "Nothing ever works out for me," start saying, "Everything is working in my favor, even if I can't see it yet." Sounds simple? It is. And yet, it's one of the most powerful shifts you can make.

Take Inspired Action: Shifting your energy isn't just about thinking differently it's about doing differently. Success isn't about motivation; it's about momentum.

Start with one small action that aligns with the frequency you want.

Want abundance? Give generously. Want love? Be love. Want success? Start acting like the person who is already successful.

The Secret Sauce: Emotional Mastery

Tony Robbins refers to this as "peak state" - the practice of taking control of your emotions rather than letting them control you. Your frequency is directly linked to how you feel, and how you feel is something you can influence. The key lies in your physiology. Emotions are closely tied to physical state. For instance, a person feeling sad may slouch, breathe shallowly, and exhibit low energy, while a confident individual stands tall, breathes deeply, and exudes vitality.

To alter your frequency, start by changing your physical state:

- Stand up straight.
- Breathe deeply.
- Move with energy.
- Speak with conviction.

Try it now: adjust your posture, take a deep breath, and notice the immediate difference. This isn't magic - it's neuroscience. Your body sends signals to your brain about how to feel, and your brain adjusts your frequency accordingly.

The Law of Alignment: The Missing Piece in the Manifestation Puzzle

Many discuss the Law of Attraction, focusing on drawing desires toward oneself. However, the Law of Alignment emphasizes becoming the person who naturally attracts those desires. To attract wealth, align with the frequency of abundance, not desperation. For love, embody self-worth rather than neediness. Success comes from exuding confidence, not hesitation. Consider: who is more likely to seize opportunities - the individual doubting themselves or the one radiating assurance? The universe responds to your state of being, not merely your wishes.

The Choice Is Yours. - So, here's the question: Are you going to keep tuning into the same old frequency, attracting the same results, or are you ready to shift? Because the truth is, you are the dial. You've always been. And the moment you decide to turn it toward a higher frequency - the moment you stop reacting to life and start creating it - everything changes.

17

THE ART OF ALIGNMENT

"You don't attract what you want. You attract what you are."
Wayne Dyer

Once you understand the FTBA formula, you realize that you already have everything you need to create the life you want. Success, love, abundance - it's not something you chase. It's something you align with. Many people live as if they are in a constant state of waiting. Waiting for the perfect moment. Waiting for a sign. But the moment you align your thoughts, beliefs, and actions, you stop waiting. You step into your power. You are not searching for a missing puzzle piece - you are the puzzle. You don't need to wait for success to show up. You don't need to wait for love to find you.

You already have it.

Love: It's Already Inside You

So many people think, "I'll feel loved once I meet the right person." But love isn't something external - it's a frequency you emit. When you truly love yourself, you send out that energy, and it comes back to you in abundance. Align your thoughts ("I am worthy of love"), beliefs ("I deserve deep, fulfilling relationships"), and actions (self-care, openness to connection), and love flows to you effortlessly.

Health: You're Not Chasing It, You're Embodying It

Health isn't something you struggle for. It's an energy. If you constantly think, "I'm always tired," your body will respond to that frequency. But when you align your thoughts ("My body is strong"), beliefs ("I deserve to feel good"), and actions (healthy habits), health becomes second nature. You're not fighting for it - you are it.

Success Isn't External: It's Internal

Most people think success is something external -achievements, money, recognition. But real success starts inside. When you align your energy with success, it doesn't matter what the world says. You already are successful because you own that energy. Ever noticed how when you're in a negative headspace, everything seems to go wrong? That's because your energy is attracting more negativity. But when you shift your frequency - when you think and act like someone who is successful - success starts showing up effortlessly.

Dancing with the Flow of Life

Now that you understand alignment, it's time to embrace the rhythm of life. Imagine your life as a dance - one where every step is guided by the energy you radiate. When your thoughts, beliefs, and actions are in harmony, the dance becomes effortless. You're no longer resisting. You're flowing. Like any great dancer, you must practice. The more you align, the more natural it becomes. Soon, you'll find yourself in sync with the very pulse of the universe.

Turning Up the Volume on Your Energy

To keep the flow going, turn up the volume on your frequency.

Imagine you're tuning into a radio station that plays success, love, and abundance 24/7. The more you align, the stronger your signal.

Think Big -

- Dream as if the world is already at your feet.
- Believe with Unshakable Confidence
- Your belief system is the foundation of everything you create.
- Take Inspired Action
- Move boldly in the direction of your desires.

Let Go of the Need to Control

Life has a natural rhythm, an invisible current that carries us forward. But so often, we resist it. We fight against it, trying to force outcomes, micromanage every detail, and predict every twist and turn. The harder we try to control life, the more exhausted we become. True freedom, however, comes when we learn to let go. Imagine floating down a river. The water knows its course - it flows smoothly, sometimes gently, sometimes swiftly, but always moving forward. Now picture yourself in that river, but instead of relaxing into the current, you're paddling furiously against it, trying to steer it in a direction it was never meant to go.

That's what controlling every aspect of life feels like. It's exhausting, frustrating, and ultimately ineffective. Letting go doesn't mean giving up or being passive. It doesn't mean abandoning your dreams or letting life simply "happen" to you. It means trusting that things are unfolding as they should. It means recognizing that you don't have to force everything into place - sometimes, the best things come when you step back and allow them to find you.

The Invisible Power!

There was a time in my life when I tried to control everything - my work, my relationships, my future. I thought that if I just worked harder, thought more, planned more, I could make life bend to my will. But all that control only left me feeling drained. The turning point came when I finally let go. I stopped obsessing over every detail and allowed life to flow. And that's when things truly began to change. Suddenly, opportunities started appearing effortlessly.

Conversations felt more natural. The stress that had once weighed me down began to lift. I realized that life wasn't against me - it had been waiting for me to align with it. The more I trusted the flow, the more I noticed the beauty in the small, imperfect moments. Letting go is not about losing power; it's about gaining freedom. It's about shifting from fear to trust, from struggle to ease. When you release the need to control, you make space for better things - things beyond what you could have ever planned. Life becomes lighter, and you start experiencing joy, not because everything is perfect, but because you've stopped resisting the imperfections. So, take a deep breath. Let go of the need to force things. Trust that life is carrying you exactly where you're meant to be.

Celebrate Every Step

Every moment of alignment is a moment worth celebrating. Progress, not perfection, is the goal. The universe responds to the energy you put out - so celebrate your wins, big or small. What once felt impossible will start happening effortlessly. That's the magic of alignment at work. I used to be caught up in a cycle of waiting. Waiting for the perfect moment, the perfect achievement, the perfect version of myself before I allowed myself to feel joy. But life doesn't work that way. One day, I asked myself - what if I started treating every little step forward as a victory?

What if I stopped waiting for some grand milestone and simply celebrated my journey, as raw and imperfect as it was? So, I made a shift. Instead of criticizing myself for not being 'there' yet, I began appreciating where I was. I decided to reward myself for showing up, no matter how small the step seemed. Some days, it was as simple as telling myself, "You did great today" and enjoying my favorite chocolate as a treat. Other days, it was about allowing myself to take a break without guilt - maybe watching a movie I loved or going for a walk with no agenda other than to breathe and exist.

Fake It till You Make it!

I remember a time when my body felt uncomfortable, like I was out of place in my own skin. It wasn't just about work; it was a deeper, more unsettling feeling. I didn't understand why I felt that way, but I knew I didn't want to stay stuck in it. That's when I started affirming, "I am already happy. I am already healthy. I am in love with my body."

Did I believe it at first?

Not entirely.

But I kept repeating it.

And with each repetition, something shifted. Instead of fixating on what wasn't working, I began focusing on the reality I wanted to create. I started living as if those affirmations were true, and soon, they became my truth. Instead of seeking love outside of myself, I affirmed, "I am loved. I am desirable enough to be loved by all." I stopped saying, "I want to be the best speaker in India," and instead declared, "I already am."

That's the power of celebrating every step. When you acknowledge and reward your progress, you create momentum. The universe sees your joy, your gratitude, and it responds by giving you more reasons to celebrate. Alignment isn't about reaching a final destination - it's about embracing the journey, trusting the process, and knowing that every small step counts. So, celebrate yourself today. Not for being perfect, but for showing up, for trying, for believing - even when it's hard. The more you acknowledge your progress, the more effortless your growth becomes. That's the magic of alignment at work.

18

THE FREQUENCY OF LOVE

"You yourself, as much as anybody in the entire universe, deserve your love and affection." - Buddha

For the longest time, I believed that love was something other people had - something I wasn't worthy of. It started in school. I was the girl who never got invited to sleepovers, the one who sat alone at lunch, watching groups of friends laugh over inside jokes I wasn't a part of. I told myself it was fine. I convinced myself I liked solitude. But deep down, it chipped away at me. Then came high school, where having a boyfriend wasn't just a status symbol - it was validation. If someone loved you, you mattered. If someone wanted you, you were beautiful, special, worthy. But me? I was the girl who watched from the sidelines. No love notes in my locker, no stolen glances in the hallways, no one nervously asking for my number. I laughed it off with my friends, pretending I didn't care, but inside, a darker narrative formed: *If no one chooses me, maybe I'm not meant to be chosen.* This belief followed me into adulthood. I carried it like an invisible weight, allowing it to dictate how I saw myself. I craved love but never expected it to find me. My heart ached to be seen, but I hid behind self-deprecating jokes and an armor of indifference. And the worst part? I thought this was normal.

The Wake-Up Call: Love Starts with You

One day, I came across a quote that changed everything: *"Love recognizes no barriers. It jumps hurdles, leaps fences, penetrates walls to arrive at its destination full of hope."* - Maya Angelou. For the first time, I asked myself - *What if love wasn't something I had to earn? What if it was already within me, waiting to be acknowledged?* I had spent years waiting for someone to give me love, to tell me I was enough. But love isn't a prize you win. It's a frequency you tune into. And I was vibrating at the frequency of lack, of unworthiness. So, I decided to shift. If love wasn't coming to find me, I was going to create it within myself.

Step 1: *Self-Love Isn't Just a Buzzword*

I started with the mirror. At first, it felt ridiculous. Standing in front of my reflection, saying things like, *"I am worthy of love. I am beautiful. I am enough."* My mind fought back. It whispered, *"But are you?"* The years of loneliness, of not being picked, of feeling invisible - they didn't disappear overnight. But I repeated the affirmations anyway.

Day after day, I spoke to myself with kindness. Instead of criticizing my body, I thanked it. Instead of replaying old wounds, I imagined a future where I was loved effortlessly. And slowly, my energy changed.

Step 2: *Breaking Free from* **Old** *Beliefs*

I realized that my belief system was the real barrier. I had been conditioned to think love was something given to you by others. But what if love was a state of being? What if I was already whole? I started questioning my past experiences. Maybe the kids at school weren't rejecting me - maybe they just had their own insecurities. Maybe the boys who never noticed me weren't proof of my unworthiness - maybe they just weren't my match. Perspective changed everything. I wasn't unloved; I was unaligned. And alignment begins with self-worth.

Step 3: *Seeing Love Everywhere*

I began looking at love differently. Instead of focusing on romantic love, I started noticing the love that already existed in my life. The friend who checked in on me. The barista who smiled and remembered my order. The stranger who held the door open. Love was all around me - I had just been too focused on what I *didn't* have to see it. I practiced gratitude every day, writing down three things that made me feel loved. It was a small shift, but it rewired my mind to see abundance instead of lack.

Step 4: *Attracting Love By Becoming Love*

One of the most powerful lessons I learned was this: You don't attract what you want. You attract what you are. When I was desperate for love, I repelled it. I came across as needy, insecure, always looking for external validation. But when I started living in a state of love - treating myself well, believing in my worth, radiating joy - everything changed. People were drawn to me in a way they never had been before. It wasn't about my looks or my status. It was my energy. I had stepped into the frequency of love, and love had no choice but to respond.

The Lesson: *Love Was Never Missing - It Was Waiting*

If I could go back and tell my younger self one thing, it would be this: You are not unlovable. You were never unlovable.

Love isn't something you chase -it's something you become.

And the moment you stop searching outside yourself and start embracing the love within, everything changes.

"Love is not something you earn.

It's something you embody. And when you do, it finds you in ways you never imagined."

19

HEALTH IS THE REAL WEALTH

"Health is not just about what you're eating. It's about what you're thinking and saying." - Richard Baker

Just Like Love, Health is a Frequency For the longest time, I struggled with my health. It wasn't anything drastic - just constant fatigue, bloating, low energy, and a sense that my body wasn't at its best. No matter how much I rested or what I ate, something always felt off. I had started accepting it as normal, convincing myself that maybe I was just built this way. But deep down, I knew there had to be another way. One day, I stumbled upon a simple yet powerful idea: just like love and money, health is also a frequency.

The way I thought about my body, the emotions I associated with it, and the beliefs I carried were shaping my physical reality. If I constantly told myself I was tired, my body would respond with exhaustion. If I believed I had a weak digestive system, my gut would obey that command. I realized I had been tuning into the wrong station. It was time to adjust my frequency to wellness.

Shift to Wellness: The Power of Mindset

The first thing I had to change was my perception of myself. I had spent years reinforcing the belief that my body was fragile. I'd say things like, "I always feel drained" or "My stomach is sensitive to everything." It was no surprise that my body reflected exactly what I believed.

So, I made a shift. I started telling myself a new story. Every morning, I would stand in front of the mirror and say, "I am healthy and strong. My body is resilient. I am full of energy." At first, it felt forced. A small, skeptical voice inside me whispered, "You're just saying words." But I kept going, repeating these affirmations until they didn't just sound true - they felt true.

Affirmations: Reprogramming My Health

Affirmations became my daily ritual. I didn't just say them; I embodied them. I imagined every cell in my body absorbing these words, aligning themselves with health and vitality. I told myself:

- "I am vibrant and full of life."

- "My body is a vessel of strength and healing."

- "Every part of me is thriving."

The more I repeated them, the more I started noticing small shifts. I woke up feeling a little lighter. My energy levels improved. My digestion felt more at ease. It was as if my body was finally receiving the message I had been sending it all along.

Visualize Health: See Yourself Thriving

One night, I took it a step further. I sat down, closed my eyes, and imagined the healthiest version of myself. I pictured myself waking up refreshed, feeling energized, moving through the day effortlessly. I saw myself eating my favorite foods without discomfort, my body processing everything with ease. I did this every night before bed. And something incredible happened. My body started catching up to the vision. The bloating became less frequent. My energy levels soared. My digestion improved. It was as if my body was aligning itself with the reality I had visualized.

Self-Care and Positive Habits: Aligning Actions with Health

Of course, mindset alone wasn't enough - I had to take action.

If I wanted to vibrate at the frequency of health,

I needed to back it up with daily habits that reinforced that energy.

1. **Eating Nutritious Foods** – Instead of focusing on what I "couldn't" eat, I started nourishing my body with foods that supported my healing. I embraced vibrant, whole foods - fresh fruits, leafy greens, lean proteins, and plenty of water. Every meal became a love letter to my body.

2. **Exercising Regularly** – Movement became my medicine. Whether it was yoga, a morning walk, or just stretching, I made sure to stay active. With every movement, I imagined my body growing stronger, more resilient.

3. **Getting Enough Rest** – I finally prioritized sleep. No more scrolling late at night, no more sacrificing rest for productivity. I created a nighttime routine - reading, journaling, deep breathing - to signal to my body that it was time to heal and restore.

4. **Practicing Relaxation** – Stress had been my silent enemy for too long. I made relaxation a priority. Deep breathing, meditation, even just taking a few minutes to be present - it all helped shift my body from a state of tension to one of healing.

Tuning Into Wellness

The more I committed to these changes, the more effortless they became. I realized that health wasn't something I had to chase - it was something I had to tune into. The same way I could turn a radio dial to find the right station,

I had to turn my mental and emotional dial to the frequency of wellness. It wasn't overnight magic. But little by little, my body transformed. I felt lighter, stronger, more alive than I had in years. And it all started with a decision - to see myself as healthy, to believe in my body's ability to heal, and to align my thoughts, emotions, and actions with that belief.

The Frequency of Healing: A Journey to Wellness

Looking back, I see that my body was never the problem. The problem was the frequency I had been operating on.

Once I tuned into health, everything changed. Now, whenever I feel out of balance, I don't panic.

I listen. I adjust. I return to the habits, the affirmations, the visualizations that realign me with health. Because I know now - wellness isn't something outside of me. It's already within me. It always was.

And if I can shift my frequency to health, so can you.

Do This Prayer today

Thank You Prayer for All My Body Parts

Dear Divine Creator,

I come before you with deep gratitude, acknowledging the miracle that is my body.

Thank you for my mind, which holds my thoughts, dreams, and wisdom, guiding me each day.

Thank you for my eyes, which open to the world and reveal its beauty in every moment.

I thank you for my ears, which allow me to hear the melodies, voices, and sounds that fill my life

Thank you for my nose, which helps me breathe and enjoy the scents of the earth.

I am grateful for my mouth, for enabling me to speak, eat, and express love and kindness.

Thank you for my teeth, which help me chew and break down nourishment for my body.

Thank you for my tongue, which lets me taste the food you provide and communicate with others.

I thank you for my neck and throat, allowing me to speak, swallow, and breathe with ease

Thank you for my shoulders, which support my body and help me carry burdens with strength

I appreciate my arms, hands, and fingers, which create, touch, and offer care to those around me

Thank you for my chest and ribs, which protect my heart and lungs, the center of my being

I am thankful for my heart, beating with love, pumping life through my veins.

Thank you for my lungs, which provide me with every breath, nourishing my body with air.

I thank you for my stomach, which processes and nourishes me with the food I take in.

Thank you for my liver, kidneys, and intestines, working tirelessly to detoxify and cleanse my body.

Thank you for my spine, which holds me upright, allowing me to stand tall and move freely.

I am grateful for my muscles, bones, and joints, giving me strength, stability, and flexibility.

Thank you for my legs, feet, and toes, which carry me through this life, grounding me with each step.

Thank you for my reproductive organs, which allow the continuation of life and the gift of creation.

I am thankful for my skin, which protects me, regulates my temperature, and connects me with the world.

Every part of me is a divine blessing, working in perfect harmony.

Thank you, Divine Creator, for my magical, sacred body. May I always honor, care for, and love it as you have lovingly designed *Amen.*

20

SUCCESS IS ALREADY YOURS

"The only limit to your impact is your imagination and commitment." - Tony Robbins

When I began my journey, there was one mantra I always followed: *success is my birthright*. I firmly believed that if I didn't succeed, no one else would be able to achieve it for me. So, I reprogrammed my mind to think and believe that if I didn't succeed, it wouldn't happen at all. I would erase all those limiting beliefs and the negative conditioning I had carried from my childhood. I would stand in front of the mirror and give myself a motivational speech, reminding myself, *you can do it*.

The words that I longed to hear from others, the ones that would calm my soul and push me forward, I began saying them to myself. This simple, yet powerful, practice became my daily ritual. I would look into my own eyes, as if I was speaking directly to my future self, telling myself that I was capable and deserving of everything I wanted to achieve. This became my way of increasing my self-love and confidence, guiding myself through every obstacle, and always choosing to believe in my own power.

The mirror technique not only boosted my self-esteem, but it also became a constant reminder that I was in control of my own destiny. The more I practiced it, the more it became ingrained in my belief system. I wasn't just waiting for validation from the outside world - I had learned to validate and encourage myself, which made all the difference in my growth.

The Frequency Shift: A Journey to Success

I had always wondered - why did success seem effortless for some while others struggled endlessly? Was it luck, hard work, or something beyond the visible? My journey into the world of mindset transformation began on a rainy evening when I stumbled upon the idea of tuning my frequency to success. It sounded mystical at first, but the more I explored, the more I realized - success was not just about talent or effort; it was about alignment. If I could shift my mindset, align my thoughts, and take inspired action, success would become inevitable. And so, I embarked on an experiment, using techniques that had transformed countless lives.

Future Pacing

Every morning, I stood before my mirror, looking deep into my own eyes. It wasn't just about vanity - it was about connection. I had read about the Mirror Technique, where one speaks affirmations with confidence, making the subconscious believe in their power.

With a determined gaze, I spoke:

- "I am worthy of success."

- "Success flows easily and effortlessly into my life."

- "I am confident, successful, and unstoppable."

At first, it felt awkward. But the more I did it, the more conviction I infused into those words. Slowly, my self-perception changed. I no longer saw someone *hoping* for success - I saw someone who *expected* it. And that expectation led to action.

The Power of Visualization: Living Success Before It Happens

I decided to take visualization seriously. Every night, I closed my eyes and imagined my future self - successful, confident, and fulfilled. I saw the emails congratulating me on my achievements, the phone calls offering incredible opportunities, the joy of standing in a place I once only dreamed of.

The key wasn't just seeing it - I had to feel it.

So, I let my emotions flow. I felt the exhilaration of success, the warmth of accomplishment, and the confidence of someone who had already *made it.* My mind couldn't tell the difference between imagination and reality, and soon, my actions began aligning with this new identity.

Inspired Action: The Missing Piece of the Puzzle

Shifting my mindset wasn't enough - I needed to act. But not just any action. I had to take inspired action - the kind that felt effortless, intuitive, and driven by belief rather than desperation. Instead of forcing myself into endless work with uncertainty, I started asking myself:

What would my successful self-do today?

Would they hesitate? No.

Would they wait for the perfect moment? Never.

Would they take bold, confident steps toward their goal?

Absolutely. I followed that guidance.

Each day, I took one step - one phone call, one proposal, one courageous decision. And each step built momentum. Opportunities that once seemed distant started appearing effortlessly.

Tuning into Success: The Frequency Shift

I realized that just like a radio needs to be tuned to the right station, my mind needed to be tuned to the frequency of success. Negative thoughts? I replaced them with affirmations. Self-doubt? I drowned it with visualization. Hesitation? I countered it with inspired action.

The result?

A complete transformation. I was no longer someone *trying* to be successful - I was already successful in my mindset, and reality had no choice but to catch up. Doors that once seemed locked flung open. Conversations turned into collaborations. Dreams turned into reality.

Conclusion: The Inevitable Success

Success was never a distant dream - it was always within me, waiting to be unlocked. By shifting my mindset, aligning with the frequency of success, and taking action from a place of belief, I had rewritten my story. The best part? Anyone can do it. Success is not about chance; it's about choice. Tune into the right frequency, and the universe will respond.

Your success is waiting.

Are you ready to align with it?

21

THE ABUNDANCE MINDSET

"Abundance is not something we acquire. It is something we tune into." - Wayne Dyer

I had always believed that money was hard to come by. Growing up, I had heard phrases like "Money doesn't grow on trees" and "You have to work endlessly to be rich." These beliefs settled deep into my subconscious, shaping how I approached life and finances. But then, everything changed when I decided to shift my perspective and embrace an abundance mindset.

Shifting to Abundance

One evening, as I sat on my couch scrolling through social media, I stumbled upon a video about the Law of Attraction. The speaker talked about money as energy - something that flows to those who align with it. I was intrigued. Could my financial struggles be a reflection of my inner beliefs? Determined to test this theory, I began by identifying my limiting beliefs. I wrote down every negative thought I had about money:

- "I will never be rich."

- "Making money is exhausting."

- "Wealth is only for lucky people."

Once these thoughts were on paper, they seemed absurd. Who said wealth was only for the lucky? Who decided money was scarce? The only person holding me back was me. So, I made a commitment - to change my mindset and reprogram my beliefs.

Affirmations: Reprogramming My Mind for Wealth

Each morning, I stood in front of the mirror and spoke affirmations aloud.

- "I am open to receiving money."

- "Wealth flows easily and effortlessly to me."

- "I deserve and welcome financial prosperity."

At first, it felt awkward, as if I was lying to myself. But after a week, something strange happened. My energy shifted. I started feeling lighter, more optimistic. The negativity I once

associated with money began to fade. I realized that affirmations weren't just words - they were commands to my subconscious.

Visualizing Prosperity: Seeing to Believe It

One night, I sat quietly, closed my eyes, and imagined my ideal financial future. I pictured myself paying my bills with ease, booking first-class flights, and even surprising my family with generous gifts. The key wasn't just seeing it - it was feeling it. I imagined holding a check with my name on it, feeling the weight of crisp bills in my hands, experiencing the joy of financial freedom. The emotions were powerful. I was tuning into the vibration of abundance. The next morning, I felt a surge of motivation. Something inside me had shifted - I was ready to take inspired action.

Taking Inspired Action

While mindset shifts were crucial, I knew that action was equally important. So, I asked myself, "What can I do right now to move closer to financial abundance?"

I took four key steps:

1. Improving My Skills

I enrolled in an online course to enhance my expertise. The more valuable I became, the more opportunities would come my way.

2. Creating Opportunities

Instead of waiting for success, I created it. I started freelancing, networking, and even working on a side project that aligned with my passions.

3. Budgeting Wisely

I tracked every dollar I spent and created a financial plan that helped me save, invest, and grow my wealth.

4. Investing in Myself

I prioritized self-growth - reading books, attending seminars, and surrounding myself with successful individuals who had an abundance mindset.

As I took action, things started changing. I landed new clients effortlessly. Unexpected financial opportunities appeared. Money, which once felt distant, began flowing easily into my life.

Money Flowing with Ease

One day, I received an email - an unexpected bonus from work. The very next week, a friend referred me to a high-paying project. Coincidence? Not at all. I had shifted my energy, and the universe was responding. I no longer saw money as something scarce. Instead, I viewed it as an endless resource, circulating freely and coming to me in ways I could never have imagined.

The Universal Manifestation Cheque

Excited by my transformation, I decided to try one last experiment. I took out a blank check and filled it out:

- Pay to the order of: *My Name*

- Amount: *₹1,00,00,000* (or any amount I desired)

- Memo: *For achieving my financial dreams*

- Signed by: *The Universe*

I placed the check in my wallet and looked at it daily, imagining the moment I would cash it. It wasn't about the money itself - it was about aligning my energy with financial abundance.

Energy Exercise for Success An

To reinforce my new mindset, I developed a daily energy alignment exercise:

1. Placing my right hand over my heart, I closed my eyes and affirmed, *"All is well."*

2. With my left hand, I traced the arc of a rainbow, saying, *"Life is magic."*

3. I clenched my left fist, then drew it down with force, declaring, *"I am unstoppable."*

This practice filled me with confidence and strengthened my belief in abundance.

Conclusion: The Abundance Mindset

By rewiring my beliefs, taking inspired action, and aligning my energy with prosperity, I transformed my relationship with money.

It no longer felt like a struggle but flowed naturally into my life. The key lesson I learned is that abundance begins within. When you shift your mindset, the world shifts with you. Wealth isn't reserved for the lucky or chosen few; it's available to anyone willing to attune to it.

Today, I encourage you to embrace abundance. Speak affirmations, visualize your wealth, take inspired actions, and trust that the universe is working in your favor.

You are worthy of financial freedom.

You deserve prosperity.

Most importantly, you are abundant.

22

THE SECRET WEAPON OF SUCCESS

"Success isn't always about greatness. It's about consistency. Consistent hard work leads to success. Greatness will come."

-by Dwayne Johnson

I still remember the first time I whispered an affirmation to myself. "I am powerful. I am limitless. I am destined for greatness." It felt strange at first, like I was trying to convince myself of something too big, too bold. But then... something changed. The words sank in. My energy shifted. Suddenly, I wasn't just saying it - I was believing it. And let me tell you, that's where the magic happens.

Affirmations: The Magic Spells you Cast Daily

Think of affirmations like tiny sparks of magic that light up your life. They're not just pretty words - they're power. They shape your reality, command the universe, and set you up for unstoppable success.

Goal-Oriented Affirmations – These are the big, bold declarations of your future. "I am living my dream life, traveling the world, financially free!" Say it, see it, FEEL it. When your mind locks in on the goal, the universe listens. Action-Oriented Affirmations – These push you into motion. "I am confident and capable of taking bold steps toward my dreams!" This is the kick-in-the-pants energy that moves you from thinking to DOING. **Alignment-Oriented Affirmations** – These are the secret sauce. "I am worthy of all the abundance the universe has to offer." When you embody the energy of your dreams, you become a magnet for them.

Cycle of Manifestation: Affirm, Act, Align

Picture this: You declare your goal (affirm), you take inspired steps (act), and you keep your vibe sky-high (align). That's the cycle. That's the formula. And if you stick with it, your dream life will go from vision to reality faster than you ever imagined.

But here's the deal - affirmations aren't a one-time wish. You don't just plant the seed; you have to water it daily. And that's where the next powerhouse tool comes in...

Vision Boards: Your Dreams in Full Color

There was a time when I felt lost. Life felt like a series of dead ends, but then, I created my first vision board. I still remember hanging it on my bedroom wall, watching my dreams take shape - pictures of places I wanted to visit, the kind of home I craved, the life I was determined to live.

Every night, I stared at that board, letting it sink into my subconscious. Even on the hardest days, when doubt crept in, that board reminded me of who I was becoming. I fought for that vision. I pushed through the noise of the world telling me to settle. And guess what? That vision board wasn't just decoration - it was the map to my future.

Creating Your Ultimate Vision Board

This isn't just a random arts and crafts project - this is your soul speaking. Your vision board is a declaration of your wildest dreams. So grab a board, magazines, scissors, glue, and get ready to craft your destiny.

Go Digital or Old-School – Whether it's a Pinterest board or a giant poster on your wall, make sure it's something you see every day. Choose with Intention – Don't just slap on pretty pictures. Every image should ignite something inside you. That dream house, that business empire, that travel adventure - it all has to mean something.

Feel It Deeply – If your board doesn't make your heart race, you're not dreaming big enough. Adjust, refine, and pick images that truly set your soul on fire. Put It Where You'll See It – Your vision board is your daily dose of inspiration. Hang it where you'll catch a glimpse of it every morning. Let it sink in. Let it work its magic.

The Ultimate Manifestation Hack: Combine Affirmations with Your Vision Board

Here's where things get really spicy. Imagine standing in front of your vision board, looking at that dream vacation, that business success, that thriving life, and saying:

"I am traveling the world, experiencing new cultures, and living in abundance!"

"I am a champion, and success flows to me effortlessly!"

"I am financially free, and money flows to me with ease!"

Feel that? That's the power of merging words with visuals. When you link affirmations to your vision board, you supercharge your manifestation game.

Evolve, Update, And Keep the Energy Fresh

Your dreams will grow. Your goals will shift. That's the beauty of life. At the end of each month, take a moment to refresh your vision board. Remove what no longer excites you. Add new dreams. Adjust your affirmations to match your evolution. Keep it dynamic, keep it powerful, and watch how fast things start moving.

Do It Now! Your Future Self Will Thank You

No more waiting. No more doubting. Today is the day. Set aside some time, grab your supplies, and create the vision board that will define your next chapter.

Stand in front of it every morning, say your affirmations out loud, and FEEL the energy of your future self.

You are capable.

You are worthy.

You are unstoppable.

And the life you desire?

It's already on its way.

Affirm + Visualize = Manifest.

Let's go!

23

THE SIMPLE MAGIC OF APPRECIATION

"Gratitude is not only the greatest of virtues, but the parent of all the others." – Marcus Tullius Cicero

Gratitude is one of the easiest yet most powerful tools available to us for aligning our energy and frequency. Why? Because **gratitude is the direct gateway to positive energy.** When you express gratitude, you align yourself with a high-frequency vibration that attracts more of what you want into your life. It's like tuning into a radio station: when you focus on things you're grateful for, you align with the frequency of abundance, joy, and positivity.

Why Gratitude is Important

Gratitude is a powerful practice that shifts your focus from what's missing in your life to the abundance that already exists. In a world where it's easy to become preoccupied with worries, doubts, or the pursuit of more, gratitude allows you to pause and recognize the richness of your current circumstances. This simple yet profound practice rewires your mindset, opening your energy to receive additional blessings. Instead of feeling depleted or dissatisfied, gratitude fosters a sense of completeness and contentment, even as you strive toward future goals.The magic lies in this: when you concentrate on what you have, you attract more of what you desire. It's as if the universe acknowledges your appreciation and responds by providing more. Gratitude naturally aligns your energy with the frequency of abundance, facilitating the manifestation of health, wealth, love, and more. It's not merely about acknowledging the positives but also about opening yourself to receive an even greater share of life's gifts. As Melody Beattie eloquently stated, "Gratitude unlocks the fullness of life. It turns what we have into enough, and more.

By embracing gratitude, you transform your perspective, leading to a more fulfilling and abundant life.

How to Practice Gratitude: The Simple Steps

So, how do you harness the magic of gratitude? It doesn't have to be complicated. Here's an easy method to get started:

Start with a Gratitude Practice: Every day, take a moment to express gratitude. You can do this in the morning when you wake up, or in the evening before you go to bed.

Write down three things you're thankful for, no matter how small. It could be as simple as "I'm grateful for the sunshine today" or "I'm grateful for my health." The key is to focus on the present and what you have right now. Smile While You Do It: Don't just think about the things you're grateful for - feel the gratitude. When you express gratitude, smile. It might feel a little odd at first, but smiling instantly raises your energy, making you feel more alive, positive, and ready to attract even more to be grateful for. Smile as you say or think about the things you're thankful for, and feel your energy shift. It's a simple but effective way to raise your frequency. Practice Gratitude Throughout the **Day**: Gratitude doesn't have to be limited to a few minutes in the morning or before bed. Try to find moments during the day when you can express thanks - whether it's for a friendly interaction, a beautiful moment in nature, or even for a simple cup of coffee.

The more you can train yourself to be grateful in small, everyday moments, the more naturally gratitude will flow through you. Gratitude Journaling: Create a dedicated gratitude journal where you can write down at least three things you are grateful for each day.

You could also reflect on what went well that day or what you've learned from a challenging situation. Over time, you'll start to see a shift in your thinking, and your energy will begin to align with a higher frequency. A gratitude journal is an easy way to track your journey of growth and manifestation.

Why Gratitude Attracts More Positive Energy

The law of attraction states that like attracts like. So, when you vibrate with the energy of gratitude, you attract more things to be grateful for. Think of it like a magnet: the more you express appreciation for what you have, the more the universe will send your way.

This is because gratitude sends out a clear message that you are open to receiving more. By practicing gratitude, you're putting out an energy that says, "I am ready to receive more of life's blessings."

For example, let's say you express gratitude for your health. By focusing on the health, you already have, you align your energy with the vibration of wellness. In turn, this can attract even more health and vitality into your life.

If you're grateful for your relationships, your frequency aligns with the energy of love and connection, and you may find that your relationships flourish.

The Bottom Line: Gratitude is a Game-Changer

Gratitude is more than a feel-good habit; it's a transformative practice that can profoundly change your perception of the world.

By focusing on what you're thankful for, you elevate your vibrational frequency, aligning your energy with abundance and attracting more of what you desire. This simple yet powerful shift in mindset rewires your brain, fostering a sense of contentment and openness to life's blessings. As you cultivate gratitude, you naturally invite more positive experiences into your life, enhancing your overall well-being and satisfaction.

The Art of Manifestation Through Magic Water

Imagine waking up each morning, feeling deeply connected to your goals, dreams, and desires. What if, with each sip of water, you could channel the energy of your dreams into your body? Picture yourself drinking a glass of water infused with your intentions and watching the magic of manifestation unfold. Welcome to the world of *Magic Water* - a simple yet profound ritual that has the power to align your energy and bring your desires to life.

The Water That Healed Me: A Story of Intention, Belief, and Manifestation

For the longest time, I struggled with my gut health. No matter what remedies I tried, no matter how many diets I followed, nothing seemed to work. My stomach issues persisted, leaving me feeling helpless and frustrated. Doctors prescribed medicines, nutritionists suggested meal plans, but deep down, I knew there had to be something more - a missing piece that science alone couldn't provide.

That's when I stumbled upon the idea of Magic Water. It sounded simple, almost too simple to be true. But something in me, a quiet yet persistent voice, told me to give it a try. I started with a small ritual: each night, I would take a glass of water, place it over a piece of paper where I had written my intention - "My gut is strong, healthy, and healed." I would let it sit overnight, believing that the water was absorbing my words, my energy, my desire for healing.

Every morning, I drank that water with absolute faith. With each sip, I visualized my gut growing stronger, my digestion becoming effortless, and my body embracing perfect health. I spoke to the water before drinking it, whispering my gratitude as if the healing had already happened. At first, it felt like just a ritual - one that brought me peace, if nothing else. But as days turned into weeks, something incredible happened.

My symptoms started to fade. The constant discomfort that had been a part of my life for so long began to lessen. My energy levels rose. I felt lighter, stronger, and, most of all, healed. It wasn't just the water that did this.

It was my intention, my belief system, and the little extra effort I put into aligning my mind with my body's healing. Science might not fully explain it, but I experienced it. What medicine couldn't completely fix, my belief, my words, and my energy did. That experience changed how I see life. If water could carry my intentions and help me heal, what else could it do? What other dreams, desires, and goals could I manifest simply by aligning my energy with them? Water is not just a liquid - it's a messenger.

Every drop absorbs what we speak, what we think, and what surrounds it. It holds the potential to heal what seems unhealable, to achieve what seems impossible, and to turn our deepest desires into reality.

So, if there's something in your life that you've struggled with, something that seems just out of reach, I invite you to try this. Speak to your water. Infuse it with gratitude, with belief, with the certainty that what you desire is already on its way. And then, watch the magic unfold - one sip at a time.

What Is Magic Water?

Magic Water is more than just a refreshing drink - it's a powerful tool for manifestation. It involves infusing water with the energy of your intentions and desires.

Water is a medium that can carry energy, and when you program it with affirmations or goals, you tap into a force that helps you align with what you want. Writing down an affirmation or goal actively charges the water with the energy of your dreams, signaling to the universe that you are ready to receive what you desire - one sip at a time.

The Ritual: How to Manifest with Every Sip

Step 1: Write Down Your Affirmation or Goal

Begin by writing down a clear affirmation or goal that resonates with you. This could be anything you want to manifest - whether it's love, abundance, health, success, or peace. Some examples include:

- *"I am financially abundant and open to receiving money."*

- *"I am healthy, vibrant, and full of energy."*

- *"Love flows effortlessly into my life."*

Be specific and positive with your wording. Choose something that truly excites you and feels real.

Step 2: Charge Your Water

Once your affirmation is ready, it's time to prepare your *magic potion.* Take a clean glass and fill it with fresh water. Place the paper with your affirmation under the glass and let it sit overnight. During this time, the water absorbs the energy of your intentions, making it a charged vessel for your manifestation.

Step 3: Drink with Intention

The next morning, drink the water mindfully. With each sip, visualize your affirmation coming to life. Imagine the energy of your desires flowing into you, infusing every cell of your body with the frequency of your dreams. Feel the positive vibration filling you up, bringing you closer to the reality you've envisioned.

The Science Behind Magic Water: The Power of Energy

Water is an incredible medium that absorbs and holds energy. Scientific studies have shown that water molecules can be influenced by their environment, a phenomenon known as molecular memory.

Research in quantum physics and experiments by Dr. Masaru Emoto suggest that water responds to thoughts, words, and emotions, forming unique molecular structures based on the energy it receives. When you charge your water with intention, you are programming it to carry that energy into your body, influencing your thoughts, feelings, and actions.

Think of it this way - every sip you take is a conscious act of transformation. With every drop, you are aligning yourself with your deepest desires, reinforcing your belief system, and strengthening your connection with the universe.

Magic Water is not just about manifestation; it is about gratitude, trust, and the power of the unseen forces that shape our reality. What medicine couldn't heal, belief did. What seemed impossible, intention made possible. This practice is a reminder that the answers often lie in the simplest of things - the air we breathe, the thoughts we think, and the water we drink. When you combine gratitude with intention and action, you tap into a force far greater than yourself.

So, the next time you hold a glass of water, remember - it's more than just water. It's a vessel for your dreams, a carrier of your energy, and a reminder that you are the creator of your own reality. You have the power to shape your life, one sip at a time.

Drink with purpose. Believe with conviction. And watch the magic unfold.

24

TIME FOR DOUBLE HAPPINESS

Lift Your Mood, Lift Your Life -Meharr

Have you ever noticed that when you're feeling down, everything seems to go wrong? It's like the universe just piles on more and more problems. And the more you focus on them, the worse they seem to get. This happens because when you're feeling low - whether it's sad, stressed, or frustrated - your energy is at **a** low frequency, and like attracts like. Simply put, the lower your mood, the more problems you'll attract. But here's the secret: You can change your frequency. You don't have to stay stuck in that low mood. When you're feeling down, it's the perfect time to raise your energy and bring in happiness, even if it feels forced at first. This is the power of Double Happiness.

Low Frequency = More Problems

Think of yourself as a radio station. If you're tuned to a low frequency (like 90 FM, full of negative thoughts and feelings), all you're going to get are more low-energy experiences. More problems, more stress, more reasons to feel sad. When you're feeling down, it's like you're sending out signals to the universe that you want more of the same: more things to worry about, more things that make you upset, and more reasons to feel stuck. But here's the good news: You can change the station.

The Power of Double Happiness: Shift Your Energy

When you're in a low mood, that's the perfect moment to double up on happiness. The goal is to shift your energy from negative to positive, and here's how you do it:

Acknowledge the Feeling, But Don't Stay There

It's perfectly human to feel sad, frustrated, or overwhelmed at times. Our emotions are a reflection of our experiences, but they don't have to define us. Allow yourself to feel whatever arises - whether it's a wave of sadness, frustration, or even anger - but don't allow that feeling to take root in your heart. Simply recognize it, honor it, and then gently let it go.

With a deep breath, say to yourself, "I won't let this moment rule me. I choose to step beyond this feeling and open myself to something better." You have the power to move through emotions without staying trapped in them.

Say "Time for Double Happiness!"

There is magic in words, in the intention behind them. When you say, "Time for Double Happiness!" out loud, it's not just a phrase - it's a powerful command to your mind. You are telling yourself, "It's time to shift, to change, to embrace a new energy."

Imagine it like flipping a switch: one moment you're caught in negativity, and with a simple declaration, the next moment you're ready to invite joy, peace, and optimism. It's a playful, yet intentional act of reclaiming your inner peace and joy.

Do Something That Brings You Joy

The next step is crucial - feed your soul. Joy isn't something that happens by chance; it's something you actively choose. When life feels heavy, engage in something that makes you feel alive. Maybe it's moving your body to a song that fills you with energy, dancing like no one's watching. Or perhaps it's a quiet moment of laughter shared with a friend over the phone, a funny video that brings lightness to your spirit. Go outside and let nature remind you of its calming power - the crisp air, the rustling of leaves, the warmth of the sun on your skin. Or take a pause to write down a few things you're grateful for. Gratitude is like a gentle hug for the heart, a reminder that even in tough times, there's beauty and abundance surrounding you. These small acts have the potential to reset your entire state of mind and bring a radiant energy into your day.

Smile!

It may feel strange at first, but try it anyway: smile. Even when you don't feel like it. Your brain doesn't distinguish between a genuine smile and one that's simply willed into existence - it responds to both. The simple act of smiling sends signals to your brain, activating a flood of feel-good chemicals, lifting your mood, and releasing any tension you're holding. It's like a tiny spark of joy that you ignite within yourself. And as you smile, you may notice that the world around you begins to feel just a little bit lighter, a little bit brighter. Smiling becomes a way of showing up for yourself - no matter the circumstances.

Affirmations for Happiness

Now, it's time to anchor your newfound energy with affirmations. These words are more than just positive statements; they are declarations of self-love and empowerment. As you breathe in the fresh air, feel the joy coursing through your body, and smile with intention, repeat to yourself:

- *"I choose happiness right now."*
- *"I am capable of handling anything life brings me."*
- *"I am worthy of joy and good things."*
- *"I release negative energy and embrace peace."*

Each affirmation is a seed you plant in your mind, nurturing it to grow into a beautiful garden of positivity, confidence, and peace. These words serve as gentle reminders that you have control over how you respond to life, and you have the power to create your own happiness

Why Double Happiness Works?

When you're feeling sad or frustrated, it can feel hard to break out of that cycle. But remember: your mood is like a magnet. When you're sad or upset, you're attracting more things that make you feel sad and upset. But when you choose to **raise your energy**, you start to attract more positive things, too. When you do something that makes you happy, like dancing or laughing, your energy goes up. And that higher energy attracts better things into your life - more opportunities, more good vibes, and more positive situations.

Let's say you're having a tough day - maybe work is overwhelming, or things didn't go as planned, and your mind starts spiraling into negative thoughts. Here's how you can practice Double Happiness to turn things around: First, catch yourself thinking something like, "Nothing ever goes right for me," and immediately say, "Time for Double Happiness!" Then, even if it feels a little silly, get up and dance to your favorite song for five minutes.

As you move, you'll feel your energy shift, even if it's just a little bit at first. Smile, even if it's forced, and repeat an affirmation like, "I am grateful for today, and I choose to be happy." Just like that, your mood will begin to lift.

That small shift in energy creates space for better things to come your way. Instead of attracting more stress, you might notice the rest of your day flowing more smoothly. A new opportunity could pop up, or you may even get some good news.

That's the power of consciously raising your frequency and choosing happiness, even in tough moments.

The Moment Everything Changed

I remember the exact moment I stumbled upon the power of **Double Happiness**. It wasn't in a book or a motivational video - it was in the middle of what felt like one of the worst days of my life.

A Series of Setbacks

It started with a series of setbacks. I had just received an email that a project I had poured my heart into was being delayed indefinitely. My phone buzzed with a message about an unexpected expense that threw my budget into chaos. And to top it off, I spilled coffee all over my notes for an important meeting.

My mind immediately spiraled into negativity:

"Why does this always happen to me?"

"Nothing ever goes right."

I could feel the weight of frustration sinking in, dragging me down like quicksand.

A Defiant Decision

But then, something inside me snapped - not in defeat, but in defiance. I had read about how energy attracts energy, and I knew if I kept feeding this downward spiral, the day would only get worse.

That's when I decided to put Double Happiness to the test. I stood up, took a deep breath, and said out loud, "Time for Double Happiness!" - even though, at that moment, I didn't feel remotely happy.

It felt a little ridiculous, but I committed to it anyway.

The Shift Begins

First, I played one of my all-time favorite songs - the kind that makes it impossible to sit still. At first, I just tapped my foot, but within seconds, I was dancing. I told myself, "For five minutes, I'm going to forget everything and just move." My frustration didn't vanish instantly, but something shifted. I felt lighter. My mind started clearing. Then I smiled - a real smile, not a forced one. And as I danced, I repeated: "I am grateful for today, and I choose to be happy."

Energy Creates Reality

The shift in energy was undeniable. Suddenly, my problems didn't feel as crushing. My mind, which had been stuck in a loop of negativity, started opening up to solutions.

- Instead of sulking about the delayed project, I drafted a new approach to present to my team.

- Instead of stressing over the unexpected expense, I found a way to adjust my budget without feeling overwhelmed.

- And the coffee-stained notes? I rewrote them - more clearly and concisely than before.

The Universe Responds

Then, something unexpected happened. A client, whom I thought had lost interest in working with me, emailed out of the blue with a new proposal - one that was even better than the project that had just been delayed. Later that evening, a friend sent me a random uplifting message, just when I needed it most. It was as if the universe was responding to my energy shift in real-time.

The Power of Choice

That day, I learned something profound: when you take control of your energy, you take control of your reality. Double Happiness isn't just about pretending to be happy - it's about consciously choosing to shift your state, even when it feels impossible. It's about breaking the cycle of negativity and creating space for better things to flow in.

A Lifelong Practice

Since that day, I've used Double Happiness every time I feel myself slipping into frustration, doubt, or overwhelm.

And every single time, it works.

Maybe not instantly, but always in ways that remind me that I am the one steering my experience.

Happiness isn't something that just **happens** -

it's something

we **create,**

amplify,

and attract.

25
CANCEL, CANCEL: REPROGRAMMING YOUR MIND

"Your thoughts create your reality. When you change your thoughts, you change your world." – Norman Vincent Peale

One of the simplest yet most powerful tools for shifting your frequency is the practice of saying **"Cancel, Cancel"** when you catch yourself speaking or thinking negative thoughts.

This technique is like a reset button for your mind, interrupting the negative energy before it has a chance to take root. It may sound a little quirky, but the effects are profound when used consistently.

What Does "Cancel, Cancel" Mean?

The idea is simple: whenever you say something negative, whether out loud or in your head, immediately say **"Cancel, Cancel"** to interrupt the flow of that thought or statement.

It's like hitting a mental "delete" button, telling your subconscious mind that you don't want to hold onto that energy).for example, if you catch yourself thinking,

"I'm always broke," you'd quickly say "Cancel, Cancel" and then replace that thought with something positive like, "I am open to receiving abundance in all forms."

This technique is incredibly powerful because your words and thoughts create your reality. Every time you think or speak, you're sending out energetic vibrations into the universe, and these vibrations can attract similar energy back to you. If you're constantly saying negative things, you're attracting more negativity into your life.

Why Does This Work?

Your brain is like a playground where thoughts play and connect with each other. When you think something, your brain makes a little path to remember it. If you keep thinking sad or angry thoughts, your brain makes more and more paths for those thoughts.

But if you stop and say "Cancel, Cancel!" and think something happy instead, you're making new, better paths in your brain. Over time, your brain gets better at thinking happy thoughts, and that makes you feel better!

Also, there's something called the "Law of Attraction." It's like this: when you think happy thoughts and say nice things, good things start coming to you, like fun friends, toys, or happy moments. But if you keep thinking bad thoughts, more bad things come your way.

So, when you choose to think happy thoughts, you start bringing happiness into your life! By saying "Cancel, Cancel," you're consciously choosing to block out negative energy and replace it with something better. This shift not only changes your mood but also elevates your vibration, making you more aligned with positive outcomes.

One of my clients, a highly ambitious entrepreneur, walked into our session, frustration written all over his face. "I know what I need to do," he said, shaking his head, "but I just can't stop overthinking. I analyze everything to death, and by the time I'm done, I feel drained and do nothing." I could see the exhaustion in his eyes - the result of carrying the weight of endless "what ifs" and worst-case scenarios.

His energy was being wasted in a loop of doubt and hesitation rather than action and results. That's when I introduced him to a simple but powerful tool: **"Cancel, Cancel."** At first, he was skeptical. "Just saying 'Cancel, Cancel' will stop my overthinking? That sounds too easy," he said. But I assured him, "It's not about stopping the thoughts entirely - it's about interrupting them before they spiral out of control and replacing them with something empowering."

The Shift Begins

I gave him a challenge: For the next 24 hours, every time a doubtful or negative thought entered his mind, he had to say 'Cancel, Cancel' out loud or in his head. Then, he had to replace it with a thought that moved him toward action.

He agreed to try it. The first few times, he caught himself thinking:

"What if I fail?" → Cancel, Cancel. → *"Every challenge is a lesson. I grow and succeed."*

"I don't know if I'm ready." → Cancel, Cancel. → *"I am prepared, and I take action now."*

By the afternoon, he messaged me: *"This is weird. I actually feel lighter. I'm catching myself before I spiral."* By the evening, something incredible happened. He had been delaying an important business decision for weeks - stuck in analysis paralysis. But that night, he made the call. No more overthinking, no more hesitation. He simply acted. The next day, he walked into our session with a completely different energy. "I can't believe how much mental space I freed up just by doing this for one day," he said. "It's like I unplugged a drain that had been sucking all my energy."

Results Over Overthinking

That one day of practice was enough for him to realize just how much his overthinking had been holding him back. Instead of wasting energy on doubts and fears, he began directing it toward execution. Within a week, he had launched a new initiative in his business, something he had been putting off for months. All because of two simple words: Cancel, Cancel.

The Lesson?

Overthinking is just energy wasted in the wrong direction. When you take control of your thoughts, you take control of your actions. My client learned in one day what most people never realize in a lifetime: the power of consciously choosing your thoughts. So, the next time your mind starts spiraling into doubts, fears, or endless "what-ifs," remember this: Cancel, Cancel. Replace. Act.

And watch how your life transforms.

The Science Behind the "Cancel, Cancel" Technique

To reprogram your mind, start by catching negative thoughts as they arise. Be mindful of your inner dialogue, and whenever you notice yourself thinking something negative, immediately say "Cancel, Cancel." For example, if you think, "I'll never be successful," stop right there and replace it with a positive affirmation like, "I am capable of achieving anything I set my mind to."

This simple interruption helps shift your focus. After saying "Cancel, Cancel," replace the negative thought with a positive affirmation that aligns with your goals. By doing this, you're creating new neural pathways that will help positive thinking become your default mindset over time.

However, positive thinking alone isn't enough - action is also key. As you replace negative thoughts with positive ones, your actions will begin to shift as well, naturally aligning with your new mindset. Taking inspired action will open up more opportunities, boost your self-confidence, and lead to better results, helping you move closer to your goals. When you start using "Cancel, Cancel," you're creating a positive feedback loop.

Here's how it works:

Negative thought → You say "Cancel, Cancel" → Replace with a positive affirmation → Your frequency shifts → You attract more positive situations → Your subconscious begins to accept positive thoughts more easily → Your life begins to reflect your higher frequency.

This feedback loop trains your mind to focus on the **positive** and stop dwelling on the negative. Over time, you'll notice that your thoughts become more empowering, your actions become more aligned with your desires, and your life will begin to reflect the positive changes you've made in your energy.

Real-Life Examples:

Example 1: Self-Doubt

Let's say you're about to make a big decision and you think, "I'm not good enough for this." The moment that thought enters your mind, you say **"Cancel, Cancel"** and replace it with something like, "I am fully capable and deserving of success." You shift your focus from insecurity to self-assurance, raising your frequency in the process.

Example 2: Fear of Failure

Imagine you're trying something new, like starting a business or moving to a new city, and the thought arises, "What if I fail?" Instead of letting this fear control you, you quickly say, **"Cancel, Cancel"** and replace it with, "Every challenge is an opportunity for growth. I learn and succeed in everything I do." By regularly practicing this technique, your mindset becomes more positive and proactive, and your reality begins to shift in ways that support your growth and goals.

Final Thoughts:

"Cancel, Cancel" isn't just a fun mantra - it's a scientifically backed tool for changing your frequency and rewiring your brain. By consistently interrupting negative thoughts and replacing them with positive affirmations, you're taking control of your inner dialogue and consciously creating the life you want. The more you practice, the more you'll align with your desires and attract the positive energy that's already waiting for you.

Today, take control of your mind by actively canceling every unwanted thought that arises. Thoughts are powerful, but you hold the power to choose which ones you engage with. Start by becoming aware of your thoughts. Whenever an unwanted thought enters your mind - whether it's negative, self-doubting, or simply unhelpful - immediately say "Cancel, cancel, cancel" in your mind. Visualize this thought disappearing as you replace it with a more positive, empowering one. Make this your mantra for the day: "I am in control of my thoughts, and I choose positivity." Each time a negative or unwanted thought arises, mentally say "cancel" and then replace it with something affirming and empowering. For example, if you think, "I can't do this," immediately replace it with, "I am capable and confident."

Or, if you have a self-doubt, replace it with, "I trust my abilities and my worth." This practice is not just about eliminating negativity; it's about choosing to fill your mind with thoughts that elevate you. With each "cancel," you are reinforcing your power to create a positive mental environment. By staying consistent, you'll train your mind to focus on what serves you, allowing peace and clarity to flow into your day. Keep practicing this throughout the day, and notice how quickly your mindset shifts. At the end of the day, reflect on how many unwanted thoughts you were able to cancel and replace. Celebrate your progress, knowing that you have the power to direct your mind towards what you want to manifest.

PART 3

HEALING YOUR MIND, BODY AND SOUL

Dear Readers,

In this part, I will embark on a journey to heal your mind, body, and soul. True healing is not just about mending what is broken but about rediscovering your wholeness. You will learn to release the past, nurture your present, and embrace the future with strength and clarity. Let this be the moment you choose yourself - your peace,

26

THE HEALING JOURNEY

"The wound is the place where the Light enters you." *Rumi*

Healing is never about silencing one part of myself for the sake of the other. It is not about choosing safety over freedom, or logic over passion. Healing came when the two forces - heart and mind - came together, not as adversaries, but as partners. My heart led me to the adventure, and my mind ensured I was prepared.

Together, we created a life that was vibrant, meaningful, and authentic. The storms of doubt and fear still came, but now, I knew how to face them, with both heart and mind guiding me forward. In the end, my journey was not just one of discovery, but one of integration. Healing happens when I allow the heart's spontaneity and the mind's clarity to work together. It's when I listen to both sides of myself and allow them to guide me in a way that's balanced, thoughtful, and full of love. So, next time I find myself torn between the heart's desire for freedom and the mind's need for safety, I'll remember my story. Healing isn't about choosing one over the other - it's about bringing them together. When the heart and mind align, the possibilities are endless. In the dance of life, let both the heart and mind be my partners.

Together, they'll guide me to the shores of my deepest potential, where joy, peace, and purpose awaiting.

Navigating the Universe of Emotion

Imagine you're in a spaceship, soaring through the universe of your emotions. Inside, you have two co-pilots: the Heart and the Mind. The Heart is the adventurous one, constantly urging you to chase new dreams, take risks, and dive into the unknown. The Mind, however, is more cautious, analyzing each move and weighing the consequences, ensuring you stay grounded and safe.

To successfully navigate this cosmic journey, you need to balance both forces - trusting the Heart to push you toward growth and listening to the Mind when you need direction. Together, they help you chart a course through the stars of possibility and avoid the black holes of fear and uncertainty. In this vast emotional cosmos, the Heart is the beacon of adventure, always pushing you to explore the unknown. It feels first, thinks later, embracing the thrill of new experiences, the exhilaration of love, the mystery of connection. The heart is the dreamer, the artist, the poet.

The Mind, however, is the engineer. It designs, builds, and strategizes. It wants to understand the patterns of the universe, to make sense of the chaos, to keep you grounded. The mind is the one who calculates, who plans the route, who demands you measure every step.It prefers the tried and tested, the safe and familiar. Both the mind and the heart have their own strengths, but when they don't align, the result can be a storm of confusion, doubt, and conflict.

The Unknown Battle

Let's imagine the collision that happens when emotions are suppressed, and the tension between heart and mind grows too intense. When the mind tries to suppress the feelings of the heart - when it dismisses the whispers of passion and desire in favor of control - something starts to shift. The pressure builds, like a spaceship with too much fuel ready to explode. Suppressing emotions, ignoring your true feelings, trying to be "diplomatic" at all costs, can cause a chain reaction.

The internal conflict between your heart and mind doesn't just stay inside; it leaks out. You begin to feel it in your body. You might experience sudden bursts of anger, perhaps in a moment when it feels completely out of place - yelling at a friend or partner over something trivial. Or, maybe you feel that familiar knot in your stomach, an overwhelming anxiety that you can't explain.

Your body is reacting to the suppressed emotions, the unresolved battle within your inner space. Perhaps your headaches become more frequent, or your back aches with tension, as though the universe itself is trying to remind you that the journey of suppressing emotions comes at a cost. Your spaceship - the vessel of your body and mind - becomes damaged as the inner storm rages on.

A Journey Beyond Conflict

What if, instead of suppressing or battling these forces, you could navigate this inner space with balance, allowing the heart and mind to work together, as one crew, on the same mission? Imagine your inner space as an uncharted galaxy. The Heart has the power to explore the unknown, to see the beauty in the stars, to follow the gravitational pull of your desires. But the Mind, the strategist, is essential to help you avoid black holes of regret and detours into emotional turbulence. You need both.

Mind: *"I know you're scared, but think about the rewards. What if this is the breakthrough you've been waiting for?"*

Heart: *"I trust this journey. The universe has led me here for a reason. I feel alive in this moment - let's follow that feeling."*

Together, they can work in harmony - the heart feeling the path ahead, the mind charting the course.

The Key to Healing and True Happiness

In this world of inner space, healing happens when the mind stops trying to control everything, and the heart stops suppressing its desires. Healing happens when both forces understand their roles in your life and work together. Healing is the integration of the heart's spontaneity and the mind's clarity. By embracing this balance, you find freedom. You free yourself from the chains of doubt, fear, and hesitation. You can step into your own power, aware that you don't have to choose one over the other - you can have both.

The Heart Knows: The Treasure of Life is in the Journey

In your spaceship of life, the true treasure isn't just the destination. It's the journey itself - the moments of joy and sorrow, the peaks and valleys, the fears and the courage. It's in the small victories and the growth that happens when you embrace both your heart and mind. As you move through this vast inner universe, remember: life is finite, a single voyage through the stars. Why waste it stuck in indecision, when you can learn to explore, to feel deeply, to make decisions from a place of alignment?

The battle between the heart and mind doesn't have to be a war. It can be the greatest adventure of all.

The treasure lies not in escaping this inner space, but in embracing it fully - living with your heart wide open and your mind focused, allowing the ship of your life to sail smoothly through the galaxies of joy, growth, and possibility.

A Journey of Inner Harmony

Imagine a vast, endless ocean stretching before you. The sun is setting, casting golden hues across the water, turning it into a shimmering blanket of warmth. A small boat is gently bobbing on the waves, rocking ever so slightly. The boat is you, and the sea is your life - vast, unpredictable, and full of potential. Now, as you sit in this boat, you notice something incredible. Two winds are blowing.

One is warm, gentle, and filled with the sweet scent of freedom and adventure. It comes from the heart. The other is cool, clear, and steady, keeping you on course, guiding your way with a calm certainty. This wind comes from the mind. At first, the two winds seem to be at odds. The warm, free-spirited wind of the heart wants you to set sail without a map, to explore the unknown with nothing but hope as your compass. The cool, steady wind of the mind insists on planning every route, ensuring there are no storms ahead, no rocks to crash into.

How Does Healing Happen?

But what if both winds could work together? What if healing, real healing, happens when the heart's spontaneity and the mind's clarity come into perfect alignment? The heart's passion, mixed with the mind's wisdom, allowed me to navigate the journey of self-discovery, step by step. When I learned to trust my heart, it was as if the universe opened up. Every opportunity, every new challenge was no longer something to fear but something to embrace.

And all the while, my mother's faith in me served as the steady anchor, reminding me that even when the winds seemed at odds, she was there, holding me steady. She taught me that dreams don't have to be perfect from the start. It's okay to stumble along the way. In fact, those stumbles are often the moments that shape you the most. It wasn't easy, but as I began to trust both the heart's impulse and the mind's caution, the path forward became clearer.

And when I took that first step - saying "yes" to becoming a Coach and Speaker, to helping people transform their lives - I didn't just take a leap of faith. I took the first step toward a reality I had only once dared to dream about. I realized that everything begins with a thought, but it's the courage to act on it, to blend heart with mind, that turns those dreams into something real.

Who am I really, without all these external labels?

But the fear of the unknown gripped me. What if I failed? What if my dreams were too big, too unrealistic? What if, despite all my affirmations and mindset shifts, the universe had other plans for me? But this time, I made a choice. Instead of retreating into my old patterns of fear and insecurity, I decided to do something radical: I embraced the uncertainty.

The Power of Letting Go of Control

Here's the thing about healing: We all have this deep-rooted need for control. We want to know exactly how things are going to turn out. We want a guarantee that our efforts will lead to success. But life doesn't work like that.

Healing doesn't come with a step-by-step guidebook. It's messy. It's unpredictable. I learned to let go of my need to control everything. I didn't know what the future would look like, but I chose to trust the process.

I chose to surrender to the unknown. In my time of uncertainty, I rediscovered what made my heart come alive.

And slowly, I realized that my life wasn't about finding the right job or chasing the next achievement. It was about finding meaning and purpose, doing things that made me feel fully alive. Acting as if you have already achieved it make you believe in your capabilities even more even in times of challenges.

A New Way of Being: The Shift from Doing to Being

As I continued my journey, something shifted inside me. The more I stopped doing and allowed myself to simply be, the more I aligned with my true self. I stopped measuring my worth by how much I could achieve or how much I could control.

This is the deeper, more profound level of healing: the shift from doing to being. For so many of us, we define ourselves by what we do.

We are the successful one, the ambitious one, the hardworking one. But what if you were to strip all of that away?

What if you were to embrace the space between the doing - the moments of stillness, of contemplation, of being - and trust that this stillness is just as important as the hustle?

Healing Means Stepping Back

Healing doesn't always require action. Sometimes, it's about taking a step back and simply being present with what is. I discovered that my worth wasn't tied to my achievements.

I didn't need to prove anything. In the absence of external validation, I found my own inner peace.

Now,

Reflect on the balance between your heart and mind. Imagine them as two co-pilots in your life. What does your heart desire most at this moment?

What concerns or cautions is your mind raising? How can you let both your heart and mind guide you harmoniously?

27

THE ART OF LETTING GO

"We must be willing to let go of the life we have planned, so as to have the life that is waiting for us." - E.M. Forster

I remember walking through the halls of school, surrounded by so many people, but always feeling alone. I didn't have many friends, and the ones I did have were few and far between. I had just one best friend, and that was only in my tenth or twelfth grade. I would look around at groups of friends and wish, with all my heart, that I could be a part of something like that. I longed for the feeling of belonging, of having a group that truly understood me. I promised myself that when I reached college, everything would be different. I dreamed of having an amazing group of friends, people who would accept me, people who would laugh with me and stand by me.

Anything I couldn't do in school, I would do it in college - I would live those moments I had always wanted. When I finally stepped into college for my B.Com course, I felt like this was my chance. But life, as it often does, had other plans. I was given a choice between two sections - A and B. By mistake, I was allocated to Section B, and even though I was offered a chance to change, I didn't. I had already spent a few days in Section B, had formed a group, and I felt comfortable. So, without thinking too much, I stuck with it.

All things Perfect?

At first, everything seemed perfect. I was in a group, I had people to talk to, and I thought things were finally looking up. But soon, the group I was in started to show its true colors. It wasn't the friendship I had dreamed of. They were bullies, and I couldn't understand why they treated me this way. I never had the courage to ask them why they were so indifferent to me, why they made me feel small.

The question lingered in my mind: "Was I not lovable enough? Was that the reason I never had school friends? Was that why I was always alone? "These thoughts began to cloud my mind like a thick fog, and I felt lost. It felt as though everything I believed about myself was being challenged. The pain of not having closure was consuming me. I had never understood how important closure was until then. Without closure, without answers to the questions that plagued my mind, I felt emotionally drained. I didn't know what was real anymore, and I didn't know how to fix it.

But then, something clicked. I asked myself a question that changed everything: "Am I really unlovable, or is it that I am operating on a different frequency than they are, and our energies just don't align?"

That's when it hit me - I had spent so much time questioning my worth, but maybe I was just in the wrong place with the wrong people. Maybe, just maybe, what I thought I wanted wasn't actually right for me. I also asked myself,

"If I could go back in time, would I choose to repeat those friendships? Would I want to relive those relationships?" And my mind answered with a resounding "No." In that moment, I realized that I didn't need those toxic friendships.

I didn't need to keep questioning myself or seeking validation from people who didn't understand me. This was my sign to move on.

The Art of Letting Go

Letting go wasn't easy. It's one thing to know in your heart that you need to move on, but it's a whole other thing to actually do it.

The idea of letting go sounds beautiful in theory, but in practice, it's one of the hardest things you'll ever do. It's exhausting, it's emotional, and it's scary. But sometimes, it's the only way to find the love and acceptance you've been searching for - within yourself.

And so, I took that step. I let go of the people who didn't value me. I stopped blaming myself for not being "good enough" and started realizing that I didn't need anyone else's approval to know that I was worthy of love. This was the beginning of my journey to self-love.

The process wasn't quick, and it wasn't easy. But with every day, I grew stronger. I started focusing on myself, my passions, and my goals. I began to see my own worth, and that was the key.

I started attracting the right energy, the right people. And most importantly, I found a deep love for myself. That was the love I had always been searching for.

That was the ultimate moment of realization for me - the love and belongingness I had been searching for was actually within me all along. It wasn't out there, in the friendships or the groups I had tried to be a part of. It wasn't in the validation I thought I needed from others. It was already inside me, waiting to be uncovered.

And as I embraced this truth, I began to evolve, not just as a person, but as a stronger, more self-aware individual. The emotional hardships, the struggles, the feelings of rejection - they all played a role in shaping who I was becoming. And with that realization, I asked the universe to guide me.

I surrendered my doubts, my fears, and asked for the clarity I needed. I wanted to be in a space where I could grow, surrounded by the right energy and the right people. And just like that, things started to shift.

The Violet Flame of Letting Go

There are moments in life when the weight of the past lingers too heavily on our shoulders - moments when regrets, fears, and anxieties cloud our ability to move forward. In these times, we must remind ourselves of the power of release, of surrendering what no longer serves us We can also learn the art of letting go, using the transformative energy of the Violet Flame and the practice of Violet Breathing to cleanse the soul and renew the spirit.

A Journey into Healing

Imagine stepping into a space of complete serenity, where the past no longer haunts you, and the future feels light with possibility. This space exists within you, waiting to be unlocked. All it takes is a deep breath and the willingness to let go. Sit or lie down in a quiet place where you won't be disturbed. Close your eyes and take a deep breath in, feeling the cool air filling your lungs. As you breathe out, imagine releasing the tension gripping your body, the worries weighing on your mind. Slowly, the air around you begins to shift, infused with a soft violet glow - a color of transformation, spirituality, and renewal. With each inhale, visualize drawing in this radiant violet light.

See it entering your nostrils, filling your lungs, and spreading through every cell of your body. The warmth of this light soothes you, cleansing away negativity, fear, and emotional blockages. As you exhale, imagine all the burdens you carry turning into wisps of gray smoke, dissolving into the violet energy surrounding you. With every breath, you feel lighter, freer.

The Power of the Violet Flame

Now, picture a beautiful violet flame flickering in front of you - gentle yet powerful, radiant yet calming. This flame is no ordinary fire; it does not burn but rather transforms. It holds the energy of renewal, capable of dissolving pain and clearing the path ahead. See this flame growing larger, surrounding you in its cocoon of light and warmth. Within its embrace, there is no fear, no self-doubt, no regret - only pure transformation.

Take a moment to bring to mind something you wish to release - an old fear, a lingering doubt, a memory that holds you back. Envision this thought entering the violet flame, watching as it dissolves completely, leaving behind nothing but clarity and peace. The past does not define you. The pain you have carried is not meant to be a lifelong burden. As the violet flame works through you, feel the shift - your heart lighter, your mind quieter, your spirit freer. This is the power of letting go.

Returning to the Present

As you slowly bring your awareness back to the present moment, take a deep breath. Wiggle your fingers, move your toes, and when you're ready, gently open your eyes. The world around you may look the same, but something within you has changed. The Violet Flame is always with you, a reminder that transformation is possible at any time. Whenever you feel burdened, whenever the past weighs too heavily, return to this practice. Breathe in the light, breathe out what no longer serves you. Release. Heal. Transform. You are free to move forward, lighter, stronger, and filled with the energy of renewal.

Embracing New Beginnings

As I let go of the past and embraced the lessons it had taught me, I realized that life was offering me a fresh start. It was like turning the page to a new chapter, one where I could write my own story with confidence and clarity. The first step in embracing this new beginning was learning to trust myself. Trusting that the decisions I made would lead me to the right places and the right people. I began to understand that my journey was unique, and I didn't have to follow anyone else's path. College, once a place I saw as the answer to my longing for connection, became a platform for self-exploration. I started participating in activities that excited me, things I had always been curious about but never dared to try.

Whether it was joining a club, volunteering for events, or simply taking a walk alone to reflect, these small steps helped me discover more about myself than I ever thought possible. During this phase, I came across people who truly inspired me - people with kindness in their hearts and dreams as big as the sky. These weren't always the loudest or most popular people in the room. In fact, many of them were quiet yet profound in their presence. They taught me the value of depth over numbers, of quality over quantity, when it came to relationships. For the first time, I began to see friendship in a new light - not as a group to fit into but as a bond that naturally forms when energies align. I learned to nurture the connections that felt right, without forcing anything.

And while I still had moments of doubt or loneliness, they no longer consumed me. This was the beginning of a new phase - one filled with hope, gratitude, and the courage to step into the unknown. I wasn't the same person I was in school or even in the early days of college. I had grown, not in ways that everyone could see, but in ways that I could feel. And that was enough.

Cultivating Authentic Connections

As I ventured deeper into self-discovery, I recognized the profound importance of authentic connections. These bonds, rooted in genuine understanding and mutual respect, became the cornerstone of my personal growth. In the past, I often sought validation from external sources, yearning to fit into predefined molds. However, this journey taught me that true connection arises not from conforming, but from embracing one's authentic self. By being genuine, I attracted individuals who resonated with my true essence, leading to relationships that enriched my life. Engaging in open and honest conversations allowed me to share my vulnerabilities and listen to others' experiences without judgment.

This mutual exchange fostered trust and deepened our bonds. I learned that it's not the quantity of relationships that matters, but the quality. Even a few meaningful connections can provide immense support and joy. Through these authentic relationships, I discovered the beauty of mutual growth. We celebrated each other's successes and provided solace during challenges.

These connections became a mirror, reflecting my strengths and areas for improvement, guiding me toward continuous self-improvement.

In essence, embracing authenticity not only transformed my relationship with myself but also enriched my interactions with others. It taught me that when we present our true selves to the world, we invite genuine connections that nurture our soul and contribute to our collective journey of growth.

Embracing the Journey Ahead

Reflecting on this transformative journey, I've come to understand that life is a series of continuous evolutions. Each phase, with its unique challenges and rewards, contributes to our growth and self-awareness. Letting go of past constraints allowed me to embrace new beginnings with an open heart. By trusting myself and seeking authentic connections, I navigated the complexities of life with renewed confidence. As I move forward, I carry with me the lessons learned: the importance of self-trust, the value of genuine relationships, and the courage to embrace change.

Life's journey is unpredictable, but with resilience and authenticity, I am prepared to face whatever comes my way. In the words of an insightful article, "Change is a constant companion on the road of life, guiding us through uncharted territories and presenting opportunities for growth and self-discovery."

Embracing this perspective, I look forward to the adventures ahead, ready to write new chapters filled with hope, learning, and authentic experiences. As I embraced this new beginning, I made a promise to myself: to never again compromise my peace or my sense of self for the sake of fitting in.

Life was too short to be anything other than authentic, and I was finally ready to live it on my own terms.

28

THE HEALING POWER OF FORGIVENESS

"Forgiveness is the greatest gift you can give yourself. It's not just about forgiving someone else; it's about freeing yourself from the past." – Maya Angelou

Forgiveness is one of the most profound acts of healing. It's not about condoning someone's wrongs or letting them off the hook - it's about freeing yourself from the chains of resentment, anger, and hurt. Holding onto past wounds can weigh heavily on the heart and mind, blocking your ability to move forward and experience peace. By forgiving, you release the grip of these emotions, allowing space for healing, growth, and emotional freedom. Why is forgiveness so important?

When we choose to forgive, we reclaim our power. The person who wronged us may never be able to change the past, but we have the ability to change how we respond to it. Forgiveness shifts the focus from the wrongdoer to our own well-being. It's a choice to heal, to let go of the emotional baggage that keeps us stuck, and to create a life filled with peace rather than pain. It's not always easy, but it is always worth it.

My Journey of Transformation

Once, I stood at the crossroads of my life, feeling a sense of fulfillment. I had poured my heart into something meaningful - teaching people the powerful mind tools that aren't part of traditional schooling. I had unlocked the secrets of the Law of Attraction and watched, almost in awe, as my dreams unfolded into reality.

My career soared, relationships blossomed, and success seemed to flow effortlessly toward me like a river finding its way downstream. But as I reveled in the richness of the life I had created, something deeper was brewing beneath the surface - a quiet unrest, like a faint hum of discomfort, that I could never quite ignore.

Despite the wealth of achievements, there was a weight I carried, a shadow that lingered in the corners of my mind. Guilt. Regret. The ghosts of choices I couldn't undo. They were like invisible shackles around my soul, preventing me from fully embracing the present moment. I had the tools to manifest my desires, to create, to build - but I couldn't shake the heavy emotions that seemed to follow me wherever I went.

A Dance with the Past, the Present, and Freedom

I remember one evening, sitting alone in my study, the soft glow of the lamp casting long shadows over the books and papers scattered across the desk. The room was quiet, yet my mind was far from it. I could feel the toll that unresolved emotions had taken on me. My stomach, once steady and strong, now churned with unease.

Every morning, I woke up with a heaviness in my chest, as though an invisible weight was pressing down on me. I became sick more often, my energy waning. The energy I had so carefully cultivated was now drained, and no amount of positive thinking could fill the void. In that stillness, it became clear to me: I couldn't move forward while holding on to the past. The guilt and regret that lived inside me weren't just emotional - they were manifesting physically. It was as if the unresolved energy had built a wall around my heart, a wall I couldn't tear down with just intention or willpower. It felt like handcuffs that bound me to a version of myself I no longer wanted to be.

A Glimpse of Light

Then, one serendipitous day, as if the universe knew exactly what I needed, I stumbled across something that seemed to call my name. It was a small book, titled "Ho'oponopono: The Hawaiian Art of Forgiveness." The moment I saw those words, a spark lit up inside me. I wasn't sure what it was, but I knew it was important. Ho'oponopono - a practice of reconciliation, responsibility, and healing.

I began to read about it, and the words spoke directly to my soul. It was simple yet profound, an ancient practice that promised freedom from the very emotions that had been holding me hostage for so long. Without hesitation, I enrolled in a course to learn more. The moment I signed up felt like stepping onto a path I was always meant to walk. That day - an ordinary day turned extraordinary - became one of the most magical days of my life. I had found the key to my liberation.

The Four Sacred Phrases

In the course, I learned the four sacred phrases of Ho'oponopono, each one carrying its own magic:

- "I'm sorry."

- "Please forgive me."

- "Thank you."

- "I love you."

At first, these words seemed so simple, almost too simple. But as I spoke them - whispering them gently to myself, letting them reverberate through my being - I felt something begin to shift.

I'm Sorry

The first phrase, "I'm sorry," wasn't about seeking external forgiveness. It was about taking responsibility for the energy I had carried. I wasn't blaming myself, but rather acknowledging that I was the creator of my reality, even in my pain.

Sorry to Myself

I begin with these words, not to others, but to myself. I say sorry to the parts of me that have been neglected, ignored, or harmed in ways I never fully acknowledged. I apologize for the times I've mistreated my body, mind, and soul - knowing that something wasn't good for me, but still choosing it. I've eaten things I knew weren't healthy, like that burger I devoured despite knowing how it would weigh me down. I've scrolled endlessly through Instagram, staring at screens when I knew my eyes needed rest.

I've chosen convenience over well-being, comfort over growth, and in those moments, I've neglected the deep care I deserve. I say sorry to the tired parts of me that needed sleep but were kept awake by distractions.

I apologize to my heart for the times it ached because I didn't listen, when I chose to ignore the gentle whispers of self-love in favor of external validation. I'm sorry for all the moments where I didn't honor my own needs, for the times I chose the easy way rather than the healing way. I'm sorry for the self-judgment, the guilt, and the guilt I've placed on myself - when all I needed was grace.

Sorry to Others

I'm sorry to others, too, for the ways I may have unknowingly caused pain. I have to acknowledge that even though my intentions were never to hurt, sometimes my actions, or lack thereof, led to suffering.

The words I spoke in haste, the silence when I should have spoken up, the moments I didn't show up as my true self - these have rippled out, affecting the lives of those around me. I say sorry for the misunderstandings, the times I may have let someone down, for any unintentional harm caused. I recognize that even with the best intentions, we all create karmas that can echo back in ways we don't foresee. I apologize for the imprints I may have left on others, for every careless action, and every missed opportunity to be more mindful.

Sorry to Universe

And as I say sorry to myself, and to those around me, I expand this apology to the universe itself. Before I close my eyes each night, I send out a deep, heartfelt apology to everyone I may have hurt, knowingly or unknowingly.

I apologize for every time my actions or my energy contributed to pain, suffering, or negativity, whether it was someone close to me or someone I've never met. I ask for forgiveness from the world, from the people I may have crossed paths with, from the souls whose paths I touched in fleeting moments but may have left behind a trail of sadness.

Sorry to Control Everything

I let go of the belief that I am perfect or that I can control everything around me. Instead, I recognize my humanity, my mistakes, and my deepest wish for healing. I apologize for all the karma I may have unknowingly created, for all the times I allowed the ego to lead instead of compassion, for all the judgments I've passed, and for the actions that have perpetuated pain.

I send my apology out with no expectation, no demand for forgiveness, but simply as a release - an offering of peace. A reminder that I am always in the process of learning, growing, and transforming, and that in each moment, I can choose to align with love, kindness, and understanding. I am sorry. I forgive myself, and I forgive others. I thank you, and I love you.

Please forgive me

"Please forgive me" was a surrendering of the past, an offering of forgiveness not only to others but to myself. It is a powerful request for release from guilt and negative energy. It's an invitation to let go of past actions and emotions that may have caused harm, consciously or unconsciously.

By saying this, we acknowledge our responsibility in creating our reality and seek inner healing. It is not just about asking for forgiveness from others but also forgiving ourselves. This phrase helps us release burdens, create peace, and allow love to flow into our hearts.

In saying these words, I open my heart to the immense healing that forgiveness offers. I ask for forgiveness, not only from others but from myself. I recognize the times I have fallen short, when my actions, however unintentional, have caused harm or hurt to those I love, and to myself.

Forgiveness for the Past

I ask for forgiveness for the moments I failed to show up as my highest self, when I acted out of fear, doubt, or confusion. I acknowledge the energy I've held within me - resentment, regret, or judgment - and I release it now.

Please forgive me for the times I've allowed my wounds to dictate my reactions, for the moments I let my past mistakes shape my present, instead of embracing the wisdom they offered. I seek forgiveness for the pain I caused with my words, or the things left unsaid that could have healed. I ask for forgiveness for not recognizing the interconnectedness of all beings, for when I failed to act with compassion, understanding, and empathy.

Forgiveness for the Imperfections

Asking for forgiveness is an act of surrender, a letting go of the burden I've carried for too long. It's a request to free myself from the weight of guilt, from the shadows of the past that have clouded my vision. It's an invitation to release the grip of old stories, old wounds, and to open up to the possibility of renewal and peace.

Please forgive me, for I am not perfect, but I am committed to learning, growing, and becoming more aligned with love. I ask for forgiveness not as a sign of weakness, but as a declaration of strength - the strength to release what no longer serves me, to move forward with grace, and to embrace the love that resides within me and around me. May this forgiveness heal the broken places, mend the gaps, and guide me back to the truth of who I am - a being of love, of light, and of infinite potential. Please forgive me, and in doing so, may I forgive myself, allowing my heart to soften and my soul to be free.

Thank You

"Thank you" - a quiet yet powerful reminder of gratitude for the lessons, for the healing already taking place. "Thank you" holds a deep, transformative power. It is an expression of gratitude for the healing that is already happening within us.

When we say "Thank you," we are acknowledging that the process of releasing negative emotions and shifting our energy has begun. It's an affirmation that we trust in the process of healing, even before we see its results.

Gratitude opens the heart and soul to the flow of love, and by saying "Thank you," we invite more peace, understanding, and healing into our lives. It's a way of honoring the lessons learned and the growth that comes from every experience.

Thank You to Yourself

I open my heart to the transformative power of gratitude. I express my thanks, not only to others but to myself. I recognize the times when I have doubted, when fear and confusion have clouded my path, and when I failed to see the lessons in my struggles. I thank myself for the strength to grow through each challenge, and for the resilience that has guided me through even the hardest of times. Though I've made mistakes, I honor myself for the willingness to learn and evolve with each experience.

Thank You for Each Moment

Thank you for the moments when I fell short, for they have been opportunities for growth. I am grateful for the lessons I've learned, even when they came through hardship. I thank the pain and the joy, the light and the dark, for each one has taught me something profound. I hold space for the energy I've carried - regret, guilt, or judgment - and I release it with gratitude, knowing that each emotion has served its purpose.

Thank You for The Wounds

Thank you for the wounds, for they have revealed the places within me that needed healing. I appreciate the wisdom they have offered, and I honor the journey of self-discovery that has come from those challenges.

I am grateful for the opportunities to act with compassion, even when I stumbled.   I thank myself for the courage to continue, despite moments of doubt or hesitation.

Thank You for The Imperfections

In the process of gratitude, I acknowledge my imperfections and the lessons they bring. Gratitude is not just a practice, but a deep surrender - a willingness to let go of the burdens I've carried. I thank myself for the strength to release what no longer serves me, to free myself from the shadows of the past, and to embrace the clarity that comes with a heart full of appreciation. By offering this gratitude, I open the door to the infinite possibilities that await.

Thank your for The Love Around ME

Thank you for the love that surrounds me, for the people and experiences that have enriched my life. I am grateful for the moments of connection, of understanding, and of love that I have shared with others. I thank the universe for guiding me toward growth, peace, and healing. I am grateful for the person I am becoming - more aligned with my true essence, more aware, and more compassionate. May this gratitude heal the broken places within me, mending the gaps and guiding me back to the truth of who I am - a being of love, light, and infinite potential. Thank you, and in doing so, may I continue to honor and love myself, allowing my heart to expand and my soul to be free, knowing that I am on a path of endless growth, healing, and transformation.

I Love You

And finally, "I love you" - the most profound of all. It was a message of deep, unconditional love for myself, a promise to heal, to forgive, and to embrace peace. "I love you" is the most powerful expression of healing and transformation. It is a declaration of love not just for others, but also for ourselves. When we say "I love you," we are offering unconditional love to the parts of us that need healing - the wounds, the fears, the doubts. It is a reminder that love is the ultimate force that can heal all things.

This phrase allows us to connect with our deepest essence, which is love, and helps us release judgment and embrace compassion. By saying "I love you," we invite a sense of unity, peace, and divine healing, not only for ourselves but for everyone and everything around us.

In saying these words, I open my heart to the immense power that love offers. I declare my love, not only for others but for myself. I recognize the times I have doubted, when fear and insecurity held me back, and when I failed to show up fully as the loving being I am meant to be. I acknowledge the moments when I didn't honor my own worth, and I embrace the love within me now.

Love for the Past

I offer love to the moments I've struggled, when I acted out of fear, uncertainty, or confusion. I honor the lessons of my past and release any judgment or regret I've carried with me.

I choose to love myself even in my imperfections, recognizing that every challenge and every mistake has been an opportunity for growth. Please love me for the times I've allowed my wounds to cloud my vision, for the moments I let my past define who I am, instead of using it to fuel my evolution. I invite love into the places where I've been hardest on myself, and I embrace the wisdom that my experiences have provided. I ask for love for the things I may have said or done that caused harm, and for the unspoken moments where love could have healed.

Love for The Wounds

I love you, even if you have hurt me. In the depths of my heart, I choose to see beyond the pain, beyond the actions that caused me sorrow. I understand that sometimes we hurt others because of our own wounds, our fears, or our struggles.

And even though your actions may have left scars, I release the anger and resentment, choosing instead to send you love. I love you not because of what you did or didn't do, but because love is the only way to truly heal and move forward.

I let go of the past and hold onto the peace that comes from forgiving, for I know that holding onto pain only hurts me further. You are a part of my journey, and in loving you, I free myself from the burden of bitterness.

I love you, not as a sign of weakness, but as a way to reclaim my peace, my strength, and my ability to move forward with an open heart. As I repeated these phrases, I felt a subtle but powerful shift. It wasn't immediate, but over time, I began to feel lighter. It was as if with each repetition, I was shedding layers of pain, guilt, and regret, like leaves falling from a tree in autumn.

Each word was like a brushstroke of light, painting over the dark corners of my mind. The handcuffs began to loosen.

A Prayer for Loving Myself

I stand before the mirror, and in my eyes, I see,

A soul that's been searching, longing to be free.

I offer this prayer to the heart within me,

To embrace every part, and let my spirit be.

I thank you, dear heart, for your courage and grace,

For your strength, for your kindness, in each tender place.

I release all the doubts, the fears that I've known

And welcome the love that has always been my own.

May I honor my journey, the path I have walked

And love every step, even when I have talked,

Harshly to myself, or doubted my worth,

May I forgive and remember my infinite birth.

I ask for the wisdom to love what I see,

To nurture and cherish the person I'll be.

For I am a being of beauty and light,

A soul deserving of love, pure and bright.

May I hold my heart softly, with gentle embrace,

And walk through this life with a smile on my face.

For in loving myself, I set my soul free,

To live fully, to shine, and to simply be me.

Amen.

A Letter to Divine Presence

Dear Divine Presence,

I come before you with a heart heavy with regret and self-doubt. I acknowledge the times I have fallen short, the moments I have been harsh with myself, and the choices I have made that no longer serve me. Please help me release the weight of guilt and shame that I have carried for so long. I ask for the strength to forgive myself for the mistakes I've made, for the times I've hurt others or failed to show up as my highest self.

I recognize that I am human, and in my humanity, I have learned lessons, sometimes through hardship, sometimes through pain. Help me see these moments as opportunities for growth, not as reasons to judge or condemn myself. Grant me the grace to let go of the past, to release the burdens I've placed on my heart, and to embrace the beauty of my imperfections.

Teach me to love myself as I am - flaws, scars, and all - knowing that I am deserving of healing, peace, and forgiveness. I forgive myself for the times I doubted my worth, for the moments I held myself back, and for the times I didn't trust in my own strength.

I forgive myself for not always showing love to the person I am, for not always being kind to my heart.

May I walk forward with compassion for myself, knowing that each step I take is a step toward healing, growth, and self-love. I release the past and embrace the present moment with open arms, ready to move forward with the wisdom and grace I have gained.

Thank you, Divine Presence, for the gift of forgiveness. Thank you for guiding me back to my own heart, to peace, and to the love that resides within me.

Amen.

29

THE TRANSFORMATIVE POWER OF HO'OPONOPONO

"Healing is about taking responsibility for everything that comes into your life. When you clean the memories that create suffering, you open yourself to divine inspiration and true freedom." - Dr. Ihaleakala Hew

The more I practiced, the more I noticed how Ho'oponopono began to weave itself into every corner of my life. Every time I felt even the slightest discomfort - physical, emotional, or mental - I would turn to the four phrases. When a fever tried to creep in, I whispered them quietly to myself. When I felt fear or anxiety, I called upon the healing words. Every time, I felt a wave of peace wash over me. My body relaxed. My mind cleared. The discomfort would fade away like morning fog under the warm rays of the sun. But it wasn't just my body that was healing. My relationships began to transform. When misunderstandings arose with loved ones, I used Ho'oponopono to clear the energy. I would say the words, and it was as if a veil had lifted, creating space for deeper understanding and forgiveness. The more I used the practice, the more I felt connected - not only to others but to myself. Even the simplest things - like when my phone or laptop wasn't working - became opportunities for healing. I would speak the four phrases, and it was as if the universe itself responded, helping things align and flow.

The Freedom of Now

In the end, Ho'oponopono didn't just heal my past - it became a way of life. It taught me to forgive myself, to love myself, and to embrace the present moment fully. The invisible handcuffs that once held me captive were no longer there. I was free - free to live, free to love, and free to create with an open heart. Each phrase, a key to unlocking my own liberation. Now, whenever life feels challenging, whenever I'm faced with pain or uncertainty, I turn to those four sacred phrases. They are my constant companions, my guides, and my healing balm. I've learned that true freedom comes not from controlling the external world but from healing and releasing the energy within. And in that healing, I've found a peace deeper than I ever imagined.

This is my story - a journey from regret to freedom, from guilt to love. And it is only the beginning.

Ho'oponopono is a beautiful practice that invites us to take responsibility for the energy we carry within ourselves. It is a reminder that the world we experience is deeply connected to our inner state. Every challenge, every conflict, and even our health, is in some way influenced by the thoughts, emotions, and actions we harbor. When we hold on to resentment, anger, or hurt, we create negative energy that not only affects us internally but also perpetuates these feelings in the world around us.

At the heart of Ho'oponopono lies the understanding that the healing of any situation begins with us. The practice doesn't ask us to blame others for our suffering, but instead encourages us to look within, recognizing that we have a part to play in everything that happens in our lives. It's about taking ownership of our emotions and releasing the grip they have on us, inviting peace and transformation in their place. The practice of Ho'oponopono, as popularized by Dr. Ihaleakala Hew Len, offers a simple yet profound way to heal ourselves. It revolves around four powerful phrases - each one a step toward releasing negativity and embracing love.

How Ho'oponopono Can Help You Heal

Ho'oponopono works by shifting your mindset and emotional state, helping you release the negative energy you may be holding onto. It teaches that you are responsible for your own feelings and experiences, even if they involve others. By applying the mantra to situations where you feel hurt, angry, or blocked, you begin to dissolve negative emotions and bring yourself into alignment with peace and forgiveness.

The beauty of Ho'oponopono is its simplicity. Whether you are dealing with personal struggles, challenging relationships, or inner turmoil, the practice encourages deep self-awareness and compassion, helping you heal from within.

It's a reminder that healing often starts not with changing others, but by healing ourselves and shifting our own energy. Through regular practice of the Ho'oponopono mantra, I begin to feel more at peace, let go of past hurts, and foster greater emotional resilience. It served as a powerful reminder that forgiveness, love, and gratitude are transformative forces in our lives. For me This is more than just a technique - it's a philosophy, a way of life that emphasizes personal responsibility, love, and healing. It encourages us to heal our hearts and minds, to restore our inner balance, and to approach the world with compassion and forgiveness.

Healing Relationships with Ho'oponopono

I never thought four simple phrases could change my life. *"I'm sorry. Please forgive me. Thank you. I love you."* But when I discovered the practice of Ho'oponopono, I realized that healing relationships wasn't about fixing others - it was about healing myself first. There was a time when my relationship with a close friend had become strained. Misunderstandings piled up, and unspoken resentment created a wall between us. Every conversation felt forced, every silence heavy with things left unsaid. I told myself that it wasn't my fault - that if they truly cared, they would reach out. But deep down, I knew that holding onto blame was only keeping me stuck.

Each day, I sat in a quiet space, closed my eyes, and thought of my friend. I repeated the mantra:

"I'm sorry. Please forgive me. Thank you. I love you."

I wasn't saying it to them directly - I was saying it to myself, to the energy of our relationship, to the emotions I had been holding onto. At first, it felt awkward, like I was just repeating empty words. But as the days passed, something shifted. I began to see where I had contributed to the distance between us. Maybe I hadn't expressed my feelings clearly, or perhaps my own fears had caused me to misinterpret their actions. More importantly, I realized that by holding onto resentment, I was only hurting myself. As I continued the practice, I felt lighter. The anger and frustration I had carried for so long started to fade. And then, something unexpected happened - my friend reached out. Our first conversation was hesitant, but there was a softness that hadn't been there before. Slowly, we started to rebuild our connection, and before I knew it, the friendship that had once felt lost was rekindled. That experience taught me a powerful lesson: healing doesn't always come from demanding apologies or proving who was right. It comes from letting go, from taking responsibility for our own emotions, and from allowing love and forgiveness to take the lead. Now, whenever I face conflict - whether with a friend, a family member, or even myself - I return to those four simple phrases. Because sometimes, the key to healing isn't changing others. It's changing the way we hold them in our hearts.

Manifesting Abundance with Ho'oponopono

A few years ago, I found myself stuck in a cycle of financial struggle. No matter how hard I worked, money seemed to slip through my fingers like sand. Unexpected expenses always popped up, opportunities felt scarce, and deep down, a quiet but persistent voice whispered: *"Maybe I'm just not meant to be wealthy."* I didn't realize it then, but I was carrying a lifetime of limiting beliefs about money. I grew up hearing phrases like *"Money doesn't grow on trees"* and *"You have to work twice as hard to make ends meet."* I believed that wealth was for others, not for me. Initially, I thought, *What does forgiveness have to do with money?* But something about it called to me. So, I decided to try.

I sat in a quiet space, closed my eyes, and repeated the four phrases:

"I'm sorry. Please forgive me. Thank you. I love you."

At first, I directed them toward my financial past - the mistakes, the bad investments, the times I felt powerless. Then, I turned inward. I asked forgiveness from myself for believing I wasn't worthy of abundance. I apologized for holding onto scarcity, for doubting my own ability to attract wealth.

Days turned into weeks, and something shifted within me. The anxiety that once gripped me when checking my bank balance began to fade. Instead of seeing obstacles, I started noticing opportunities. Unexpected sources of income appeared - a freelance project, a refund I had forgotten about, even a random bonus at work. It felt as though, by clearing my inner blocks, I had finally allowed money to flow freely into my life.

One day, out of nowhere, I received a call about a business opportunity I had never even considered. A friend, unaware of my financial struggles, recommended me for a project that not only paid well but also aligned with my passion. It felt like the universe was finally responding to my openness.

Looking back, I realize that Ho'oponopono didn't magically bring me money - it removed the barriers I had built against receiving it. The moment I let go of my old beliefs, abundance found its way to me. Now, whenever I feel stuck or doubtful, I return to those four simple phrases. Because abundance isn't just about money - it's about allowing ourselves to receive, to trust, and to believe that we are worthy of all the good the universe has to offer.

Healing My Heart Through Ho'oponopono

For years, I carried an invisible weight - one made of past regrets, heartbreak, and self-blame. It wasn't something I spoke about, but it was always there, lingering in the quiet moments. I had made mistakes, been hurt, and, in some ways, hurt others too. No matter how much time passed, the memories stayed, replaying in my mind like an old record. Ho'oponopono, promised healing, not by changing the past, but by changing how I held onto it. Skeptical yet desperate for relief, I decided to try.

I sat in silence, closed my eyes, and softly repeated the four phrases:

"I'm sorry. Please forgive me. Thank you. I love you."

At first, the words felt foreign, almost meaningless. But as I continued, something inside me stirred. I directed them toward the version of me that had made mistakes - the one who didn't know better at the time. I spoke them to the moments where I had been hurt, to the younger me who had carried burdens too heavy for her to bear.

"I'm sorry for holding onto this pain for so long."

"Please forgive me for being so hard on myself."

"Thank you for surviving, for enduring."

"I love you. You are enough."

Tears streamed down my face, but with each repetition, the weight on my chest grew lighter. The memories were still there, but they no longer held power over me. I wasn't erasing the past - I was making peace with it.

Over the weeks, I kept practicing. Slowly, I noticed a shift. The self-judgment softened. The tight grip of anger and regret loosened. I found myself waking up with a little more lightness, a little more gratitude. I started treating myself with the same kindness I had always given others. One day, I looked in the mirror and, for the first time in a long time, saw not someone broken, but someone healing. Someone worthy of love - not just from others, but from herself. That's when I knew: Ho'oponopono had given me the greatest gift of all - inner peace. And with that peace, I could finally move forward, lighter and freer than ever before.

When to Use Ho'oponopono

Ho'oponopono is a powerful tool to clear negative energy and restore peace, and there are several moments when it can be particularly effective. During conflict, whether it's anger, resentment, or miscommunication, repeating the mantra helps dissolve negative emotions and promotes healing. If you feel stuck in any area of your life - be it your career, relationships, or health - It clears the emotional blocks that are holding you back, allowing you to move forward. Using the mantra before sleep can also be highly beneficial, as it helps release the tensions of the day, bringing you into a peaceful state for rest and renewal. Additionally, incorporating this into your meditation practice enhances your inner peace, aligning you with your higher self and deepening your connection to the present moment.

Creating the Space for Healing

To begin practicing this, find a quiet and comfortable space where you won't be disturbed. Take a few deep breaths to center yourself. Close your eyes and focus on the issue you wish to heal. It could be a person, a situation, or even yourself. As you bring the issue to mind, allow yourself to feel the emotions associated with it. Don't judge or analyze - simply acknowledge and be present with those feelings. This is the first step of healing: allowing yourself to feel and accept what is present. And repeat "I am Sorry, Please Forgive me, Thank You and I love You "

Power Of 108 Times

The number 108 is deeply sacred in many spiritual traditions, symbolizing unity and the connection between the mind, body, and spirit. In the practice of Ho'oponopono, repeating the mantra 108 times amplifies its healing power, aligning the practitioner with universal energy and facilitating deeper forgiveness, love, and emotional release.

When reciting *"I'm sorry, Please forgive me, Thank you, I love you"* 108 times, you magnify the energy of the words, helping to clear negative emotions, limiting beliefs, and past wounds. This repetition creates a meditative state, allowing you to release tension and cultivate peace, love, and gratitude.

The number 108 acts as a container for your healing, guiding you toward transformation by helping you surrender to the process of forgiveness. With each repetition, you open yourself up to deeper levels of emotional freedom, healing, and self-love, ultimately manifesting a more abundant and joyful life. Through this sacred practice, you not only heal past hurts but also invite positive energy into your present and future, allowing the universal flow of love and healing to guide you toward peace and inner harmony.

Why Say Thank You for the Negative?

Negative experiences often carry valuable lessons, hidden opportunities, and clues about the areas in life that need attention or improvement. When something unpleasant happens, it's easy to get frustrated, angry, or upset. But the real power comes from recognizing that everything serves a purpose, even the things that seem negative at first. Here's why saying "thank you" for negative situations is a game-changer. When you choose to thank the negative experience, you're actively changing your mindset. Instead of seeing it as a setback, you begin to see it as a lesson or a stepping stone toward something better. Resisting negativity only keeps you stuck in it longer. When you accept it and thank it, you let go of the resistance. This frees up energy and allows you to move forward with greater ease. Also, every time you respond with gratitude instead of frustration, you strengthen your mental resilience. You learn to face adversity with a positive attitude, and that makes you stronger and more equipped to handle challenges in the future. The major benefit is

Complaining or focusing on the negative tends to keep us stuck in a loop of problems. But when you thank the negative, you shift your focus toward solutions and open up space for new ideas to flow in. It's like telling the universe, "I'm ready for growth, what's next?"

How to Say Thank You for the Negative

Here's a simple way to incorporate this practice into your daily life:

When Something Goes Wrong, Pause:

Instead of reacting with frustration, stop for a moment and acknowledge the negative situation. Take a deep breath, and center yourself before proceeding.

Say "Thank You":

You don't have to mean it right away, but say it. It could be something like:

"Thank you for this challenge. I know it's here to teach me something."

"Thank you for showing me where I need to grow or change."

"Thank you for helping me become stronger."

Reflect on the Lesson

After you've said thank you, take a few moments to reflect.

Ask yourself, what is this experience teaching me?

What can I learn from this?

Sometimes the answer will be clear, and other times it might take a bit of time to see the lesson.

Find the Opportunity

Look for the hidden opportunity in the situation. Maybe a negative experience shows you where you need to improve, motivates you to take a different path, or helps you appreciate what you already have.

Examples of Saying Thank You for the Negative

Let's take a look at some real-life examples of how you can apply this rule:

Financial Setback

Let's say you lose money or face a financial setback. Instead of stressing out, say: "Thank you for this experience. It's showing me how I can be more mindful with my money, and it's encouraging me to find new ways to create wealth."

Relationship Problems

If you have a disagreement or problem in a relationship, instead of holding on to resentment, say: "Thank you for this challenge. It's helping me understand what I need from this relationship and teaching me how to communicate better."

Career Stagnation

If you feel stuck in your job or career, instead of complaining about your circumstances, say: "Thank you for this situation. It's making me realize that I need to take action toward something I truly love. I'm now ready to pursue new opportunities."

Health Issues

If you're facing a health challenge, you might say: "Thank you for this experience. It's teaching me to take better care of my body and prioritize my well-being. I'm becoming healthier every day."

Reframing Negativity with Gratitude

Saying "thank you" for negative experiences is a powerful tool that can help you shift your energy and attract more positivity into your life. By learning to see challenges as opportunities, you train yourself to respond with grace and gratitude instead of resistance. In doing so, you open yourself up to personal growth, greater success, and deeper abundance

So, the next time life throws you a curveball, instead of reacting with frustration, pause and say, "Thank you." It's in these moments that you empower yourself the most. Embrace the challenges, and watch how the universe aligns to give you exactly what you need to grow.

30

Embracing the Flow –
A Journey of Surrender and Self-Love

"Surrender to what is. Let go of what was. Have faith in what will be."   - Sonia Ricotti

Ho'oponopono for Surrender

Preparation: Grounding into the Present Moment
Take a deep breath in… hold it for a moment… and slowly exhale.

Feel the rise and fall of your chest as you breathe

Allow your body to relax, your mind to quiet down, and your heart to open.

Whatever you are carrying - worries, expectations, doubts - set them aside for now.

This is your time to surrender, to trust, and to heal.

Step 1: Acknowledging Resistance

Sometimes, I find myself holding on too tightly - trying to control outcomes, fearing the unknown, and struggling against life's flow.

I acknowledge that this resistance does not serve me, but I have been afraid to let go.

I recognize the moments when I have doubted the process, questioned my own journey, or felt impatient with divine timing.

Now, gently place your hand on your heart and repeat:

"I am sorry, Universe, for the times I have resisted your flow and held onto fear instead of faith."

"I am sorry for trying to force things to happen in my way and in my time instead of trusting your perfect divine timing."

"I am sorry for the moments I let worry take over, forgetting that I am always guided, protected, and supported."

Breathe deeply and allow the weight of control to loosen. You are safe in surrender.

Step 2: Releasing the Struggle

I now see that my need to control is only an illusion, a barrier between me and the peace I seek.

Holding on so tightly has only drained my energy and made me feel disconnected from my true self.

I no longer wish to carry the burden of needing all the answers right now.

I choose to release the struggle, the tension, and the fear that things might not work out.

With deep sincerity, say:

"Please forgive me, Universe, for forgetting that everything is already working in my favor, even when I cannot see it yet." "Please forgive me for resisting growth, change, and divine intervention, believing that I knew what was best for me."

"Please forgive me for allowing doubt to cloud my heart when deep down, I know I am always being taken care of."

Feel the tension in your body dissolve as you release control. Let it go.

Step 3: Trusting Divine Timing

I understand now that surrendering is not giving up - it is allowing life to unfold as it is meant to.

I trust that everything is happening for my highest good, even when the path ahead is unclear.

I welcome the unknown, knowing that it holds possibilities far greater than anything I could ever imagine.

I choose to be patient, to trust, and to let the Universe guide me with love and wisdom.

With gratitude in your heart, affirm:

"Thank you, Universe, for always aligning things perfectly, even when I do not understand them in the moment."

"Thank you for removing obstacles that are not meant for me and redirecting me toward the opportunities that will truly serve my highest self."

"Thank you for teaching me that trust is not about seeing the whole picture, but about knowing in my heart that I am exactly where I need to be."

Let a wave of gratitude wash over you, filling you with peace and acceptance.

Step 4: Fully Surrendering with Love

I choose love over fear, faith over doubt, and surrender over resistance.

I release the need to figure everything out, to rush, or to control.

I allow myself to flow like water, trusting that the current of life is leading me to something even better than I imagined.

I surrender my fears, my worries, and my expectations. I surrender fully, completely, and with love.

With your whole heart, say:

"I love you, Universe, and I trust your divine wisdom to lead me exactly where I need to go."

"I love you for always taking care of me, even when I cannot see the bigger picture."

"I love you for holding me in your embrace, guiding me gently, and reminding me that I am never alone on this journey."

Take a deep breath in… and exhale…

Feel the lightness in your heart as you surrender completely.

Closing: Embracing Peace & Divine Flow

There is nothing more for you to do right now.

You have spoken your truth, you have released your fears, and you have returned to trust.

You are safe. You are loved. You are free.

Whenever doubts arise, return to these words:

"I trust. I surrender. I receive."

Now, gently open your eyes when you are ready.

Move forward with ease, knowing that everything is unfolding exactly as it should.

Ho'oponopono For Self-Love

Step 1: Set Your Intention

"Today, I choose to connect deeply with myself. I choose to release self-doubt, heal past wounds, and embrace unconditional self-love. I honor myself and the beautiful journey I am on."

Take a deep breath in, filling your body with light, and exhale, letting go of any tension or resistance.

Step 2: Begin the Practice

Start by visualizing your inner self - your heart, your soul, the essence of who you are. Imagine this part of you standing in front of you, looking at you with love, understanding, and compassion. Now, slowly begin to repeat the four Ho'oponopono phrases.

"I'm sorry."

"I'm sorry for the times I've been too hard on myself.

I'm sorry for not loving myself the way I deserved.

I'm sorry for ignoring my needs, my dreams, and my feelings.

I'm sorry for the times I doubted my worth, compared myself to others, or felt like I wasn't enough.

I'm sorry for carrying guilt, shame, and pain that I didn't deserve to hold onto.

I acknowledge my mistakes, my fears, and my struggles. I am human, and I am learning. I am deeply sorry."

Take a deep breath and allow yourself to feel the weight of what you're releasing.

"Please forgive me."

"Please forgive me for the times I didn't honor my own boundaries.

Forgive me for neglecting my own happiness while trying to please others.

Forgive me for the harsh words I've spoken to myself, for not seeing the beauty and strength in who I am.

Forgive me for doubting my potential, for playing small, and for not believing in myself. I ask for forgiveness for carrying patterns, beliefs, or habits that have held me back. I now release them with love. Please forgive me."

Take another deep breath, and with your exhale, feel the forgiveness washing over you.

"Thank you."

"Thank you for standing by me, even when I didn't appreciate you.

Thank you for every breath, every heartbeat, and every step I've taken on this journey.

Thank you for the strength you've shown me during difficult times and the lessons you've taught me along the way.

Thank you for being resilient, for holding onto hope, and for never giving up, even when things felt impossible.

Thank you for allowing me the opportunity to heal, to grow, and to transform into the person I am becoming. Thank you for loving me, even when I didn't love myself."

Feel a deep sense of gratitude for your body, mind, and soul as you take another deep breath.

"I love you."

"I love you for who you are and who you are becoming.

I love your flaws, your imperfections, and your quirks.

I love your strength, your courage, and your kindness.

I love you for surviving, for thriving, and for always seeking the best, even in the hardest moments.

I love you because you are worthy of love - just as you are. I love you because you are deserving of joy, peace, and abundance. I love you because you are me, and I choose to love myself unconditionally."

As you repeat "I love you," imagine your entire body being filled with a warm, glowing light - pure love radiating from within.

Take a few moments to sit in this feeling of self-love and healing. Imagine any heaviness, negativity, or self-doubt dissolving into the light, leaving you feeling lighter, freer, and more aligned with your true self. Say these words to yourself as you close:

"I honor myself. I trust myself. I am worthy of love, peace, and happiness. Today, I choose to love and accept myself unconditionally."

Take three deep breaths, gently bring your awareness back to the present moment, and open your eyes when you're ready.

A Prayer of Healing & Forgiveness to My Younger Self
Take a deep breath. Close your eyes. Place your hands over your heart.

Now, imagine yourself stepping into a vast space filled with a soft golden glow. The air is warm, gentle, comforting - like love itself. As you walk forward, you see a small crib before you, and inside it… is you - your younger self, just born.

So tiny. So pure. So innocent.

Their tiny fingers curl and uncurl, their chest rises and falls with each soft breath, their eyes - still untouched by the burdens of life - flutter open for a moment. And in that moment, your heart swells. This is you, before the weight of expectations, before the struggles, before the pain. You kneel beside the crib, tears welling up in your eyes. With a trembling voice, you whisper:

"I'm sorry."

I'm sorry, my love, for all the times I didn't protect you the way I should have.

I'm sorry for letting the world make you believe you weren't enough.

I'm sorry for the pain I let you carry, for the wounds that never should have been yours.

I'm sorry for not always listening when your body, your heart, and your soul cried for rest, for love, for care.

I'm sorry for forgetting how precious you are.

A soft breeze flows through the room, and you feel a shift - a warmth, an opening. Your younger self stirs, their tiny hand reaching toward you. You gently take it in yours and whisper:

"Please forgive me."

Please forgive me for not always honoring the miracle that you are.

Please forgive me for doubting your strength, for not seeing the beauty in you when you needed it the most.

Please forgive me for the harsh words, the self-judgment, the moments I stood in front of the mirror and wished you were different.

Please forgive me for the pain I let you endure, for the love I withheld from you - the love you always deserved.

Tears spill down your cheeks, but they are not heavy. They are cleansing, releasing. And as they fall, you feel something changing within you - a deep, unshakable gratitude rising like the sun.

You place your hand gently on your younger self's chest and say:

"Thank you."

Thank you, my beautiful soul, for carrying me through every storm, even when I didn't acknowledge your strength.

Thank you for never giving up on me, for healing me in ways I never even noticed.

Thank you for your resilience, for your heartbeat, for every breath that kept me alive.

Thank you for reminding me - again and again - that I am worthy of love, of care, of peace.

A golden light begins to glow from within the tiny body before you, growing brighter and warmer until it surrounds both of you. It is love - pure, unconditional, eternal.

You lean in, pressing a gentle kiss to your younger self's forehead, and with all the love in your heart, you whisper:

"I love you."

I love you, my dearest, exactly as you are.

I love you for your scars, for your imperfections, for your strength.

I love you for being my home, my light, my guide.

I love you with all that I am, in this moment and forever.

As you embrace them, the golden light wraps around you both, merging your past and present selves into one. The weight of years, of wounds, of regrets dissolves, leaving only peace, healing, and wholeness.

You are safe. You are loved. You are whole.

Take a deep breath. Feel this truth settle within you.

And when you are ready, open your eyes - reborn in love, in forgiveness, in gratitude.

A Ho'oponopono Healing Prayer for Your Inner Child

Close your eyes. Take a deep, slow breath in… and exhale gently. Feel your heart beating, steady and strong. Now, imagine yourself walking down a path bathed in soft golden light. The air is warm and comforting, filled with a sense of peace and love.

As you walk, you notice a small figure sitting in the distance - a child. As you step closer, your breath catches in your throat. It's you.

Your younger self sits there, knees hugged to their chest, eyes filled with questions, with pain, with the burdens they have carried for so long. You feel an ache in your heart as you realize how much this child has endured - how much of your pain, fear, and self-doubt they still hold.

You kneel before them, gently reaching out your hands. With deep emotion, you whisper:

"I'm sorry."

I'm sorry, my love, for the times I abandoned you when you needed me the most.

I'm sorry for not listening to your cries, for pushing aside your emotions, for forcing you to be strong when all you wanted was to be held.

I'm sorry for the pain you carried in silence, for the wounds that were never acknowledged, for the love you longed for but never received.

I'm sorry for not treating you with the kindness, patience, and care you always deserved.

A single tear rolls down your younger self's cheek. They look at you, searching, waiting… hoping. You take their small hands in yours and say:

"Please forgive me."

Please forgive me for ignoring your needs, for suppressing your voice, for pretending you were fine when you weren't.

Please forgive me for the moments I looked in the mirror and criticized us instead of celebrating who we are.

Please forgive me for the unhealthy choices I made, for the times I neglected my body, my health, my well-being.

Please forgive me for believing I wasn't enough, for the years of self-doubt, for the times I let fear and pain define us.

Your younger self's fingers tighten around yours. A shift happens - subtle, but powerful. A warm, golden light begins to glow between your hands. A feeling of release, of peace, of understanding fills the space between you.

With deep gratitude, you smile through your tears and say:

"Thank you."

Thank you for holding on, for surviving even when the world felt too heavy.

Thank you for keeping my heart beating, for allowing my body to heal even when I didn't take care of it.

Thank you for your resilience, for your innocence, for the love that never truly left us.

Thank you for reminding me that I have always been whole, even when I believed I was broken.

The golden light expands, flowing from your hands into your younger self's heart, filling every wound, every scar, every space that once held pain.

Now, with every ounce of love within you, you place your hand on your younger self's cheek, look into their eyes, and whisper:

"I love you."

I love you for everything you are and everything you have been.

I love you for your courage, for your softness, for your unwavering hope

I love you for the way you kept dreaming, even when life tried to make you forget how.

I love you unconditionally, forever, in all forms, in all moments.

Your younger self lets out a soft, contented sigh. Their body relaxes. The sadness in their eyes begins to fade, replaced by warmth, by trust, by love.

As the golden light surrounds you both, it begins to merge you together - not in loss, but in unity. The child within you has never left. They are still here, still alive within your heart, and now, they are finally healed, whole, and free.

Take a deep breath. Feel this peace, this love, this healing settle deep within you.

And when you are ready… open your eyes.

You are safe.

You are whole.

You are loved.

Guided Meditation for Healing Your Body

Find a quiet place where you won't be disturbed. Sit or lie down comfortably. Close your eyes. Take a deep, slow breath in… hold for a moment… and gently exhale.

Feel your body begin to relax.

With each breath, let go of any tension, any heaviness, any worries. Allow yourself to sink deeper into a state of peace, a state of healing.

Now, bring your attention to your heart. Imagine a warm, golden light glowing at the center of your chest. This light is pure love, pure healing energy - a source of deep restoration within you.

With your next breath, let this golden light begin to expand… slowly… gently… filling your entire chest.

Now, whisper in your mind:

"I'm sorry."

I'm sorry for any stress or pain I have caused you.

I'm sorry for the times I ignored your signals, your needs, your cries for rest.

I'm sorry for carrying worries, fears, and emotions that have weighed you down.

As you breathe in, feel this golden light growing warmer, softer - responding to your words with love and understanding.

"Please forgive me."

Please forgive me for not always nourishing you, f or neglecting you, for doubting your strength.

Please forgive me for the unhealthy choices, the self-criticism, the moments I did not honor you.

Please forgive me for forgetting that you are my greatest gift.

Now, feel the golden light flowing beyond your heart, spreading into your shoulders, arms, and hands… traveling down into your belly, your legs, your feet. Every part of you is bathed in healing energy, in forgiveness, in love.

"Thank you."

Thank you, my body, for everything you do for me - every breath, every heartbeat, every step.

Thank you for carrying me through life, even when I took you for granted.

Thank you for healing, for regenerating, for always working to bring me back into balance.

The golden light glows even brighter now, flowing into every cell, every organ, every muscle. Feel it dissolving pain, washing away discomfort, filling you with strength, harmony, and renewal.

"I love you."

I love you, my body, exactly as you are.

I love you for your resilience, your beauty, your ability to heal.

I love you, and I promise to listen, to nurture, and to honor you from this moment forward.

Take a deep breath in… and as you exhale, feel every part of your body embraced in peace, in warmth, in wholeness.

You are healed.

You are whole.

You are loved.

When you're ready, gently bring awareness back to the present moment. Wiggle your fingers, your toes. And when you feel ready, slowly open your eyes.

Carry this **healing energy** with you.

Know that at any moment, you can return to this space - to love, to forgiveness, to deep healing.

Ho'oponopono For Health

Take a deep breath, close your eyes, and place your hands gently over your heart. Allow yourself to be fully present in this moment. Now, begin the practice:

"I'm sorry"

I'm sorry for any pain or imbalance I've caused my body.

I'm sorry for not always listening to your needs, for ignoring the signs you've shown me.

I'm sorry for the times I let stress, fear, or unhealthy habits take over.

I'm sorry for holding onto thoughts, emotions, or patterns that don't serve my health and well-being.

"Please forgive me"

Please forgive me for not nurturing you the way you deserve.

Please forgive me for the moments I doubted your strength and ability to heal.

Please forgive me for neglecting the care and attention you've needed.

Please forgive me for holding onto guilt or shame about my body or my health.

"Thank you"

Thank you for supporting me every single day, even when I haven't treated you well.

Thank you for your resilience, for healing me in ways I may not even realize

Thank you for carrying me through life, for every breath, every heartbeat, and every step.

Thank you for reminding me that I have the power to choose health and well-being.

"I love you"

I love you, my body, for everything you do for me

I love you for being my home, for holding my spirit, and for carrying me through life's journey.

I love you for your ability to heal, regenerate, and adapt.

I love you unconditionally, no matter what.

Visualization:

Now, imagine a soft, golden light filling your entire body, starting from your heart and radiating outward. This light carries love, forgiveness, and healing energy to every part of your body - your organs, muscles, cells, and even your thoughts.

As this light flows, feel it dissolving any blockages, pain, or negativity, leaving only peace, health, and balance in its place.

Take a few more deep breaths. When you're ready, open your eyes and say:

"I honor my body, my health, and my journey. I am whole, I am healed, I am at peace."

Ho'oponopono Abundance Meditation & Visualization

Find a quiet space where you won't be disturbed. Sit comfortably, close your eyes, and take a deep, calming breath in… hold for a moment… and gently exhale.

Breathe in abundance… and exhale all doubts.

Breathe in wealth… and exhale any resistance.

Breathe in gratitude… and exhale any fear.

Now, in your mind's eye, imagine yourself standing under a vast, open sky - endless, bright, and filled with golden energy. You feel a warm breeze on your skin, carrying with it the scent of prosperity, of new possibilities. Suddenly, the sky begins to shimmer, and you see cash flowing down from the Universe - softly, gently, like golden rain. The notes are crisp and new - ₹500, ₹1000, ₹2000 - floating around you like blessings from the Divine.

They swirl in the air, surrounding you, touching your hands, filling your pockets, landing at your feet. Now, look up. In the sky, you see a number forming - a number that represents the exact amount of money you wish to receive. It is clear, bright, shining like pure light. It is yours. It is already on its way to you.

With deep emotion, you place your hand on your heart and whisper:

"I'm sorry."

I'm sorry for the times I blocked my own abundance.

I'm sorry for believing I was not worthy of wealth.

I'm sorry for carrying limiting beliefs about money, about success, about receiving.

I'm sorry for any fears, doubts, or struggles I held onto.

Now, the golden notes fall even more abundantly around you, touching your skin, filling your hands with wealth. The Universe is responding, forgiving, aligning with your desires.

You take another deep breath and say:

"Please forgive me."

Please forgive me for ever doubting my own prosperity.

Please forgive me for not trusting that wealth is my birthright.

Please forgive me for any negative thoughts I have held about money.

Please forgive me for the times I rejected the flow of abundance.

The cash flow intensifies - it is endless, limitless. More and more currency flows to you, into your wallet, your bank account, your life. **You are being showered with divine wealth.**

Now, with deep gratitude in your heart, you smile and say:

"Thank you."

Thank you, Universe, for your infinite generosity.

Thank you for always supporting me, always providing for me.

Thank you for the wealth that flows to me easily and effortlessly.

Thank you for aligning me with prosperity, for opening all doors to abundance.

The number in the sky glows even brighter now. It is real, solid, already yours. Money is no longer something you chase - it flows to you naturally, continuously, abundantly.

Finally, with deep love, you open your arms wide, feeling the energy of wealth surround you. You whisper:

"I love you."

I love you, money, for being a tool of freedom and joy.

I love you, abundance, for flowing into my life in endless ways.

I love myself, for knowing that I am always supported.

I love the Universe, for blessing me with more than I could ever imagine.

Take a deep breath in... feel the golden notes resting gently in your hands. This is real. It is happening. You are wealthy.

With a final exhale, let all resistance go. Feel the energy of pure abundance settle within you. You are aligned with wealth. You are the magnet for infinite money.

And when you are ready... slowly open your eyes.

The Universe has already begun its work.

Wealth is yours.

Abundance is flowing.

It is done. It is done. It is done.

This meditation is designed to remove money blocks, align you with abundance, and allow you to receive effortlessly. You can do it daily to shift your energy toward wealth and prosperity.

Ho'oponopono Meditation & Visualization for Career Success

Find a quiet space where you won't be disturbed. Sit comfortably, close your eyes, and take a deep, calming breath in… hold for a moment… and gently exhale.

As you relax, imagine yourself standing at the entrance of a beautiful golden door - the gateway to your dream career, your highest potential.

You place your hand on your heart and whisper,

"I am ready. I am stepping into my greatest future."

Now, take a deep breath and step forward through the door.

As you cross the threshold, you find yourself in a bright, powerful future. You are no longer just dreaming of success - you are already living it.

See yourself in your ideal career.

Where are you?

What are you wearing?

Who are you working with?

What kind of work are you doing that excites and fulfills you?

Look around - your dream office, your thriving business, your stage, your clients, your projects - everything is exactly as you desire.

Feel it.

Breathe it in.

This is your reality.

Now, hear the applause of success, the recognition, the gratitude of those you've impacted. See the wealth, opportunities, and success flowing effortlessly into your life.

Your **future self** walks toward you. They are powerful, confident, and glowing with success. They look into your eyes and smile.

They whisper:

"Welcome home.

This is yours.

You have always been meant for this."

Ho'oponopono Prayer for Career Success

With deep emotion, you lace your hand on your heart and say:

"I'm sorry."

I'm sorry for the times I doubted myself.

I'm sorry for believing I wasn't good enough.

I'm sorry for the moments I hesitated, feared, or let opportunities pass me by.

I'm sorry for any limiting beliefs I held about success, money, or my worth.

As you say this, a golden light begins to shine from within you, breaking away all fears, all doubts, all self-sabotage.

You take a deep breath and say:

"Please forgive me."

Please forgive me for the times I didn't believe in my own power.

Please forgive me for not trusting my abilities, my path, my journey.

Please forgive me for letting fear hold me back.

Please forgive me for thinking I was not meant for greatness.

Now, feel a wave of forgiveness and pure, unconditional acceptance washing over you. Your future self-places a hand on your shoulder, reassuring you that all is well.

The past is gone.

The struggles no longer define you.

You are FREE.

You smile and say:

"Thank you."

Thank you, Universe, for aligning me with my dream career.

Thank you for every lesson, every opportunity, every challenge that shaped me.

Thank you for my skills, my passion, my vision, my unique gifts.

Thank you for the success that is already mine.

The golden light around you **grows even brighter**. Success, wealth, and abundance flow effortlessly toward you. Doors open. Opportunities arrive. The right people come into your life.

And now, you whisper the most powerful words of all:

"I love you."

I love you, my career, for allowing me to serve and shine.

I love you, my path, for guiding me toward my highest potential.

I love myself for being brave, for believing, for stepping forward into my dreams.

I love the Universe for blessing me with endless success and joy.

Anchoring Your Future Success

Your future self takes your hands and smiles.

"You are already this. You don't need to chase it - it is already yours."

Now, imagine merging with your future self - becoming that powerful, successful, limitless version of you.

Feel the energy shift.

Feel the confidence settle in.

Feel the certainty that you are already living your dream career.

You turn back and see that the golden door is gone - because there is no separation anymore.

This is your reality.

This is who you are now.

Take a deep breath in… and as you exhale, feel this success, this alignment, this unstoppable energy settling within you. When you're ready, gently open your eyes.

It Is Done. It Is Yours.

From this moment forward, you are walking, acting, and thinking as the successful person you have just embodied.

Doors will open.

Opportunities will come.

You are now fully aligned with your highest career potential.

It is done. It is done. It is done.

Closing the Prayer: Sealing the Energy

As you take this final breath, feel the warmth of love, healing, and abundance embracing you.

Know that you have been heard.

Know that you are already transformed.

Know that your desires are now aligning with divine timing.

The past no longer defines you.

The future is already yours.

All that remains is this sacred moment - where you are whole, complete, and at peace. With gratitude in your heart, whisper one last time:

"I release, I trust, I receive."

And so, the prayer is complete. And so, the energy is sealed.

And so, it is... **The chapter closes. A new one begins.**

31

HEALING THE INNER CHILD

"The wounded inner child contaminates your present life by replaying old scripts, but healing comes when you listen, acknowledge, and nurture that child within you." - John Bradshaw

The Storm Within

I remember being a teenager, caught in a storm of emotions I couldn't quite name. There were days when everything felt too overwhelming - like a silent scream trapped inside me, unheard and unrecognized.

I longed for someone to understand, to listen, to acknowledge the feelings that I didn't even have the words for.

Sometimes, it felt like there was a voice deep within me, a small fragile one, wanting to be heard - a baby longing to be pampered, reassured, and held. But I didn't know how to make sense of it.

A Chance Discovery

One evening, in the midst of one of my restless searches for peace, I found myself scrolling through YouTube, looking for meditation videos to calm my anxious mind. That's when I stumbled upon a title that seemed odd yet intriguing: "Heal Your Inner Child." At first, I scoffed. It sounded ridiculous. Inner child? What did that even mean? But curiosity got the better of me, and I clicked. That click led me down a path I never expected - one of deep healing and self-discovery.

Meeting My Inner Child

As the video played, the guide spoke about the wounded child that lives inside us, the one who carries our past pains, unmet needs, and unexpressed emotions. The idea struck me like lightning. It explained so much - why I sometimes reacted so strongly to small things, why certain words cut deeper than they should, why I often felt an inexplicable sadness or anger.

The more I listened, the more I realized that the pain I was experiencing wasn't just about the present - it was echoes from my younger self, still waiting to be heard. I learned that, as children, we are incredibly vulnerable. A stern look from a parent, a harsh word, or simply feeling ignored can leave wounds that stay with us for years.

Sometimes, these wounds become so deeply buried that we forget they exist, but they continue to shape the way we see the world, the way we trust, and the way we respond to love and rejection.

The First Step

The video introduced a practice - a meditation technique to connect with this inner child. At first, I was skeptical. Talking to my "inner child" felt strange, even silly. But I was desperate to feel better, so I gave it a try. I closed my eyes, took a deep breath, and followed the guide's words:

Breathing in, I see myself as a five-year-old child.

Breathing out, I smile with compassion at the child within me.

At first, nothing happened. I felt awkward, even resistant. But as I continued the practice, something shifted. In my mind's eye, I saw a little version of myself - small, lonely, and longing for reassurance. Tears welled up in my eyes. This was the part of me I had ignored for so long. And in that moment, I felt an overwhelming sense of tenderness toward that child. I wanted to hold them, to tell them they were safe, loved, and that they mattered.

The Transformation

The more I practiced this meditation, the more I noticed changes within me. I started understanding my emotions instead of running from them. I became kinder to myself, more forgiving of my past, and more patient with my healing. It wasn't an instant fix - healing never is - but it was a beginning. I also realized that my parents, too, had once been five-year-old children. They carried their own wounds, their own unspoken hurts. Understanding this didn't erase the pain of the past, but it helped me find compassion.

If they had been hurt children once, perhaps they simply didn't know how to love me in the way I needed. This understanding softened something in me, allowing forgiveness to take root - not just for them, but for myself.

That's why sometimes she may have behaved unkindly with me.

If you can see your mother as a fragile five-year-old girl, then you can forgive her very easily with compassion. The five-year old girl who was your mother is always alive in her and in you. Breathing in, I see my mother as a five-year-old girl. Breathing out, I smile to that wounded five-year-old girl who was my mother. Mother, five years old. Smiling with compassion.

Embracing Self-Compassion

Over time, I learned to check in with my inner child regularly. I imagined holding their hand, listening to them, offering them the love and safety they had always needed. I found ways to nurture myself - through self-care, journaling, and practicing self-compassion.

The voice that had once been desperate to be heard was no longer screaming. It was finally being listened to. Healing the inner child isn't about blaming our past - it's about acknowledging the pain that shaped us and offering ourselves the love we didn't always receive. If I could tell my younger self anything, it would be this:

You are seen. You are heard.

And you are enough.

32

LISTENING TO MY INNER CHILD

"It is never too late to have a happy childhood." - Tom Robbins

I remember the day I first sat down to talk to my inner child. It felt strange at first, like stepping into an unfamiliar territory within myself. But something inside told me this was a conversation I had been avoiding for far too long.

It started when I noticed patterns in my life that kept repeating - fears that held me back, doubts that whispered I wasn't enough, and an unexplained sadness that lingered despite my achievements. I had read about the concept of the inner child before, but it had always seemed abstract. One day, in a moment of quiet reflection, I decided to try. I closed my eyes, took a deep breath, and imagined my younger self sitting in front of me - a small child with wide, searching eyes, waiting to be heard.

A Dialogue with My Past

I looked at her - the little girl who had faced moments of loneliness, who had longed for reassurance, who had learned to hide her pain behind a bright smile. I spoke softly, "I see you. I know you're there. And I'm here now to listen." At first, there was silence. Then, almost like an unlocked floodgate, emotions I hadn't acknowledged in years started to surface. Memories of feeling unheard, misunderstood, or not enough poured out. I let my inner child speak, and I simply listened. I felt her fears, her desires, her need to feel safe and loved. And as I listened, something shifted within me - I no longer felt separate from her. She was still a part of me, and she had been waiting for me to acknowledge her.

The Healing Process

From that day forward, I made it a practice to connect with my inner child every day. Sometimes, it was through meditation; other times, it was as simple as taking a walk and imagining her by my side. I reassured her, "We have grown. We are strong now. We are safe." The more I practiced, the more I realized how much my inner child had influenced my present self - the way I reacted to challenges, the way I sought validation, the fears I held onto. I once read a story about a woman who carried deep wounds from her childhood.

She had been abandoned by her parents, left feeling unworthy of love. As an adult, she struggled with relationships, fearing rejection at every turn.

One day, she decided to confront her past. She wrote letters to her younger self, offering the words of comfort she had never received. Over time, she noticed changes - her relationships improved, her self-worth grew, and she found a sense of peace she had never known before. This resonated deeply with me. I realized that healing wasn't about erasing the past but rather integrating it with love and understanding. I started writing letters to my own inner child, telling her all the things she needed to hear. "You are loved. You are enough. You don't have to be afraid anymore." And with each letter, I felt lighter, freer.

The Transformation

As I continued this journey, I noticed subtle yet profound changes in my life. The constant anxiety that had followed me for years started to fade. My relationships became healthier, as I no longer sought validation from external sources. I became more present, more at peace with who I was. One day, I took a walk in nature and imagined my inner child walking beside me. I reached out my hand and whispered,

"Let's enjoy this moment together." And for the first time in a long time, I felt whole. Healing is not an overnight process. It is a journey - a conversation we must continue having with the parts of ourselves that have been left in the dark for too long. If we take the time to listen, to embrace, and to heal, we will find that the peace we seek has always been within us, waiting to be rediscovered.

A Letter to the Child Within

The first time I sat down to write a letter to my inner child, I felt ridiculous. Who was I even addressing? Was this some sentimental exercise with no real meaning? But as I put pen to paper, something strange happened. Words began to flow, and with them, emotions I hadn't realized I was still carrying.

"Dear little one, I see you. I see the way you were hurt, the way you learned to hide your feelings, the way you tried to be strong because you thought you had to. I'm here now, and I promise, you don't have to carry this alone anymore."

As I wrote, a weight I didn't even know I was holding began to lift. I realized that the child inside me had been waiting for this - waiting to be acknowledged, to be told that their pain wasn't imagined, that their fears were valid. That first letter turned into another, and then another. And after a while, I wondered - if my inner child could respond, what would they say? So, I tried something different. I closed my eyes, imagined myself at five years old, and let that child write back.

"I just wanted someone to listen."

And so, a conversation began.

And this is what I wrote for the very first time:

Dear Little Me,

I see you. I see the way you curl up in bed at night, staring at the ceiling, wondering if things will ever get better. I see the way you carry the weight of the world on your small shoulders, pretending you're okay when your heart is heavy with unspoken pain. I see the tears you hold back because you're afraid no one will understand.

I wish I could hold you. I wish I could whisper into your ear that it's not your fault. None of it is your fault. The loneliness, the fear, the aching need to be loved in the way you deserve - it was never meant to be your burden to bear. I wish I could tell you that you are not broken, even on the days when you feel like the world has shattered you into a million unfixable pieces.

I know you feel invisible. I know you wonder if anyone will ever truly see you, hear you, love you for who you are. But listen to me, my love: one day, you will meet people who do. One day, you will no longer have to shrink yourself to fit into spaces that were never meant for you. You will bloom in the light of your own becoming, and it will be so, so beautiful.

I wish I could stop the hurt before it reaches you. I wish I could stand between you and every cruel word, every moment of doubt, every heartbreak that will make you question your worth. But even though I can't, I promise you this - you will survive it. You will take every scar and turn it into something breathtaking. You will find strength in the places you thought only held pain. And one day, you will look back and see how far you've come, and you will be proud. You are loved. You are enough. You always have been. And I promise you, little one, the best is yet to come.

With all the love in my heart,

Me

Sharing Joy with the Child Within

Healing wasn't just about acknowledging pain; it was also about rediscovering joy. I started inviting my inner child into the present. When I climbed a hill, I imagined my younger self running up alongside me, laughing at the wind in our hair. When I sat beneath a sunset, I let them marvel at the colors. When I tasted my favorite childhood treat, I invited them to savor it with me. It felt silly at first, but over time, it became second nature. I wasn't just reliving memories - I was creating new ones, ones where my inner child wasn't afraid, wasn't alone, wasn't burdened with sadness. And as I did this, something profound happened: the part of me that had once been so wounded began to heal.

Finding Strength in Others

There were days when the weight of the past felt too heavy, when old wounds reopened and I felt like I was drowning in emotions I couldn't control. It was in those moments that I learned the power of support. At first, I resisted reaching out. I had spent so much of my life believing that my struggles were mine alone to bear. But then, I found people - friends who had walked similar paths, mentors who had already done the work of healing. I sat with them, spoke my fears out loud, let them hold space for me. And I realized something vital: healing doesn't have to happen in isolation.

When I felt too weak to confront my inner child alone, they sat with me. Their presence reminded me that I wasn't alone in this journey. Their strength became my strength. And in time, I learned that love and trust weren't just things to be longed for - they were things I could allow myself to receive.

Healing isn't a destination; it's a practice. Some days, I still hear echoes of old fears. Some nights, the past still creeps in. But I know now that I have the tools to face it. I write letters, I embrace joy, I lean on those who remind me that I don't have to do this alone. And most importantly, I keep listening to the child within me, knowing that they are finally safe.

33

BREAKING THROUGH WRONG PERCEPTIONS

"We see the world not as it is, but as we are." - *Stephen R. Covey*

There was a time when I thought the world was against me. Every glance, every whisper, every moment of silence felt like a confirmation of my deepest fear: that I was not enough.

I carried this misconception like a heavy backpack filled with stones, dragging it with me into every experience, every relationship, every opportunity. And I never questioned it.

But now, looking back, I see the flawed lens through which I viewed my life. I see the young child within me, desperate for validation, craving love but misinterpreting the world's responses.

If only I could have reached out to that version of myself and told them that everything would be okay. If only I could have shattered the walls built from wrong perceptions before they caged me in.

This is a letter to that younger me. A message sent across time to unravel the misconceptions that shaped my fears, my anger, and my self-doubt. A letter to help heal the wounds that never should have been carried alone.

Misconception #1: "They Don't Care About Me"

There was a time when I believed that silence meant indifference. I remember sitting alone in a room full of people, feeling invisible. I convinced myself that if they truly cared, they would ask how I was doing. They would notice my sadness. They would reach out first.

But they didn't. And so, I withdrew further, wrapping myself in resentment and disappointment. It took me years to understand that silence doesn't always mean neglect. That people are battling their own storms, carrying their own weights. I learned that love doesn't always come in loud declarations; sometimes, it's in the small, quiet moments - someone saving you the last piece of cake, someone remembering your favorite song, someone simply choosing to stay even when words fail.

To my younger self, I wish you had known that love isn't always obvious. I wish you had seen the kindness hidden in the spaces between words. And most of all, I wish you had learned to communicate, to reach out instead of waiting in silence for someone to read your mind.

Misconception #2: "I Am Not Good Enough"

I used to measure my worth by the approval of others. A single word of criticism could shatter me. I remember the sting of not being chosen, of not being praised, of feeling like I would always be second best. I convinced myself that I was inherently flawed, destined to never be enough. But life has taught me otherwise. Worth is not determined by external validation; it is something you cultivate within yourself.

It is found in resilience, in self-belief, in the quiet determination to keep going despite failure. I wish my younger self had known that rejection does not define you, that mistakes are proof of effort, and that true confidence is built not from applause but from knowing you are valuable even in the absence of it.

To my younger self, I wish you had realized sooner that you were always enough - just as you were.

Misconception #3: "Anger Will Protect Me"

For a long time, anger was my armor. When people hurt me, I pushed them away with coldness. When I felt vulnerable, I lashed out. I believed that if I let my guard down, I would be taken advantage of. And so, I built walls so high that even love couldn't climb over them. But I have learned that anger is not strength - it is a mask for pain.

True strength is vulnerability. True strength is choosing to understand instead of retaliate. I remember a moment when someone deeply hurt me, and my immediate reaction was to shut them out completely. But for the first time, I paused. I looked beyond my own pain and tried to see theirs. And suddenly, I saw a different story - a story of their own wounds, their own struggles. And just like that, my anger melted into compassion.

To my younger self, I wish you had known that anger is not the answer. That holding onto it only poisons your own heart. And that healing begins the moment you choose understanding over resentment.

Breaking Free: Embracing the Present with Clarity

Looking back, I see the patterns of wrong perceptions that shaped so much of my early life. I see how they dictated my reactions, my relationships, my sense of self. But I also see how I slowly, painfully, unlearned them. I learned that people who seem distant may just be lost in their own battles. I learned that worth isn't given by others but discovered within.

I learned that anger is not protection, and that forgiveness - both for myself and others - is the true key to freedom. And most of all, I learned that healing is not an overnight miracle. It is a journey. A practice. A commitment to seeing beyond the illusions of the past and embracing the truth of the present.

A Final Message to My Younger Self

Little one, if only you could see yourself now. If only you could see how much you've grown, how much you've survived, how much love you are still capable of giving and receiving.

You are not alone.

You were never alone.

And every tear, every heartbreak, every lonely night led you here - to this moment of realization, of healing, of light.

The weight is no longer yours to carry.

It never was.

With all the love in my heart,

Me

34

HEALING RELATIONSHIPS – A JOURNEY OF TRANSFORMATION

"The quality of your life ultimately depends on the quality of your relationships."   - Esther Perel

I never thought relationships could heal. Not truly, not after the kind of wounds we had inflicted on each other. Words spoken in anger, actions driven by ego, the silence that stretched far beyond mere misunderstanding - it all seemed irreparable.

Yet, life has a way of bringing unexpected lessons, and this is a story of how healing is possible, even when it feels like all is lost. It began with a realization: Healing does not come from merely forgetting the past. It does not happen because time passes. It comes when we are ready to confront our wounds, take responsibility, and choose to rebuild with sincerity.

The Breaking Point

There was time when our conversations felt like a battlefield.

Each word was a weapon, each silence a cold war. It wasn't always like this. Once, we had laughter. Once, we had an unspoken understanding. And then, life happened. Expectations clashed, disappointments grew, and before we knew it, we had drifted into different corners of our shared space, barely acknowledging each other. One day, in the middle of yet another unresolved argument, something shifted in me. I saw not just the words being spoken, but the pain behind them. I saw a person trying to be understood, just as I was. That moment of awareness was the beginning of healing.

Understanding Before Speaking

Communication is often mistaken for just talking. In reality, it is about listening - truly listening. Not just to respond, but to understand. I started practicing this. Instead of preparing my rebuttal while the other person spoke, I focused on understanding what they were truly saying. I asked myself, *What is the emotion beneath their words?* The change was subtle at first. The conversations had fewer interruptions, and the arguments softened. We still disagreed, but we began to hear each other.

The Role of Acceptance

Healing requires acceptance. Not just of the other person's flaws but of our own. I realized that in every conflict, I had played a part. Even if I felt wronged, I had contributed to the cycle of pain in some way. Accepting my role was not about taking all the blame, but about acknowledging my responsibility. When I stopped trying to prove I was right and started focusing on how we could move forward, something changed. The weight of proving a point lifted, and in its place, a space for understanding emerged.

Rebuilding Trust

Trust is fragile. It is not built overnight, nor is it repaired in an instant. It is built in small moments - choosing honesty over avoidance, choosing vulnerability over defense. Every time I showed up, every time I made an effort to be present rather than withdraw, trust started to mend itself. One evening, instead of retreating into silence, I asked, *Can we try again?* It was not about erasing the past but about rewriting the present. It was a small step, but it was a step toward healing.

Healing Together

Relationships are not just about two people existing together; they are about two people growing together. Healing is not an individual journey but a shared one. We began making conscious efforts - setting aside time for meaningful conversations, appreciating the small things, and expressing gratitude instead of criticism.

There were still moments of struggle, but the difference was that now, we faced them as a team rather than as opponents. Healing, I realized, is a continuous process. It is not a destination but a journey we choose every day. As I look back, I see that the most powerful transformation came not from waiting for the other person to change but from choosing to be the change myself. Healing relationships is not about perfection; it is about effort, understanding, and the willingness to keep trying. And so, our story of healing continues…

The Weight of Unspoken Words

For the longest time, I believed that keeping quiet was the best way to keep relationships intact. If I was hurt by something a friend said, I would swallow it. If a family member made a comment that stung, I would nod and move on. I thought confronting them would only make things worse, that they would feel hurt or offended, and I never wanted to be the cause of someone else's pain. But what I didn't realize was that, in trying to protect others, I was slowly destroying myself. Every unspoken word, every suppressed emotion, became a brick in the invisible wall around my heart. It was as if I carried an unseen weight with me everywhere I went. The resentment festered, the misunderstandings deepened, and my own emotions - valid, real, and human - were dismissed by none other than myself.

The Power of Closure: Why Speaking Heals

There came a moment when I realized that avoiding communication wasn't keeping my relationships safe - it was corroding them from within. By not speaking up, I was allowing assumptions, resentment, and silent suffering to dictate my interactions. The truth was simple: the people around me might feel momentary discomfort when confronted with my feelings, but if I kept everything bottled up, the pain would only intensify within me. That's when I learned the most important lesson about closure:

The pain of expressing yourself is temporary, but the pain of suppressing yourself lasts forever. When I finally allowed myself to communicate - to say, "Hey, that really hurt me" or "I felt ignored when you did that" - I realized that half of my pain dissolved simply by being acknowledged. Even before an apology or explanation, just saying it aloud gave my heart room to breathe. It was as if the locked doors inside me were finally opening, letting in fresh air and light.

What If They Don't Acknowledge Your Pain?

But what happens when you do communicate, and instead of understanding, you're met with dismissal? What if they say, "You're overreacting" or "You're too sensitive"?

This was something I feared deeply. It took so much courage to finally voice my pain, and the idea of it being invalidated felt like another wound altogether. But here's what I learned:

You are not over-sensitive; you are human. Sensitivity is not a flaw - it is a sign of depth, of emotional intelligence, of caring. Every human has different emotional thresholds, and just because someone else doesn't understand your pain doesn't mean it isn't real.

You are not responsible for their reaction. Your responsibility is to express yourself honestly and healthily. How they respond is beyond your control. If they are dismissive, that is their limitation, not yours.

Speaking your truth is for you, not them. Closure is not just about their reaction - it's about allowing yourself to let go of what's weighing you down. You are not communicating to win their approval; you are communicating to honor yourself.

The Relief of an Open Heart

There is a profound peace that comes from knowing you have spoken your truth. Even if the other person doesn't acknowledge it, even if nothing externally changes, the very act of expressing yourself brings an internal shift. You no longer carry the heavy weight of unspoken pain. You are free. I have learned that holding in my feelings doesn't protect anyone - it only prolongs my own suffering. The best thing I ever did for my heart was to stop assuming silence was strength. True strength is standing in your truth, allowing yourself to be seen, and knowing that your feelings matter. So, if you're holding something inside, thinking it's better left unsaid - consider this:

What if saying it sets you free?

35

EMBRACING SELF-DISCOVERY THROUGH MEDITATION

"Meditation is not a way of making your mind quiet. It is a way of entering the quiet that is already there – buried under the 50,000 thoughts the average person thinks every day." -
Deepak Chopra

While I was diligently working on building my life and focusing on my business, there was something else quietly taking root in my heart. It was an imaginary business, a business of my *karams* (actions) that I didn't realize would shape my future. This wasn't a business that needed capital, a business plan, or a product to sell.

This was a business of purpose - one that emerged out of my own thoughts, intentions, and deeds, and yet, it remained invisible to everyone around me, including myself. I remember the day vividly when my mother introduced me to BK Shivani Didi. It was during one of those rare, peaceful afternoons, where everything seemed to pause for a while.

I could feel the subtle energy around her words before even hearing them. I was unfamiliar with her at the time, but there was something undeniably magnetic about her presence. As she spoke, I found myself drawn to her - like a magnet to iron, I couldn't help but lean in. Her calmness, her way of speaking with such clarity, yet such warmth, left an impression I couldn't shake.

She became the first person I truly looked up to, the first person whose words I absorbed with the deep thirst of someone who had been searching for something they didn't yet know. Her energy, her aura, was unlike anyone I had ever encountered.

Every time she spoke, it was as if a deep silence filled my heart - a silence that wasn't empty but filled with understanding and peace. She had a unique ability to calm the storm within you, even when the outside world was chaotic. I found myself replaying her words, understanding each one, seeking to embody her wisdom in my own life.

Her words began to feel like a mirror, reflecting parts of me that I hadn't known existed. It was not just what she said but how she made me feel. It was the calm in her voice, the groundedness in her demeanor, and the energy that seemed to emanate from her with every gesture, every smile. I wanted to be like her.

I wanted to radiate the same tranquility, the same depth of understanding, the same ability to connect with people on a soul level. In that process of rediscovery, I found that the imaginary business I had once created in my mind - the one of my *karams* - was far more powerful than any material pursuit could ever be.

It was the foundation of everything that followed, the unseen force that shaped the person I was becoming.

And in that, I began to understand what BK Shivani Didi had always known: the true business is the one of the soul.

The Journey of the Soul: A Path to Inner Peace and Self-Discovery

While I was working hard on building my business and carving a life for myself, I was also nurturing another dream - one that lived deep within me, the business of my soul's evolution.

Little did I know, this wasn't just about doing well in the material world; it was about connecting with a deeper sense of purpose. The idea of success shifted in my mind from accumulating wealth to embracing peace and fulfillment.

My spiritual awakening began in the most beautiful and subtle of ways. It was during this period that I was introduced to Brahma Kumaris and BK Shivani Didi, a woman whose aura and presence spoke volumes. It was my mother who first brought up the idea, as she had been following their teachings for years.

I remember the first time I heard BK Shivani didi's voice - there was a calmness in it that instantly drew me in.

It wasn't just the words that she spoke but the way she said them. It was as if each word carried a vibration of peace, a vibration that resonated with something deep inside me.

I found myself listening intently, almost as if my soul was recognizing something familiar in her words. BK Shivani became my first true spiritual mentor.

She was the person I looked up to, the one I resonated with the most, the one I wanted to be like. The calmness, the grace, the understanding in her eyes - everything about her seemed to glow with an energy that was so soothing.

I began to realize that she wasn't just a teacher; she was an embodiment of what true inner peace looked like.

It was through her guidance that I came to understand the profound concept of the soul, and its journey - its purpose.

Who am I?

I began to learn that each of us is, at our core, a soul. The body is simply a temporary vessel for the soul's journey in this lifetime. It's easy to identify ourselves with the roles we play: daughter, wife, mother, entrepreneur. But beyond all these identities lies the true self - the soul. The soul is eternal, and while the body may change, the essence of the soul remains unchanged, untouched by time.

The question that lingered in my mind was: "If I am not just a daughter, a mother, or a professional, then who am I truly?" The teachings guided me in my quest for this answer. The soul is not defined by the circumstances or the roles it plays in a given lifetime. It's a unique spark of divinity, pure, untainted by worldly influences.

Realizing this truth helped me understand that the struggles and successes I encountered weren't who I truly was. They were experiences meant to teach me, to help my soul evolve, but they didn't define my worth. This simple yet profound realization sparked a transformation within me.

Meditation and Mindfulness

One of the first steps in understanding the soul's journey was learning about the practice of meditation. Meditation is not just about emptying the mind - it's about reconnecting with the soul. Through meditation, I started to realize how much I had been disconnected from my own essence.

Life had been so busy, so full of noise, that I had forgotten to listen to my inner voice. Sitting in silence, focusing on my breath, I began to feel a shift within. It was subtle at first, but over time, I started experiencing a deep sense of peace, as if my soul was coming back home.

Meditation helped me let go of the external pressures I had placed on myself. The pressure to constantly prove my worth, to keep chasing material success, to meet societal expectations of who I should be - these pressures had been draining me. As I practiced daily meditation, I began to shed these layers, like peeling off the mask I had been wearing for years. What was left was just me - pure, unfiltered, and at peace with myself.

Detachment and Letting Go

One of the most important lessons I learned was the concept of *detachment*. But detachment wasn't what I thought it was. It didn't mean disconnecting from the world or from the people I loved. It meant letting go of the emotional attachment I had to outcomes, to success, and to approval.

For example, if I had a business goal that I worked relentlessly toward and didn't achieve, I learned to detach from the idea that my worth was tied to that success.

Instead, I learned to trust that the Universe had a bigger plan for me - one that wasn't bound by my limited understanding. This didn't mean giving up on dreams or goals - it simply meant releasing the need to control every outcome. I learned to trust that everything that came into my life, whether good or bad, was part of my soul's evolution.

Each experience was an opportunity for growth. When I learned to let go, I found a sense of freedom that I had never known before. Through this process, I also began to understand the significance of *self-love*. In the hustle of life, it's easy to neglect the most important relationship we have - the one we have with ourselves.

Only by loving and nurturing the self can I truly love others. Self-love isn't about being selfish - it's about recognizing your inherent worth as a soul. It's about taking the time to nourish your mind, body, and spirit, so that you can give from a place of abundance rather than depletion.

Service Through Kindness

One of the most beautiful aspects of the teachings is the emphasis on *service*. Service is not just about helping others materially; it's about serving with love, kindness, and understanding. It's about being a source of peace in the lives of others. I began to realize that true service comes from a place of inner peace.

When I was at peace with myself, I could extend that peace to those around me. Whether it was a smile, a kind word, or a simple gesture of love, these acts of service had the power to change lives, including my own.

Every thought I had, every word I spoke, and every action I took was shaping my reality. The concept of *thoughts creating reality* was something that I had heard before, but now I was starting to experience it in my own life. As I learned to align my thoughts with my highest truth, I noticed the world around me changing. I felt more connected to my purpose, more grounded in my identity as a soul, and more compassionate toward others.

It's not the Destination, Rather the Journey

The journey of the soul is not a destination but an ongoing process. It's a process of shedding the layers of ego, attachment, and fear, and coming back to our true nature - peace, love, and wisdom. It's about understanding that we are not defined by the roles we play, the possessions we accumulate, or the recognition we receive.

We are defined by our essence - the divine light that resides within each of us. As I continue on this journey, I know that it's not always easy. There are days when the challenges of life make it difficult to stay centered.

But the teachings remind me to return to my soul, to return to peace. In every moment, I am reminded that the soul's journey is one of love, growth, and eternal evolution.

And with each step, I am becoming the highest version of myself.

The Script: A Scene from Your Future

Main Actor: You - standing on the precipice of a decision that will alter the course of your life.

Supporting Actor: A mentor, friend, or even a stranger who unknowingly nudges you in the right direction.

Conflict: The inner battle between self-doubt and self-belief. The hesitation that whispers, "What if I fail?" vs. the bold voice that says, "What if this changes everything?"

Climax: The moment you take action.

You send that email, make that call, stand up for yourself, express your creativity, or step onto the path you've long avoided.

Resolution: You look back - not with regret, but with pride. You stepped into your power, and the story is unfolding in ways you never imagined.

Your Story's Four Pillars

To make this real, visualize your transformation in these four aspects:

Spiritual Growth: What belief or mindset shift do you embrace today that alters the way you see the world?

Action & Courage: What one bold move do you take that you previously hesitated on?

Relationships: Who do you connect with in a new, deeper way - either by healing the past or strengthening the present?

Creative Expression: What do you create that wasn't there before - a piece of art, a new idea, a movement, a moment of beauty?

The Final Task: Write Your Own Ending

Now, take a pen or open a blank document. Write down:

- The title of your movie.

- The moment of transformation you choose today.

- The letter from your future self, thanking you for your bravery.

Then, go out and **live** that story. Let your actions today be the spark that ignites your next chapter. Let this not be the end of a book, but the beginning of a life rewritten - by you, for you.

Lights fade. The credits roll.

The audience (your future self) rises in applause.

Your story continues

PART 4

REAL LIFE HEROES WHO TRANSFORMED THEIR LIFE

In this Part, get ready to meet some extraordinary souls who turned their setbacks into comebacks and their pain into power. These are real people with real struggles, just like you and me, who refused to let life's challenges define them. From hitting rock bottom to rising like a phoenix, their journeys are living proof that no situation is ever truly hopeless.

Their stories are not just inspiring; they are a testament to the strength of the human spirit and the magic of perseverance. Their battles may be different, but the courage, resilience, and hope they carry are universal. These are the unsung warriors who faced their storms and came out stronger, teaching us that it's not about how hard you fall but how fiercely you rise.

Get ready to be inspired, moved, and motivated.

Because if they can do it, so can you.

WHERE DREAMS MEET COURAGE
By: RAMAN SINGH

I have always believed that those who dare to dream, achieve the sky. But this belief didn't come to me easily - it was forged through battles with self-doubt, fear, and a burning desire to break free from the chains of my own making. My name is Raman Singh, and this is not just my story - it's a testament to the power of rediscovery and the unstoppable force of dreaming bigger than you ever imagined.

My journey begins in a small town in Kanpur, Uttar Pradesh. Picture narrow streets lined with bustling markets, the aroma of street food in the air, and a world where tradition and expectation ruled every corner of life. I grew up in a conventional family - where high grades were worshipped, and individuality was often seen as a rebellion. School wasn't a safe haven for me; it was a maze of uncertainties. English felt like an alien language, and the fear of judgment loomed over me like a dark cloud. I was the boy who blended into the background, convinced that I was destined for an ordinary life.

But beneath the surface of self-doubt, there was a spark - a quiet yet persistent whisper that told me I was meant for something more. The moment that changed everything came after my 10th grade. In a bold, almost reckless move, I decided to form a rock band. It wasn't about impressing anyone or fulfilling someone else's dreams - it was the first time I did something purely for myself. The stage lights, the raw sound of the guitar, the adrenaline - it was far from perfect, but it was real. And for the first time, I wasn't just a passive observer of life - I was in the spotlight, alive and unfiltered.

That night ignited a fire in me. It wasn't just about the music; it was about the rush of stepping into discomfort. Suddenly, I was no longer content with blending in. I joined debates, ran for student council president, and eventually became the head boy of my school. The boy who once struggled to string together a sentence in English was now commanding stages and leading his peers. It was a metamorphosis - a living proof that growth isn't born from comfort; it's carved from chaos.

But let me tell you something - the key to daring to dream big isn't just about standing on a stage or grabbing the mic. It's about tearing down the walls you've built around yourself - the labels given to you by society, family, or even your own past mistakes. We often let the world define who we are, pushing us into boxes that suffocate our true selves. But real transformation begins when you look inward, shatter those boxes, and dare to rediscover who you really are.

When I entered college, I was known as the guy who "does it all." I was thriving - excelling in extracurriculars, seizing every opportunity, stacking achievements like trophies. I even secured a job at my so-called dream company. But beneath the surface, a question gnawed at me: Was I truly chasing my dreams, or just sprinting down a path designed by someone else?

That question became a storm in my mind, shaking everything I thought I knew. I realized my corporate job, though secure and respectable, was nothing more than a golden cage - comfortable, yet confining. The steady paycheck, the pursuit of predefined success, the expectations of society - all of it was pulling me further away from what I truly wanted.

I wanted to live authentically. To inspire, empower, and help others break free from the same invisible chains that once held me. That's when I stepped into the world of training and coaching. Right now, it may be a side hustle, but the impact it creates, the fulfillment it brings - that's what keeps me going. Because this is the dream worth chasing.

But here's the truth: daring to dream big means daring to be authentic. It's standing at the edge of your comfort zone and taking that leap of faith, even when the net isn't visible. Your dreams don't live in the safe zones - they're out there, in the wild, waiting for you to chase them.

The magic happens when you stop confining yourself to your past. Often, we let our mistakes define us - we let society's expectations chain us. But the moment you decide to rewrite your story, you open the floodgates to unimaginable possibilities. When you embrace your true self - your quirks, your flaws, your raw, unfiltered essence - you unlock a world where your wildest dreams start feeling within reach.

I adopted a simple yet powerful mindset: "I will be the best at what I do." And once I aligned my actions with this belief, the universe responded. Doors I never knew existed began to open. Opportunities didn't just knock - they broke down the walls.

But let's not romanticize the journey - it wasn't a montage of victories. It was a battlefield. There were moments of doubt, times when the road ahead was pitch dark. But every time I stumbled, I reminded myself that growth demands discomfort. Each scar was a story - a reminder that I wasn't just surviving; I was evolving.

Knowledge became my greatest weapon. The more I invested in learning - whether it was mastering new skills, understanding human psychology, or diving into spiritual wisdom - the more my confidence grew. Each piece of knowledge was a brick, building the bridge to my dreams. If you want to dream big, arm yourself with knowledge - it's the fuel that propels you beyond your limitations. And here's the most beautiful part: daring to dream big doesn't just transform your life - it creates a ripple effect. When you break free from your own limits, you unknowingly inspire others to do the same. My journey wasn't just about me - it became a beacon for others who felt trapped by their circumstances. Just like the Phoenix rises from its own ashes, I emerged stronger, and my flames of transformation lit a fire in those around me.

So, let me ask you this: What dreams have you buried under fear and self-doubt? What parts of yourself have you locked away to meet someone else's expectations? It's time to dig deep - to rediscover the raw, powerful version of yourself. Because when you do, your dreams will no longer be distant fantasies - they will become a bold, unstoppable force. You are not confined by the life you have now. The only chains holding you back are the ones you've placed around yourself. Break free. Embrace who you are. And dare - dare to dream big.

Because just like the Phoenix,

you too can rise -

and set the world ablaze...

LIVING TRUE TO MY SOUL: My Journey from Lost to Found
By: TWINKLE CHHABRA

Who was I, Twinkle Chhabra, in the old life? I often ask myself this now. Was I really living my life, or was I merely existing in someone else's world?

I was born and raised in the small town of Saharanpur. I had big dreams - dreams of making my parents proud, of earning tons of money, and achieving something everyone would admire. I was told over and over again, "Beta, padhoge likhoge to banoge nawab, kheloge kudoge to ho jaayoge kharaab." A strong belief settled into my heart: to be successful in life, one must follow the conventional path. Go to school, get a degree, work a respectable job.

This belief ran deep in me. It was reinforced by my father, who would always tell me, "Beta, business mein bohot sir dardi hai, job karo, life set ho jaayegi." And so, I did what I thought would make me happy, what I thought would make me successful. I devoted myself to my studies, worked hard, and topped my 12th CBSE boards. It led me to one of the most esteemed colleges in Delhi University - Jesus & Mary College.

For the next three years, my world was simple: college, studies, routine. I never strayed from the path. The only goal I had was to land a great job, to become financially successful, and to fulfill the dreams I had held for so long.

When I got placed at KPMG, everyone around me was ecstatic. "Wow, Twinkle! KPMG! What an achievement!" My parents beamed with pride, and I was hailed as the embodiment of success. The world saw it. But, deep down, I was dying inside. I wasn't living.

I had been assigned to a role as a business analyst, but my true self was so different. I loved speaking, engaging with people, helping others, and creating something meaningful. The work I was doing at KPMG felt hollow. I wasn't challenged. I wasn't connected to my soul's calling.

Sleepless nights became my routine. I felt confused, lost, and suffocated. A voice inside me whispered, "Twinkle, this is not your potential. You are meant for more." But no one understood. Everyone around me told me how lucky I was. "You're working at KPMG, the dream company! What's wrong with you?" They pushed me to do an MBA to "get a better package" - as if that would make me happy. But I knew in my heart that wasn't my path.

Then came the turning point - the day everything shattered.

The toxic environment at work reached its peak. My manager, the source of my suffering, humiliated me in front of my colleagues. Ridiculous accusations were made - "Twinkle doesn't flush the toilet" - and each day felt like an endless battle. The emotional toll was unbearable. There was one instance where she tracked my break time so obsessively that she came running to the canteen just to yell at me when my 30-minute break extended by a minute. I felt so small, so ashamed, so powerless.

I felt trapped. But it was in that moment of darkness that something inside me ignited. I decided then and there that I would no longer tolerate this. I refused to accept a life of misery. I took 100% responsibility for my dreams. I began working on myself. I started exploring what it meant to be an entrepreneur, to take control of my future. I found a remote job that gave me the freedom I so desperately needed. I returned home to Saharanpur, away from the noise of the city, away from the pressures of a life I had never wanted.

I no longer listened to the opinions of others. With each passing day, I invested in myself - learning new skills, taking small courses, and diving into the world of self-growth. I focused on building my confidence, understanding my worth, and mastering the qualities I needed to lead a successful life. I focused on my emotional well-being, developed a strong sense of self, and honed my skills to start a business of my own.

Two years later, on a quiet Diwali night, a voice within me screamed, "Twinkle, there are thousands of passionate souls just like you who are stuck in toxic jobs and are longing to live their dreams." That's when my soul's calling was born - ApniDuniya. A brand dedicated to helping others realize their passions and live their truth.

From that moment, everything changed. I moved forward with confidence, working on what I loved, and slowly but surely, my dream career took shape. I am now living my passion, waking up with purpose, and creating a life that truly excites me.

It's been over five years since that turning point. I am back home, living with my family, doing what I love, earning far beyond what I could have imagined before, and above all, I am fulfilled. My journey has taught me that we all have a choice in life. We can either listen to the voice within us that leads us toward our soul's true calling, or we can continue down a path dictated by others' expectations, slowly losing our sense of aliveness. The choice is ours.

If I could go back and talk to my 18-year-old self, I would tell her this: "Sweetheart, you don't need to leave your family to chase a degree. A job will not make you rich, nor will it fulfill your wildest dreams. Don't buy into the world's narrative that success comes with struggle. Trust yourself, connect with your true self, and learn the skills to build something that excites your soul." The most important thing, my dear, is whether you lived a life true to your soul.

If there is a dream deep inside you, follow it. No matter what others say. Trust that the Universe has equipped you with everything you need to make it your reality.

You reading this isn't a coincidence.

This is a sign from the Universe. It's your time to shine. Breathe.

Take that first step, and begin creating your own ApniDuniya.

THE CALLING OF A HEALER: From Darkness to Light
By: DELNA RAJESH

I've always known I was different. There was something inside me that wanted more—more understanding, more growth, more depth. It wasn't about competing with others, but about becoming the best version of myself. I wasn't trying to prove anything to anyone; I was simply trying to be the person I knew I could be. I loved myself enough to want to keep improving, to evolve, to be the best soul I could be.

As a teenager in Bombay, I would save up and buy second-hand books from the roadside—books on spirituality, self-development, and healing. I read on crowded buses and trains during my commute to work, each page feeding my curiosity and passion for deeper knowledge. It was in college that I first encountered Reiki, and I knew it was something special. I joined a group of like-minded people, all eager to grow and explore, and started practicing Reiki. Unlike some of my peers, I didn't just learn it—I let Reiki become a part of me. The energy, the principles, the way of life—I felt it in every part of me. I wasn't driven by ambition; I simply wanted to grow and live in alignment with my true self.

But then, life took an unexpected turn.

In 2004, I found myself slipping away from all the inner work I had been doing. I was young, filled with dreams, chasing higher aspirations and worldly goals. Slowly, I lost sight of what mattered most—the growth of my soul. And then, the unimaginable happened. Everything fell apart. My sense of purpose, my identity, everything I had built—it all shattered. The pain was overwhelming, and for the first time, I lost control of my life. I became lost in grief, questioning everything. I cried endlessly, sometimes without knowing why. And somewhere along the way, I convinced myself that pain was a sign of goodness—that suffering made me a better person. It was a lie I had learned from society, from stories, and from the idea that true heroes must suffer. But I wasn't a hero in a story—I was real, and I was broken.

I didn't know how to heal. All the books I had read on success and growth didn't prepare me for this. None of them taught how to handle loss, heartbreak, or despair. No one showed me how to sit with my pain, how to accept it and make peace with it. The world felt empty, and I was drowning in it.

That's when I turned to Reiki again—not for self-improvement, but for survival. Reiki, which had once been a practice of spiritual growth, became my lifeline. It was the only thing that could help me heal, though the process wasn't easy. It was painful. It was raw. It was relentless.

The 21-day healing cycles I tried to follow kept breaking. Resistance built up inside me—the fear, the anger, the unresolved pain from my past. For six long months, I struggled, trying to heal in the face of constant setbacks. It took support from two Reiki Masters just to complete one full 21-day healing cycle. I spent hours every day in self-healing, channeling Reiki, meditating, chanting, crying, and facing every piece of myself that I had long buried. Each layer of pain I uncovered was hard to confront, but necessary for healing.

Through it all, I had the guidance of my Reiki Master, Aarti Gupta. She was my beacon of light, showing me how to acknowledge my pain, to allow my breakdown, and to face my truth. With her support, I slowly started rebuilding. I immersed myself in Reiki, studying all I could - levels 1, 2, and 3, Karuna Reiki, chanting, past-life regressions, hypnotherapy, Ho'oponopono, EFT, yoga, and everything else that could help me heal. My parents, too, were there for me, supporting me through their own struggles, even as they dealt with their own fears and challenges. I spent years in this intense self-healing, studying different healing modalities and dedicating myself to coming back stronger. It wasn't quick, and it wasn't easy, but eventually, I did heal. I rose. Stronger, more resilient, and more determined than ever before. And that's when I made a promise to myself: Never again should anyone have to go through such darkness alone. Never again should someone feel like there's no way out. Never again should anyone suffer in silence.

That's when my true journey as a healer began. Not because I chose it, but because life had prepared me for it. I had been through the depths of despair and emerged with the strength to help others find their way out. I owe my recovery to my family, my master, and everyone who supported me through that dark time. And now, I am here to offer that same support to others. To anyone who feels alone in their pain—I see you. I hear you. And I promise, there is a way back. This is why I do what I do. It's not just a career it's my soul's dream and wish.

MANIFESTATION ALCHEMY: The Art of Turning Dreams into Reality

By: PREETHIKA

If you had met me in 2014, you wouldn't have seen a confident woman standing in her power. You wouldn't have seen the fire in my eyes or the strength in my voice. No, you would have seen a girl curled up in the corner of her tiny apartment, her laptop screen casting a dull glow on her depressed face. You would have seen someone who had lost faith in herself.

Outside, the world moved on, oblivious to my silent breakdown. My friends were securing high-paying jobs in top IT firms, celebrating promotions, climbing corporate ladders as if they were meant for success. And me? I was drowning in rejection emails, stuck in an endless cycle of disappointment.

The eldest daughter in a middle-class family, I was supposed to be the one who made them proud. But all I felt was the crushing weight of failure.

That night, after yet another job rejection, I opened my laptop and, with trembling fingers, typed into Quora:

"Why am I such a failure?"

A part of me expected silence. But instead, I found an answer that would change my life.

"Watch this video and thank me later!"

It was a video of "The Secret: Law of Attraction"

I scoffed at first. A documentary? About some Law of Attraction nonsense? But desperation makes you try things you wouldn't otherwise. And so, with nothing left to lose, I pressed play.

For the next ninety minutes, I sat frozen, absorbing every word. The idea was so simple, yet so profound: your thoughts shape your reality. Doubt it, and you attract failure. Believe it, and the universe aligns in your favour.

Something inside me shifted.

That night, I picked up an old notebook and wrote, in clear, deliberate handwriting, exactly what I wanted in my dream job.

A multinational company.

A gaming company.

No more than five kilometers from my home.

A team that felt like family.

I stared at the words, then closed the notebook.

For the next thirty days, I did everything The Secret said. I visualized myself in my dream job. I practiced gratitude. I refused to entertain a single negative thought.

On the thirtieth day, my phone rang.

Two interviews.

The first was with an MNC. My heart pounded as I walked in, convinced this was my moment. But within minutes, I was rejected.

The second was with an Indian company, twenty-three kilometers from home - nowhere close to what I had visualized. But I needed a job. Stability. Security. So I took it.

And then, something strange happened.

Within weeks, I found myself surrounded by the warmest, most supportive team I had ever known. The deep friendships I had asked for? They were right there.

Months later, a friend forwarded a job listing. I clicked on it, my heart stopping mid-beat.

An MNC.

A gaming company.

Five kilometers from home.

Exactly what I had written in my notebook.

I got the job.

That was the moment I realized - manifestation isn't about chasing things. It's about becoming ready to receive them.

But this was only the beginning.

The more I understood manifestation, the deeper I wanted to go. I learned that it wasn't just about asking for things - it was about becoming the person who could hold them. I had to face my fears, heal my wounds, and release the subconscious blocks that had kept me small for so long.

When my retired parents decided to move to Bangalore, we searched for a house near mine. The city's real estate market made it nearly impossible. We found a house twenty kilometers away, and my mother wanted to finalize it.

"This isn't the one," I told her. "Your house will be near mine."

She sighed, thinking I was being unrealistic. But I knew.

A month later, that house deal fell through due to legal issues. Soon after, we found the perfect home - just five kilometers from mine.

My mother stared at me when we finalized the deal. I didn't need to say anything. She finally understood.

But not everything came easily.

While my personal life flourished, my workplace remained a battlefield. I loved coding, but the pressure, the lack of appreciation, the unrealistic expectations - they drained me. The old patterns of stress and burnout returned.

That's when I met Dr. Meghna Dixit, a life coach who helped me dig deep. And what I found was something I hadn't expected.

For years, I had been carrying a childhood wound. As the eldest daughter, I had grown up under immense expectations. Be the best. Make no mistakes. Achieve, achieve, achieve. And no matter what I did, it was never enough.

That same pattern had followed me into adulthood. I had manifested bosses who treated me just like my parents had - demanding, dismissive, never satisfied.

I had to break the cycle. Through inner work, I learned to set boundaries, to stand in my worth, to demand respect without fear. And the moment I changed - so did my reality.

I was promoted. Given leadership. Valued.

And yet, something inside me whispered: this isn't where I am meant to be. I had always been fascinated by human psychology, always drawn to transformation.

So, I attended Blair Singer's program Train the Trainer thinking I wanted to get trained but I learned much more than that. I got to convert my fascination with human psychology, passion to help people manifest more productive lives into a niche. In addition to that, I also learned how to market and sell my niche.

A month later, I got my first paid client. And just like that, my new path began.

I left my corporate job. I poured my knowledge into writing The Art of Manifestation, a book designed for even non-readers to grasp the Law of Attraction. Within three days, it became an Amazon bestseller. Within a week, I had nine new clients. But success isn't just about money. It's about alignment. And soon, I faced the next challenge - scaling my business.

I realized I was playing small. Holding myself back. The same old fear of failure lurked beneath the surface. And at home, my child struggled with emotional regulation, mirroring the chaos I hadn't yet resolved within myself.

So, I went deeper. I worked with a parenting coach. I healed childhood wounds I hadn't even known I carried. I underwent feminine and womb healing. I released money blocks and emotional resistance. And everything changed. I worked less but earned double of my IT salary while working just eight days a month. My relationship with my child transformed. Life became easeful. Looking back, I see it clearly now. Manifestation isn't about wishful thinking. It's about healing, aligning, and trusting. It's about becoming the version of yourself that naturally attracts the life you desire.

And I'm just getting started. Like a phoenix, I have risen from the ashes of doubt, fear, and limitation. Reborn. Stronger. Wiser. The fire that once burned me now fuels me.

And as I spread my wings, ready to soar,

I know - this is just the beginning of my flight.

THE AWAKENED ME: A Journey to Find Purpose
By: Dr. CHARU BANSAL

I can't understand why it took me so long to see it - how life slowly drained the fire from my soul, leaving only embers of who I once was. But now, as I stand at the edge of my own rebirth, I see it all clearly.

Death isn't just when the body gives up; it happens every time a dream dies within us, every time we smother our own desires to meet the expectations of others. I have died a thousand times before this moment, each time I silenced my own voice to be the perfect daughter, the perfect wife, the perfect mother. But this time… this time, I refuse to die.

I still remember my mother's radiant smile, her bold spirit, and the way she carried herself with such grace. But when I was eleven, something changed. Her laughter became quieter, her eyes lost their light, and despair took root in the spaces where joy once lived. I was too young to understand it then, but now I know - she was drowning in her own silence. And soon, that silence swallowed her whole.

By twenty, I stepped into marriage with a heart full of hope, believing love alone would be enough to build a life. The newness of it all was intoxicating - the shared dreams, the whispered promises. But no one warned me about the invisible chains that came with those vows. I tied my happiness to the happiness of others, thinking that was what a good woman did. I became everything for everyone. Until I was nothing for myself. For seven years, I played the role of the ideal wife, mother, and daughter-in-law, nurturing a family of eighteen under one roof. From the outside, my life was picture-perfect - supportive husband, beautiful children, a secure home. But within me, there was an emptiness so vast it felt like I was being swallowed whole. I convinced myself it was just exhaustion, a passing phase. But deep down, I knew. The shadows creeping into my mind weren't just fleeting - they were consuming.

I was drowning, the same way my mother had. Nights stretched long and suffocating as I lay awake, silent tears slipping onto my pillow. I would watch my children sleep, their faces peaceful, and guilt would claw at me. How could I let them see me like this? How could I let them grow up with a mother who was merely a ghost in their home? I knew what that emptiness felt like - I had lived it after my own mother was gone.

And that terrified me. One night, as I stared at the ceiling, feeling the weight of my own despair pressing down on my chest, I heard it - a voice, small but steady, rising from the depths of my soul: *No. This will not be your story. You will not become your mother's fate. You will fight.*

The next morning, I took my first step. It wasn't grand or miraculous. It was simply *choosing* to get up and do something for myself - just thirty minutes, every single day. I started reading, learning, absorbing. I attended a gathering centered around Buddhist philosophy, where people spoke of transformation, of awakening. And for the first time, I saw something I had long forgotten - *possibility*.

The world wasn't just a place of duty and sacrifice. It could be a place of growth, of meaning, of joy. And so, I kept moving forward. I enrolled in a Bachelor's program in Education. It felt absurd at first - a mother of two, lost in depression, stepping into the world of academics. But each lesson, each book, each lecture lit something inside me that had long been dimmed. Then, I found *psychology* - and it was as if the universe had finally handed me the key to my own mind. For years, I had been at war with myself, but here was the map to understanding why. Why I felt so lost. Why my mother had drowned in her silence. Why so many women I knew were living lives that weren't their own. The deeper I delved into my studies, the more I realized - this wasn't just about me.

This was about *breaking the cycle*. I wasn't just meant to survive. I was meant to *heal*. Not just for myself, but for my children, for the generations before me who never had the chance, and for the ones who would come after me. The patterns of pain, sacrifice, and silence *had to end with me*.

Over the years, my purpose became clear. I dedicated myself to studying emotional resilience, teaching life skills, and empowering others to reclaim their own lost voices. My work extended to parents, teachers, and young minds - those who needed these tools the most. I became known as *'Mann ki Doctor'* - a healer of hearts, a guide to those struggling to find their way.

The woman who once lay awake at night, suffocated by despair, had transformed into someone unrecognizable. *I* had transformed. And if there's one thing I've learned, it's this - No matter how lost you feel, no matter how deep the darkness, the power to rise has always been within you. Sometimes, all it takes is one step. One decision. One whisper of defiance against the voice that tells you to stay broken.

So, if you are standing where I once stood, drowning in the weight of a life that feels too heavy, let me tell you - ***You are not meant to just survive. You are meant to thrive.***

The question is: will you take that first step?

RISING FROM THE ASHES: My Journey from Loss to Purpose

By: POOJA SWAMIT

Growing up in a beautiful, loving family, I was blessed with everything a child could ever dream of. My days were filled with laughter, warmth, and an overwhelming sense of security. Life felt perfect - almost like a fairy tale. But fairy tales are just that, and reality has a way of shattering illusions when you least expect it.

When I was just 17, my world was turned upside down. I lost my father to a sudden cardiac arrest. In a moment, everything changed. The pillar of our family, the man who protected and provided for us, was gone. It felt as if the ground beneath my feet had disappeared. I was lost, confused, and broken.

The only question that echoed in my mind, day and night, was, *"Why me, God? Why me?"* Why did the universe have to take away the one person who meant the world to me? The one person who was our family's strength and the sole breadwinner?

Life didn't just take my father - it took away my sense of security. We were suddenly thrust into a world of financial challenges, grief, and uncertainty. It felt as if no one was there to help us - neither emotionally nor financially. Relatives and friends drifted away, and we were left to face the storm on our own. In the depths of my sorrow, that same question kept repeating itself in my mind, *"Why us? Why this pain?"* I found myself sinking deeper into despair, unable to understand the reason behind my suffering. But then, as if guided by an unseen force, I turned to spiritual books. It was through those pages that I discovered a harsh yet universal truth - death is the ultimate reality. It is inevitable, and no one can escape it. At first, this realization was crushing, but slowly, it helped me find acceptance. I began to understand that life is not meant to be questioned; it is meant to be lived, no matter how difficult it gets.

But life wasn't done testing me yet. Just when I thought I had learned to cope with my father's loss, another devastating blow struck. After I graduated from college, I lost my mother too. Losing both parents left me shattered beyond words. My faith was shaken. I found myself questioning everything I believed in, even the existence of a higher power. It felt like the universe was cruel, unjust, and biased. I couldn't understand why I had to face so much pain and loneliness. But somewhere amidst that darkness, a tiny spark ignited. In my desperate quest to heal my mother, I had explored courses like Ho'oponopono and the Law of Attraction. What started as a way to save her gradually became a journey of self-discovery and healing for myself. The more I learned, the more I realized that the answers to all my questions were hidden in these teachings.

I learned that life is not always fair, but it is always purposeful. I began to understand that challenges are meant to be faced, not avoided. They are meant to mold us, to make us stronger, and to prepare us for a greater purpose. It was in my darkest moments that I found the light. I realized that acceptance is not about giving up; it is about moving forward with the courage to face reality. As I healed, I felt a calling - a desire to share my journey, my learnings, and my strength with others. I didn't want my knowledge to stay confined to me alone. I wanted to help others find hope and healing. And that's how my journey as a life coach began. It was a complete transformation - a 360-degree change that I never saw coming. But that's the beauty of life. Sometimes, the most painful endings are the beginnings of beautiful new journeys.

I started helping people grow, not just financially but also emotionally and spiritually. I wanted them to see that no matter how dark life gets, there is always a way out. There is always hope. I learned the true meaning of resilience - of rising from the ashes like a phoenix. I learned that life will test you, break you, and challenge you in unimaginable ways. But it will also rebuild you, strengthen you, and mold you into a better version of yourself.

Today, as I look back at my journey, I realize that every painful moment had a purpose. Every setback was a setup for a comeback. I was meant to walk this path so that I could help others find their way. Maybe that's why the universe chose me - because it knew I was strong enough to endure the pain and wise enough to turn it into purpose. Because sometimes, life's greatest challenges are given to those who are destined to inspire others. So, to anyone who feels lost, broken, or defeated, remember this - Your story isn't over yet. This is just a chapter, not the end. Keep going. Keep fighting. Because one day, you will look back and realize that the pain you thought would break you was the very pain that made you unbreakable.

This is my story - a story of loss, pain, acceptance, and purpose. A story of rising from the ashes and finding beauty in brokenness. And if I can do it, so can you.

FROM MOTHER TO MENTOR A Purpose Greater Than Myself
By: SANGEETA PURI

I never imagined that life would carve a path for me where I would stand alone - not just as a mother, but as a mentor, a guide, and at times, a warrior. When I first held my son in my arms, I vowed to give him a life built on love, wisdom, and opportunities. Little did I know, that promise would demand resilience I never thought I possessed, wisdom I had yet to acquire, and a delicate balance between being both his protector and the force that would push him forward.

Every single mother walks a tightrope between vulnerability and strength. I was no different. My story isn't just about raising a child; it's about unraveling the deep complexities of parenting a teenager, understanding the intricate dance of independence and discipline, and healing a bond that, at times, felt like it was slipping through my fingers.

Raising a son on my own was never part of the grand plan, but life seldom adheres to our expectations. From the very beginning, I knew I had to instill in him resilience and compassion, along with virtues of honesty, respect, and empathy. But words alone were not enough; I had to embody these values, to live them in the choices I made every day.

I remember the first time I saw him struggle with something bigger than scraped knees or forgotten toys. He stormed into the living room, his young face a storm of frustration and uncertainty. A fight with a friend had left him rattled. I resisted the urge to fix it, to lecture or advise. Instead, I sat beside him in silence. That moment taught me something profound - sometimes, healing begins not with words, but with presence. Not with answers, but with listening.

But as he grew, the teenage years tested everything I thought I knew about parenting. The easy closeness of childhood gave way to distance, to silences that felt heavy, to battles I didn't know how to fight. It wasn't just about him growing up - it was about both of us learning how to navigate this new world, where he sought his independence and I fought to hold on to the bond we had built.

I wasn't alone in my struggle. I saw it in the exhausted eyes of my colleagues, in the hushed conversations of other mothers at school events, in the quiet desperation of parents who had no idea how to reach their children anymore. It was then that I realized: healing was needed on both sides.

Parenting isn't just about guiding a child - it's about evolving with them, adapting, learning, and, sometimes, unlearning.

I carried my corporate experience into motherhood - discipline, structure, efficiency. But I soon learned that children don't fit into frameworks. They are not projects to be managed, but souls to be understood. That realization changed everything for me.

My journey led me into the world of education, where I became not just a parent but an advocate, a bridge between teenagers and their parents. I have worked as an educator, a principal, and a career counselor, diving deep into the world of adolescent psychology. Every day, I encountered parents who were lost, afraid they were losing their children to the pressures of modern life. I saw teenagers drowning in expectations, desperate for understanding. I remember one mother, her voice cracking as she whispered, "I don't know my daughter anymore. We used to be inseparable, but now every conversation ends in an argument. I feel like she's slipping away from me."

I understood her pain because I had experienced it. And I knew there was a way forward. In 2023, I founded The Main Character - a community born out of my personal battles and professional insights. It wasn't just about parenting strategies; it was about healing, about understanding that both parents and children deserve to be seen, heard, and valued in their own stories.

Parenting a teenager is not about having all the answers. It is about the courage to ask questions, to be vulnerable, to admit when we are wrong, and to grow together. Through The Main Character, I created a space where parents - especially single mothers like me - could find support, wisdom, and tools to rebuild their relationships with their children.

Through workshops, coaching sessions, and heartfelt conversations, I have helped mothers reconnect with their teenagers, not by controlling them, but by understanding them. Not by demanding respect, but by earning it through trust and love.

My journey was never meant to be easy. But as I look at my son now - a confident, kind, and driven young man - I know every struggle, every sleepless night, every moment of self-doubt was worth it. I didn't just raise a son. I raised a bond that will endure, a love that will never waver. And if there's one thing I've learned, it's this: we are all the main characters of our own stories. The question is - are we writing a story of connection, understanding, and healing? Or are we letting the chapters slip away, unwritten?

*** The choice is ours.z ***

RECLAIMING ME: A Woman's Silent Battle

By: Sapna Jumde

I was my father's princess once. A girl with stars in her eyes, dreams dancing in my heart. My world was limitless, a canvas I painted with ambition, courage, and a fire that refused to dim.

Then, life happened.

At 27, I met Sandeep. He wasn't the fairytale prince I had imagined, but he felt right - solid, dependable, the kind of man who could stand by me through storms. We married in 2012. Love was real, raw, imperfect. Life was spontaneous - road trips, career highs, the rush of chasing goals, the thrill of being a woman who could have it all. But there was an emptiness, an ache in the quiet moments, a feeling that something was missing.

Motherhood. I thought that was the answer.

At 37, I held my child for the first time, and my heart shattered into a million pieces of love I never knew existed. This was it. This was supposed to complete me.

But somewhere between sleepless nights and the relentless cycle of feeding, burping, and soothing, I began to disappear.

One day, I walked into my office after maternity leave, expecting to pick up where I left off. Instead, I found empty desks, unfamiliar faces, and a silence that told me everything I needed to know. My relevance had faded. No projects, no teams, no purpose.

I had become invisible. I stared at my reflection in the office washroom mirror. Who was this woman? Where was the fire, the ambition, the girl who once dared to dream beyond the horizon? My own voice, once loud and unshakable, had become a whisper drowned in the cacophony of societal expectations.

I spiraled. Days blurred into nights. The woman who once chased her dreams with relentless passion was now afraid to even acknowledge them. I convinced myself that this was just life - that all women go through it, that this was the price of love, of motherhood.

But one night, as I rocked my baby to sleep, tears spilled down my cheeks, and a voice inside me screamed:

"No. This is not it. This cannot be it."

That night, I made a choice.

I would reclaim myself.

I started small. Books. Learning. Online courses. I reminded myself of who I used to be before the world told me who I should be. It was slow, painful. Some days, I wanted to give up. But a whisper inside me kept saying, "Keep going."

In 2023, Life Coaching became my refuge, my salvation. With every session, I peeled back layers of pain, of societal conditioning, of expectations that were never mine to carry. I began helping others, guiding them towards their own light, and in doing so, I found mine.

Learning did not stop here, I wasn't feeling that content. Still waiting for my calling.

Then, I stumbled upon a video about aura reading. Energy, healing, spirituality - things I had once dismissed. But something inside me stirred. A pull I couldn't ignore. I found a mentor, Nishant Sharma, and before I knew it, I was diving deep into a world that felt both foreign and familiar, like coming home to a part of me I never knew existed.

And just like that, the fog started to lift.

In 2024, I learnt Aura reading being an inquisitive soul, which felt so right and apt for me after so many trials and failures. The world of Energy is so intriguing and amusing that I couldn't control myself but progressed further. I was drawn to Frequency Energy Healing and today I can say that with the help of Aura reading supported by Frequency Healing I have touched so many lives for the better.

Me. The woman who had once felt lost.

Today, I stand not just as a mother, a wife, or a daughter, entrepreneur, but as myself. Whole. Unapologetic. Free.

I look back at the girl who once thought marriage would fulfill her, who thought motherhood would complete her, who believed she had to shrink herself to fit into roles defined by society. And I want to hold her, tell her she was always enough. Because the truth is, we don't have to choose. We can be nurturers and warriors. Lovers and leaders. Mothers and dreamers.

We are limitless. We always have been. And we always will be.

THE POWER OF WOMEN Reclaiming Their Identity

By: Dr. SASIREKHA

I stand before you as a woman who was told countless times that I wasn't worth the effort. Born into a community that believed my only purpose was to conform, to settle, and to accept a predetermined fate. But deep down, I always felt a fire burning inside me - a fire that refused to be extinguished by societal norms or the limitations others tried to impose. I was a rebel, born to fight for what I believed in, even if that meant standing alone. I grew up in a small town, in a lower-middle-class family where educating a girl was seen as a futile investment. My father, a devout believer in astrology, was told that I would never amount to much academically, so why waste resources on my education? And so, I was sent to a government school. But as a little girl, I dared to dream bigger. I longed for that life - a life where I could go to a good school, learn, and grow.

Determined to change my path, I convinced my parents to enroll me in a private school. But soon after, my father came to my school to tell the principal that he could no longer afford the fees. His business was crumbling, and I was to be pulled out. My heart shattered. The weight of his words crashed down on me like a heavy storm. The world around me seemed to be telling me that I didn't deserve this opportunity.

But then, something unexpected happened. My principal saw something in me - a relentless determination to succeed. He believed in me when no one else did. And so, he offered my father a scholarship if I could maintain my position at the top of my class. That moment, that single gesture, became the turning point of my life. My fight for education had truly begun.

I won't lie - there were days when the weight of it all felt unbearable. I was scared, uncertain of whether I could live up to the promise I had made to myself. But each time doubt crept in, I remembered why I was doing this. Not just for me, but for the future I was carving, the future where I could stand tall and proud of everything I had overcome.

With every sleepless night, every tear shed, every exam I aced, I built a foundation for a new life. A life where my dreams weren't dictated by the limitations of the world around me. Slowly, I began to understand something powerful: the strength to rise, to overcome, to thrive, had always been within me. I had to believe it. As I moved forward, I didn't just rise for myself. I rose for my family, for my future, for my children. They were my light. The thought of them, the life I wanted to give them, pushed me to keep going, even when it felt like I was running on empty. In their eyes, I saw a reflection of my own dreams, dreams that were no longer out of reach but ready to be claimed.

I wasn't just fighting for a diploma. I was fighting for the woman I knew I could become. The woman I was destined to be. And the more I fought, the stronger I became, not just in mind, but in spirit. Today, I stand here, not just as a survivor of my struggles, but as someone who has rewritten her story. The fire inside me that once burned with fear and uncertainty now burns with purpose. The journey from doubt to purpose hasn't been easy. It hasn't been quick. But it has been mine. And every step, every hardship, every triumph has shaped me into the woman I am today. "I am not what happened to me. I am what I choose to become."

"The strongest souls are those who have faced the toughest battles. We all have stories, but it's the way we choose to write our own that makes all the difference." But as I approached my 10th grade, the weight of the world began to close in around me. My parents, especially my mother, feared that if I continued my studies, I'd never find a suitable husband. They wanted me to stay home, follow the rules, and be like the women they saw around them - quiet, obedient, and resigned. They threw every obstacle in my way - endless household chores, dressing me up in the finest clothes, scolding me into submission. But I could feel it deep inside me - a fire, a fierce resistance. I wasn't going to be that girl. I couldn't be.

I was like the rebel protagonist in a film - fighting against everything that tried to break me. With every word they said, with every door that was slammed shut, I became more determined. I had the mindset of Einstein: I used my failures, my struggles, as stepping stones to build the life I envisioned. I wasn't just fighting for an education; I was fighting for my right to be ME.

Then came the night that would change everything. After another heated argument, I was thrown out of my home. My heart shattered, but my grandmother took me in. She gave me the shelter I needed and the strength to keep going. Under her roof, I completed my 10th grade, but the pressures from my parents never stopped. They wanted to break me, make me bend to their will.

One night, I lay awake, tears streaming down my face, wondering if this was my fate. And then, like a sudden bolt of lightning, I had a moment of clarity. At 5 AM, with all the courage I could muster, I woke my mother and told her, "I will pay for my tuition classes. I will make my own way if you let me continue my studies." Her reluctant agreement marked the beginning of my fight - not just for education, but for my identity.

Today, I stand with a mission - to empower women to take control of their emotional well-being and live healthier, happier lives. Life may throw curveballs our way, but I truly believe that when life gives you lemons, it's up to you to make lemonade. It's all about the perspective you choose to adopt. The challenges we face are not a reflection of life's unfairness; they are the stepping stones that shape us. The difference lies in how we choose to look at them. I help women tap into their inner strength, to turn their struggles into triumphs. Through becoming life coaches, they don't just gain a career - they gain the power to take back their lives. I show them how to achieve financial freedom while still honoring the importance of family, love, and self-care. It's not about sacrificing who you are; it's about realizing that you have the ability to define who you become.

"Life is 10% what happens to us, and 90% how we react to it." This is the truth I've come to embrace. We are not the victims of our circumstances; we are the creators of our own story. And when we change the lenses through which we see the world, life shifts from a series of obstacles to opportunities waiting to be seized. It's time for us to stop letting the world define us. Instead, we can choose to define ourselves. And together, we'll build lives of purpose, passion, and empowerment. "You are not defined by your struggles, but by the strength with which you overcome them."

Let's rewrite the narrative,   one woman at a time.

FROM SHADOWS TO SELF-LOVE: Journey to Embracing Your True Self

By MANVI MAJESTIC

I was five years old when I first realized the world saw me differently. I stood in front of the mirror, tracing my small fingers over my cheeks, wondering why my skin didn't shine like my sister's. I didn't know the word dusky then, but I knew the weight of it. It came in the way relatives sighed when they looked at me, in the hushed comparisons whispered between neighbors, in the casual remarks about how I would look "prettier" if my skin were lighter.

I was born into a traditional Punjabi family, where love and warmth coexisted with unspoken expectations. Beauty was a currency, and I had unknowingly been handed the wrong one. My birth had been overshadowed by grief - my maternal grandfather's passing and my paternal grandmother's sudden stroke. Of course, no one blamed me, not directly. But in the way some elders sighed, in the way they looked past me, I felt it. I wasn't sure what it was, but I carried it with me like a shadow.

My father, however, was different. When my younger sister was born, he was just as happy as he had been when I arrived. He distributed sweets, beaming with pride - something not always expected when a man welcomes a second daughter. But outside our home, the world was quick to draw lines between us. My sister was fair, delicate, "beautiful." I was… something else. And so, by the time I was three, I had unknowingly absorbed these words, letting them settle into my bones like uninvited guests.

I learned early on that my worth wouldn't come from my appearance but from how well I performed. My mother often said, "Education is the key," and so I held onto it like a lifeline. I believed that if I excelled - if I became the best at something - maybe, just maybe, I could outrun the judgments. Every first-place trophy, every academic award, was my silent response to a world that had already decided my place in it. But even as I climbed the ladder of success, something was missing. I longed to be seen, not just for what I could achieve, but for who I truly was.

The turning point came in 2005 when I switched schools for ninth grade. My mother, hopeful for a fresh start, enrolled my sister and me in an all-girls school. Around that time, I overheard a conversation where someone compared me to another girl, highlighting her beauty. At just 13, my fragile self-esteem shattered. My appearance had always been a source of pain, but now it felt magnified. At my new school, I felt like a stranger, lost in a sea of unfamiliar faces, convinced that I wasn't beautiful enough to belong.

I became withdrawn. The confidence I had built through academic success crumbled. My attendance dropped, my grades plummeted, and the weight of my negative self-perception became unbearable. During this time, a boy from my tuition class started giving me attention, offering a fleeting sense of validation. His admiration felt like a lifeline, temporarily filling the void inside me. But in reality, I was chasing approval in all the wrong places, setting a pattern of seeking validation from people who made me feel like I had to prove my worth. It took a painful breakup and three years of soul-searching for me to realize that the validation I sought could only come from within. After finishing school, I attempted a CA foundation course to please my mother, but my heart wasn't in it, and I failed. For the first time, I made a decision for myself. I enrolled in a diploma course in Travel, Tourism, and Airport Handling - something that felt right to me.

This decision marked a turning point. It wasn't just about the course; it was about reclaiming my power. I excelled, scoring 90%, and for the first time, I felt a sense of accomplishment that wasn't tied to seeking someone else's approval. During this time, I also learned to drive, and my second-hand Santro became more than just a car. It was my independence, my pride, my way of taking control of my own life. The confidence I gained in that year changed everything. I was no longer chasing validation. I was living for myself. My success in the diploma program opened doors, but more importantly, it helped me rediscover my own worth. Today, as I reflect on my journey, I am on the verge of fulfilling a dream that once seemed impossible. I am working toward owning my own home - not as a material achievement, but as proof of how far I've come, from a girl seeking validation to a woman who knows her worth.

O every young girl reading this: You are enough. Your worth isn't defined by the color of your skin, your grades, or anyone's approval. The world will try to tell you who you should be, but only you have the power to decide who you truly are. Self-love isn't an overnight transformation; it's a journey. It's about choosing yourself, even when it feels impossible. It's about embracing your imperfections and celebrating your unique strengths. The validation you seek is already within you.

Trust your journey, and know that every step brings you

closer to the person you are meant to be.

ONCE, IT WAS MY OWN MESS. Now, it is my message to the world.

By ARNAB

I was taught that education was the key to success, that securing a degree meant securing my future. But what no one told me was that some lessons cannot be learned from books. Life is the real teacher, and its curriculum is far more brutal.

In 2013, I stepped out of my hometown, Kolkata, full of hope and ambition, into the world of IMS Dehradun. A new place, a new life, and endless promises - 100% placements, corporate success, a golden future. But as years passed, the illusion began to crack.

College life was a dream, but reality struck in 2017. The placement season arrived, and I walked into it confident, armed with everything I had learned. Yet, time and time again, I reached the final rounds of 45 interviews - only to be rejected. Why? Because I refused to play their game. Because I stood firm in my values when the world demanded compromise.

The truth was stark - this system was not built for dreamers. It was designed to produce workers, to mold us into cogs for a machine that glorified slavery in the name of "career growth." Titles like 'Senior Manager' and 'Vice President' were nothing but well-crafted illusions, meant to keep us running in circles.

I was different. I didn't fit the mold, and the world made me pay for it. The rejections, the loneliness, the wounds - I carried them all. And then, I finally got placed at Sairey Ventures Pvt. Ltd. I thought this was it, my breakthrough. But life had one more lesson to teach.

Two months of work. No pay. Empty promises. And then, the realization - this was a scam. A job I got through college placements, and yet, it was all a lie. That was when I learned: never trust blindly, never believe the illusions. Many of my peers got placed in flashy jobs, but how many stayed? How many realized too late that they had been sold a dream that was never theirs to begin with?

Years later, after countless struggles, failures, and heartbreaks, I finally saw it - divine timing.

The lessons life taught me were not setbacks; they were preparations. I was never meant to be just another employee. I was being shaped into something greater.

I am here to break the cycle. To help others see beyond the illusion. To show that time is bigger than money, and true success is not found in a degree or a 9-to-5 job, but in freedom.

The Universe didn't just choose me - it forged me. Every rejection, every fall, every painful lesson was shaping me into a **Quantum Leader**.

To become what we are meant to be, we must embrace the process.

We are always being redirected toward our mission, but most of us get lost in the glittering distractions of the world.

It is all about the process of inner alchemy -

A   Awareness about your Dreams and Mission

L   Letting Go of What Doesn't Serve You

C   Choosing Yourself Over Following the Herd

H   Honoring Your Principles and Values

E   Embracing Your Wounds and Pains like a Crown of Achievement

M   Manifesting Your Mission Over Your Dreams

Y   Yielding Your Efforts for the Inner World

Once, it was my own mess.

Now, it is my message to the world.

DESTINY'S CHILD: A Journey Unwritten

By: PREETHI BALADEV

It all began on a stormy day in July 1993. The sky wept as I stood in the dimly lit library of my school in Bangalore, gripping a hardbound book in my small hands. The Hardy Boys – Secret of the Old Mill. Something about it felt different - magical even. Until that moment, I had only read comics and picture books, stories meant for children. But deep inside, I had always craved something more - a world beyond my own, a place where adventure pulsed through every page, where I could escape the ordinary and live a life larger than myself.

That evening, as I devoured the book, an unspoken promise formed in my heart. One day, I will write a book that makes others feel this same unexplainable thrill - the kind that makes your pulse race and your soul awaken.

I was only a child then, but my destiny had been sealed.

I was born into a joint family of fourteen, where love and respect were abundant, but money was not. My childhood unfolded in the government quarters of Hindustan Aeronautics Limited, in a small three-bedroom house that I shared with six other children. We had a single bathroom, a vast garden filled with trees, and a grandmother, Logammal, who ruled our home with warmth and wisdom.

My parents - my father, a doctor, and my mother, a telephone supervisor - were rarely around. They worked long hours, leaving me to be raised by my grandmother and the lively chaos of my big family. I learned patience, resilience, and the art of finding joy in simplicity.

But my true love affair began in the hushed sanctuary of my school library. Those forty-minute reading periods transported me beyond the four walls of my reality. I solved crimes with detectives, fought battles in courtrooms, uncovered ancient mysteries, and traveled through time - all without ever leaving my chair.

Recognizing my insatiable thirst for stories, my father subscribed to three lending libraries and six newspapers every weekend. I read them all. One book a day, most days. Unknowingly, I was sharpening my mind, expanding my vocabulary, and fueling an imagination that refused to be contained.

Then came my first real validation. In seventh grade, my English teacher, the charismatic Mrs. Shoba Nagarajan, saw something in me that I had yet to see in myself. At the end of the school year, she wrote a note to my parents:

"Your daughter has a gift. Nurture it."

And so, the seed was planted.

But dreams don't always unfold the way we expect them to.

I took the practical path - became an engineering graduate, landed a well-paying job through campus placements, and joined a prestigious MNC as a software engineer. Four years passed. I was doing well. I had everything I was supposed to want.

But my heart felt heavy. I was suffocating in a world that did not inspire me.

Then life, as it often does, threw me a curveball.

The birth of my first daughter changed everything. I walked away from my job, leaving behind the fat paycheck with a mixture of joy and sorrow. I embraced full-time motherhood, thinking it would fulfill me completely.

I was wrong.

Postpartum depression crept in like an unseen storm. The loss of identity, the emotional isolation - it consumed me. For two years, I battled a darkness I could not name, questioning every choice I had made. I felt trapped in a life that had once seemed beautiful.

And just when I was ready to give up, the Universe intervened.

What started as a desperate attempt to reclaim myself became my salvation. I discovered the power of Yoga. I taught myself through videos, surrendering to the rhythm of my breath, the stretch of my limbs, the quiet power within. Day by day, I pieced myself back together.

One evening, my husband watched me practice and said words that would change my life again.

"You were meant for this, Preethi. This is your calling. Give back to the world."

And just like that, my purpose found me.

In 2013, I became an internationally certified yoga instructor and founded Yogashreem Center for Abundance. I trained over 50 women, guiding them toward a life of joy and fulfillment.

Then came another evolution. After the pandemic, my journey naturally transitioned toward mindfulness and meditation. I began freelancing for Nirvaan, a company that creates frequency-based music for meditation. My fascination with the power of the human mind deepened. I immersed myself in subconscious reprogramming, the Law of Attraction, and the infinite possibilities of reality shifting.

I was no longer just surviving. I was thriving.

But through it all, one love remained constant - writing.

It started small. In 2015, I wrote a raw, heartfelt piece about my C-section experience. My husband - who was not a reader by any stretch - insisted I submit it to a women's platform. I did.

The response was overwhelming. Readers connected. They resonated. They felt something.

And just like that, I had my second love affair - with the written word.

I became a freelance writer, a ghostwriter, a storyteller. And then, a challenge found me.

A nationwide short story competition under the banner of *The Times of India*. Each month, a celebrated author provided a prompt, and thousands of writers across India submitted their stories.

I entered.

I wrote.

I won.

My story was published alongside renowned authors.

I stood among the best in the literary world, and for the first time, I knew - I belonged. But something still lingered. That unfulfilled promise.

The one I made to my younger self in 1993, as she clutched *The Hardy Boys* in her tiny hands.

I had always helped others tell their stories. But what about mine?

In 2019, I finally found the courage to answer that call.

I wrote my first novel. And in 2023, "Divine Promises" was born - an action-adventure epic woven with Hindu mythology, a tale of survival, destruction, and self-discovery. It struck a chord, earning recognition and, in 2024, winning the Sahitya Sparsh Award in the Fiction – Myths & Sagas category.

If there is one word that defines me, it is learning. I am always evolving, researching, expanding. Every experience, every struggle, every triumph has shaped me into who I am today. But the greatest lesson I have learned is this: Set the intention. Believe in it. And then surrender.

The Universe is always listening. It conspires to give us what we are meant for, if only we have the courage to trust the journey. I am proof of that

.

PATH TO PURPOSE – Discovering Me

BY SALONI SHAH

Since very long time of my life I believed that life is something that happens to us, not something we could shape. But I was wrong.

I grew up in a small town in India, the second daughter in a middle-class family where people whispered that one son should be there in family. It was that Time era, when having a son truly mattered a lot. However, I was fortunate to have parents who defied societal norms. my parents' love was louder than society's voice. They nurtured and gave us the same opportunities as a boy would get in family… yet somewhere deep inside, I carried a doubt. Was I enough? Could I be more?

As a child, I was shy and introverted. The dream of studying beyond my home town started as a flicker, when I completed my school. I wanted to go for higher studies and see the world. There was a strong desire to carve my own path, as deep down I felt that's the only path to success. I started that journey with a fear …What if I fail? What if I don't belong or could not do.

Self-doubt has a way of making itself comfortable inside your mind. My relatives fed it too, reminding me that girls like me cannot survive in a hostel, away from home. But I knew I had to take the leap. My heart was already whispering: "You are meant for more."

The day I left home, something shifted inside me. It was terrifying, but also exhilarating. For the first time, I had chosen myself. The journey wasn't easy. I stepped into a world where I felt invisible and low. Every room I walked into felt like a test of my worth. Will I ever be enough that little inner voice was always behind me?

But then, I stumbled upon an idea that is self-belief. The idea that I can create my reality and I am enough. Life in the hostel was challenging, but later it became a pivotal decision that taught me resilience, hard work, and belief in my own choices. Every challenge along the way shaped the core of who I am today. I was fortunate enough to get mentors/ teachers/ friends who have helped me to reach to next level.

I earned my degree in computer science and secured a job at a multinational company. It has opened the doors I had never imagined, including abroad travel opportunities and exposure to different cultures and countries. This path shaped my journey toward success, however, the path was not very smooth. Coming from a vernacular background and being a shy person, I struggled to find my place in a competitive work environment. Office politics and critical feedback fuelled my self-doubt.

Every strong feedback felt like personal judgments. Feedback from family, friends, colleagues or seniors made me question my abilities, that time, I did not understand how to handle criticism or feedbacks and I internalized every comment as a judgment of my worth. This mindset imposed self-limiting beliefs that stayed with me for couple of years until I started my personal development journey.

The entire episode gave me one of life's most valuable lessons: Other people's opinions do not define me. What they think and say about me is their perspective, not necessarily the truth. When you have a desire to grow, life often sends you disguised angels in the form of events and people to reveal your true power.

Life has a way of testing you when you're on the verge of transformation. Just when I started embracing this new mindset, my health failed me. At first, I fell into my old patterns: "Why me? What did I do to deserve this?" But then, I realized, this wasn't a punishment it was a message.

I understood my body was speaking the language of my suppressed fears, my unresolved emotions. If my thoughts could make me sick, could they also make me whole too…

I started changing my inner dialogue. I fed my mind with gratitude, self-love, and healing. And then, something miraculous happened. I started attracting everything in life which I was waiting for? My relationships deepened. Opportunities I once thought were beyond my reach began to find me.

Every great change starts with a decision. The day I stopped waiting for someone to validate me, for success to knock on my door, for life to finally "begin," was the day my world transformed.

There are always two voices inside us. One tells us we are not enough, that we should stay small, that dreaming big is foolish. The other is softer but far more powerful. it's the voice of divinity, the voice that reminds us we are limitless. For too long, I had listened to the voice of doubt. But when I finally tuned into the divine voice within me, I found clarity, peace, and purpose.

I stopped asking, "Why me?" and started saying, "Try me."

I used to believe life was something that happened to me. Now I know the truth: Life is something I can create.

To the end, I want to give a simple message to all my readers do not be afraid to rewrite your stories and there is no right time to work on your dreams.

You don't need a miracle. You are the miracle. Change your frequency, align with your desires, and watch the magic unfold.

Everything you ever wanted success, love, health, joy, they are all inside you, waiting to be unleashed. Just align your thoughts, energy, and actions and universe will respond.

So, if you're waiting for a sign, this is it.

The question is:

Are you ready to own it?

FINDING JOY: A Journey Beyond Healing

By: MEERA

Early in life, I excelled in academics, consistently standing at the top of my class. However, at age fourteen, my life changed irrevocably when I lost a close friend to suicide. In the same period, my world was further shattered when my uncle also died by suicide, an event that deeply affected my family, particularly my mother, whose transformation into a more subdued person left a lasting impression on me. These devastating losses forced me to confront profound questions about life's purpose and human suffering at an unusually young age.

The timing of these events coincided with a school change, a transition that proved particularly challenging as I had spent my entire academic life in one institution. Despite my previous academic prowess and dreams of becoming a doctor, I found myself unable to focus on studies. It was the most horrible sensation of all - to not be able to do the one thing I knew how to do so well. I would sit with my books, paralyzed by grief and confusion, unable to turn a single page.

I endured various forms of abuse that left deep emotional scars, carried the weight of responsibilities beyond my years, developing a heightened awareness of family dynamics and emotional complexities. Despite having loving parents and material comfort, I struggled with depression, anxiety, and thoughts of suicide for over a decade - challenges that went unrecognized due to lack of awareness about mental health in my environment.

I went on to become an engineer, specializing in biotechnology. My quest for understanding led me to further studies in nutrition and food sciences, though I continued to sense a disconnect between professional achievement and emotional fulfilment. As I grew up, I developed an acute sensitivity to human behaviour and emotions. I observed how people often made life choices - in careers, relationships, and living situations - that contradicted their true desires, acting instead from fear and confusion. I noticed the striking disparity between people's internal struggles and their external presentations. Everybody was like that, everybody, it made me feel like I had nowhere to go.

A pivotal revelation came in late twenties when I discovered that not everyone experienced life as an endless struggle with thoughts of death. From a very young age, I had become accepting of the misconception that life was bad. I believed everybody struggled to live, I believed everybody lived because they didn't have the courage to die. I literally thought and believed that everybody always just wanted to die. As sad and horrible as that is, I had gotten used to it - it was the only life I knew. The shock of realizing I was alone in these feelings was like nothing I had ever experienced before. I suddenly felt betrayed by everybody to know they didn't actually feel like dying all the time. This eye-opening moment highlighted the tragic cost of mental health illiteracy - years of suffering that might have been prevented with proper awareness and intervention.

I reached a critical moment in my battle with depression. After years of always feeling like dying, one day I actually decided to give up. This moment became the best turning point of my life. I thought - even if I drowned myself, every cell in my body would fight to survive. I asked myself why, when my body wasn't ready to give up, my mind wanted to. This insight sparked a fundamental shift in my perspective - I decided that instead of living because I was afraid to die, I wanted to get to the state of mind of choosing to live because I want to live. This decision marked the beginning of my healing journey. I started with small, personal goals - singing, skating, learning Japanese - activities that were solely for my own joy and growth.

My career path took a significant turn when I began teaching, a role that brought me into close contact with children and their developmental needs. This experience prompted me to study child development psychology, deepening my understanding of human behaviour and emotional patterns. It was during this period that I discovered attachment theory, which gave me a framework to understand both my past experiences and the dynamics I observed in others.

As I healed, my perspective on past hurt transformed. I hated and resented people who brought me to that state for a long time. But as time passed, I noticed just how much my loved ones were trying for my sake. Even if they didn't know how to care for me before, I couldn't unsee just how much they tried, even if it was ineffective. What particularly struck me was the phenomenon of emotional disconnection despite mutual desire for connection. You want me and I want you, you miss me and I miss you too, I crave for your presence in my life and so do you, but we still don't look eye to eye. This observation became central to my life's mission.

Today, my work focuses on addressing this crucial gap in modern society. We as a society have learned how to do jobs, and money and cars and houses, we know how to crack exams, and job interviews, we don't know how to work with people. We learnt how to live without each other, but nobody taught us how to live with each other. I've seen my parents go decades without speaking to their siblings, living with that void every day. In countless families, parents and children, brothers and sisters exist in silence simply because they don't know how to bridge the gap. Best friends drift apart - sometimes that's natural, but when these friendships are integral to who we are, their loss can prevent us from becoming our best selves. Even lovers separate not because of irreconcilable differences, but because of miscommunications and lack of clarity - reasons that seem tragically small against the weight of a lifetime spent apart.

What troubles me is how crisis often becomes the only gateway to connection. We wait for hospital beds and surgeries to open our hearts to each other, only to retreat into silence once the crisis passes. We shouldn't need the spectre of death to draw close to our loved ones. Through my coaching practice, I teach emotional literacy using attachment theory, helping others bridge the gap between wanting connection and achieving it. My message is clear. *Get the education you need on your emotional journey. It will be challenging, but it's worth every effort. Life is too precious to spend in silence with those we love.*

The best part of my story isn't the path from darkness to light, but what came after. Healing, when complete, gives way to pure joy. The girl who once couldn't turn a page now writes love stories. The girl who carried the weight of unspoken pain now dances through life with remarkable ease. I don't carry my journey like a badge or a burden - I live in the simple pleasure of being, creating, and connecting. I laugh all the time; I make merry all the time.

Healing isn't the end of the journey -

it's the beginning of a life lived in full colour.

UNLEASHING THE POWER WITHIN:

Healing Through Thoughts

By: SAKSHI

My life once felt like a tangled mess of misfortune. The people I trusted the most - family, friends, colleagues - betrayed me, leaving my heart shattered and my soul bruised. My health was slipping away, but the worst part wasn't the physical pain. It was the mental exhaustion. Anxiety gnawed at me, consuming every waking thought. Every day, I found myself endlessly scrolling through my phone, searching for anything that might offer a solution - a glimmer of hope. It felt like the universe was conspiring against me. And then, in the middle of my darkest hour, I stumbled upon something unexpected - spirituality.

I discovered the Law of Attraction, a concept that promised the power to change my entire reality. At first, I was skeptical. How could something as simple as my thoughts transform my life? But I was desperate. So, I gave it a shot.

As I dove deeper, I realized something profound: we become what we think. My negative thoughts, my fears, my doubts - all of them were keeping me trapped in a loop of misery. But when I began shifting my focus, even slightly, things started to change. My anxiety lessened. The weight of negativity lifted. I started attracting small moments of peace, happiness, and clarity. But nothing could prepare me for what came next.

One afternoon, my world came crashing down. My mother was diagnosed with a life-threatening illness. The news struck like a lightning bolt, sending shockwaves through my entire being. I felt helpless, suffocated by fear. The doctors were grim. The air around me felt heavy, thick with despair.

I remember walking into the hospital with my mother for a follow-up appointment. The waiting room was full - children, the elderly, families - all battling their own invisible wars. Some were crying, some sat in silent exhaustion, and others carried an air of quiet defeat.

And in that moment, something inside me shifted. Money couldn't buy health. It couldn't buy happiness. It couldn't buy love. I had everything in the material world - success, a stable career, a comfortable life - but none of it mattered when my mother's life was slipping away.

I had a choice: to drown in helplessness or to fight back with everything I had. That was my turning point.

I threw myself into learning about energy healing. Reiki, visualization, manifestation - I wasn't just trying to heal my mother. I was healing myself. I was healing our family. My thoughts had power, and I was going to use them to rewrite our story. Every day, I visualized my mother healthy and radiant, surrounded by love and light. I taught her about the Law of Attraction, helping her see herself not as a victim of illness, but as a warrior reclaiming her health. And then, the miracles began.

At first, the changes were small. Subtle. A spark of energy here, a little more strength there. But then, the doctors noticed. "This is incredible," they murmured, shaking their heads in disbelief. My mother's condition improved. Her healing accelerated beyond medical explanation. It wasn't just the treatment - it was the energy, the belief, the positivity that we radiated. We were vibrating at a higher frequency, and the universe was responding.

My own life transformed before my eyes. My health improved. Relationships that once felt broken began to mend. New opportunities, both personal and professional, started flowing effortlessly into my life. It was as if the universe had been waiting for me to align my energy before it opened the floodgates of abundance.

I finally understood the truth: thoughts shape reality.

The moment I started seeing myself as worthy of health, love, and happiness, those very things started manifesting in my life. My thoughts weren't just fleeting ideas - they were the blueprint of my destiny. And so, I made it my mission to share this magic with others. I began teaching people the power of their thoughts, guiding them to shift their frequency and attract the beauty they deserve. Through Reiki, energy healing, and the Law of Attraction, I helped others awaken to their own limitless potential.

Today, my mother is healthier than ever, a living testament to the power of healing thoughts and energy. And me? I stand stronger than ever, not just as a daughter, a healer, or a teacher, but as someone who found the key to unlocking the universe's infinite abundance. Because the truth is, we all have this power within us. We just need to believe it, harness it, and watch as the universe bends to meet our desires.

The magic of thoughts is real.   And I am living proof.

A HOLISTIC VISION FOR WELLNESS By: SHRADDHA VYAS

Health is the greatest wealth. It is the foundation upon which all dreams are built. But it took losing mine to truly understand its worth.

Life is a collection of moments—some beautiful, others shattering. It's the darkest storms that forge the strongest souls, just as gold shines brightest when it faces the hottest flames. My story is no different.

Growing up, I had always known the saying, "Health is wealth." But the real meaning hit me when life threw me into a battle I never saw coming. In college, I was diagnosed with multiple lumbar disc prolapses, leading to crippling sciatic pain. At just 18, I underwent my first spinal surgery—and it failed. What followed was an avalanche of pain, despair, and nights filled with silent tears. It felt like my dreams were slipping away, one painful breath at a time. Yet, somewhere in the depths of that suffering, a spark ignited.

Flat on my back, staring at the ceiling through sleepless nights, I asked myself the hardest questions: What truly matters? Is it wealth, fame, or career success? Or is it health, love, and purpose? In those moments of raw vulnerability, I found my answers. I yearned for a life of health, of shared joy, of making a difference. I wanted to turn my pain into purpose. That desire became my lifeline.

With unwavering faith and a stubborn hope, I visualized each day - imagining the dawn of a pain-free morning. I fought with every fiber of my being, determined not just to survive but to rise stronger. My journey to recovery was long and arduous, but it became the foundation of a new beginning.

In 2018, fueled by my experiences and a deep desire to help others, I founded Appediet, an online platform dedicated to nutrition, health, and wellness. It wasn't just about diet plans or weight loss; it was about transforming lives. About giving people the strength to rewrite their own stories, just as I had rewritten mine.

My journey wasn't just shaped by pain; it was also molded by passion. I grew up surrounded by the wisdom of doctors and educators, which naturally drew me to teaching. With 17 years of experience in Life Sciences, Biochemistry, and Nutrition, I combined my academic knowledge with my personal battles to create something meaningful. I specialized in integrative nutrition, emphasizing holistic health approaches that honor each individual's culture, genetics, and lifestyle.

I've had the privilege of guiding people worldwide through challenges like weight loss, PCOD/PCOS, and diabetes management. Each success story reminded me why I chose this path. It's more than just numbers on a scale—it's about renewed confidence, restored health, and the joy of living fully.

Along this journey, I've been humbled by numerous honors, including the Global Award for Women Entrepreneurs and Educators Icons of Asia, the National Award for Best Dietitian of the Year (2023), and recognition as one of the Top 24 Women in Healthcare by She Inspire Magazine. But the awards that truly resonate are the victories of my clients—the lives transformed, the hope reignited.

My passion for learning never ceased. In 2023, I became a Certified Health and Wellness Coach from Weljii Institute under the Ministry of AYUSH. Most recently, in January 2025, I trained in Functional Medicine in Clinical Nutrition from IAFM. This journey of continuous learning is fueled by my mission to bridge the gap between traditional Indian wisdom and modern nutritional science.

I've also had the honor of presenting impactful research on topics close to my heart, including the Role of Seed Cycling and Traditional Indian Foods in PCOD Treatment (Best Paper, ICGWE 2023), the Impact of Gut Microbiota on Stress at the National Institute of Nutrition-ICMR, and Neuro-Nutrition (Best Presentation, 6th International Conference, USFN 2024).

My journey hasn't just been about professional growth; it's been about giving back. From conducting workshops on Millets in collaboration with the Government Degree College, Hyderabad, to sharing knowledge through webinars, TV, and All India Radio, my purpose has always been to empower others to live healthier, more fulfilling lives.

Today, as I stand tall—quite literally, after two major spinal fusion surgeries—I look back at the pain, the struggles, and the countless battles fought within. I see how each moment led me here, to a life of purpose, gratitude, and unshakable faith.

I am living proof of the power of manifestation, of self-reflection, hard work, and the magic of believing in a dream even when the world feels heavy. When you truly align with your purpose, the universe conspires to bring it to life.

Appediet is more than just a wellness platform. It is my tribute to resilience, my ode to hope, and my promise to every soul battling in silence: You are stronger than you think.

This journey is far from over. It is merely the beginning.

And with each step forward, I carry with me the lessons learned from pain, the strength drawn from love, and an unyielding passion to make a difference...

FROM SILENCE TO STRENGTH: A Journey to a Courageous Warrior

By: MONA

I was born into a middle-class Indian family, surrounded by love and care. Yet, despite this nurturing environment, my confidence withered as I grew older. Fear gripped me every time I tried to speak up or share my thoughts. I avoided school events, shied away from large group conversations, and convinced myself that people would judge my looks, voice, or body. A few hurtful comments from local boys about my appearance etched deep scars, making me believe I was unworthy of love and acceptance.

At home, things were no different. Sometimes my parents scolded me without explanation, and I longed for extra love and understanding from my mother. Slowly, I shut down emotionally, learning to please others just to feel accepted. I became a people-pleaser, constantly chasing external validation.

As a teenager, this need for approval only grew. I completed my B.Tech and began working at a multinational company. Despite being a high performer, my fear of speaking up haunted me. In team meetings, I froze. During performance appraisals, I couldn't advocate for my worth. Conversations about pay raises or promotions terrified me. I avoided conflict at all costs, even if it meant staying silent about my ambitions. With every unspoken word, my confidence eroded, leaving me stuck in a dissatisfying job with low pay and no career growth.

Marriage brought its own set of challenges. I loved my husband deeply, but my people-pleasing nature followed me into this new chapter of my life. I silenced my needs to keep the peace, believing that being a good wife and daughter-in-law meant sacrificing my desires. I felt emotionally unsupported and unacknowledged for all that I did for my family. Life became monotonous - a routine lived on others' terms, not my own.

Over time, my suppressed emotions and unmet expectations built up like a pressure cooker ready to explode. I felt taken for granted, unheard, and unloved. I became trapped in resentment, allowing negativity to seep into every corner of my life. And as a mother, I unknowingly repeated the cycle - releasing my anger and frustration on my child because I knew he wouldn't fight back. Guilt consumed me, but I felt powerless to change.

Then came the COVID-19 pandemic, a turning point that shook me to my core. The pressure of juggling work, cooking, and household responsibilities pushed me to the brink. Despite my husband's help, it never felt enough. Burnout spiraled into anxiety and depression, and all my unresolved issues from the past resurfaced with a vengeance. I was haunted by regrets - of not speaking up, not seizing career opportunities, not living life on my own terms.

Amid this darkness, a flicker of hope appeared. I stumbled upon a coaching masterclass by Puja Puneet. Desperate for change, I attended it. Her energy was infectious, her positivity electrifying. For the first time in years, I felt hope. Without hesitation, I enrolled in her courses, telling myself, "I've never invested in myself before - let's see where this takes me." It turned out to be the best decision of my life.

Through the program, I discovered the power of self-love and the importance of taking full responsibility for my happiness. My mindset transformed. I began prioritizing myself - my knowledge, my happiness, my relationships, and my dreams. As I changed internally, my surroundings started to change too. I learned to take a stand, to speak up for my needs. My relationship with my husband blossomed, growing more beautiful and balanced. I became a more understanding and balanced mom, nurturing my son with love and patience.

This profound transformation awakened a calling within me. I realized that I wanted to help other women on similar journeys - to break free from the chains of self-doubt and societal expectations. I became an assertiveness coach for working women, empowering them to build confidence, raise self-esteem, and make bold decisions without guilt.

I know firsthand how easy it is for women to settle for less, to feel comfortable in their struggles. But I also know that women are far more powerful than they realize. Challenges are merely mirrors reflecting our true capabilities.

Today, my mission is clear: to empower thousands of women to stand tall, be heard, and claim their worth unapologetically. Every woman deserves love, respect, and a voice. Just as I rewrote my story through courage and action, I am here to help others write new chapters in their lives. I am living proof that no matter how deep the silence, you can find your voice. No matter how dark the journey, you can find the light. And no matter how powerless you feel, you are capable of rewriting your story.

Never settle for less. You are deserving of a life that honors who you truly are.

My Mom – The OG Boss Lady

& My Guiding Light

You know how people say *"God listens when you ask with a pure heart?"* Well, my mom? She doesn't even wait for me to ask—she just *knows*. Before I even realize what I need, she's already there, handling it. If that's not god-level intuition, I don't know what is.

But this isn't just about her superpower of reading my mind. It's about how brave, fierce, and unstoppable she is. I mean, imagine being a mother to *me*—a stubborn, moody, slightly cranky (*okay, very cranky*) girl who thinks she's always right. That takes some serious courage.

Growing up, my dad treated me like a princess, and I loved every second of it. But don't be fooled—my mom is the real boss. She wasn't the overly strict kind, but she wasn't soft either. She had this rare balance—strong, wise, and *just always right*. The kind of person you don't argue with because, well...you'll lose.

The Woman Who Can Do It All

I've seen her handle everything like an absolute pro—running the house, conquering her corporate job, and managing *both* me and my sister (*two chhota packets, bada dhamaka*). She made multitasking look effortless, but it wasn't just about balancing things—it was about acing everything she touched.

And she wasn't just independent in one way—she was independent in every way. Financially, emotionally, spiritually—she never needed validation from anyone. With degrees on degrees (*I've genuinely lost count*), she didn't just *choose* one field—she dominated every single thing she put her mind to. If she decides today that she wants to be a chef, best believe she'll be running a Michelin-star restaurant by next year.

How She Shaped My Mindset

She's also the reason I even know about psychology, NLP, healing, and holistic wellness. While other moms were probably telling their kids to study math, mine was out there learning about the power of the mind and pulling me into it too.

She didn't stop at NLP. She explored energy healing, meditation, EFT (Emotional Freedom Techniques), and the mind-body connection—things that made me see healing as something way beyond just medicine. (*Also, turns out stress-eating an entire pizza is not the best coping strategy. Who knew?*)

One of the most life-changing things she did? She introduced me to Sister Shivani Didi. That wasn't just a casual "watch this" moment—it was a shift. It made me realize that being strong isn't just about fighting battles—it's about having peace within.

Why She's My Forever Inspiration

My mom isn't just a mother—she's my first role model, my biggest inspiration, and living proof that you can be powerful, independent, kind, and wise—all at the same time.

She's built a life on her own terms, stood strong in her values, and never let anyone tell her what she *couldn't* do. Watching her, I didn't just learn how to be independent. I learned how to be unshakable. From helping me figure out the unknown to quite literally making my notes when I was too swamped, my mom has been my silent backbone in ways I can't even count. There have been nights when I've dozed off mid-course, laptop still open, only to wake up tucked into bed—because, of course, she had closed everything and let me rest.

Her feedback? Brutally honest, always demanding perfection. Trust me, don't ask for her opinion unless you're ready for some next-level precision (*but let's be real, it only makes things better*). Her insights, her guidance—they've been priceless.

From her sweet, endless scoldings to those rare but precious *"I'm proud of you"* moments—every single one is a core memory.

And the best part? I started this whole venture with her.

What a powerful duo—a mother and daughter, ready to change people's mindsets and maybe even the world.

CONGRATULATIONS!

You made it. You turned every page, embraced every story, and walked through every twist and turn that this book had to offer. But here's the truth—this isn't really an ending. It's just another beginning.

Through these pages, we've danced through the storms, laughed in the face of chaos, and learned that life isn't about having it all figured out. It's about showing up anyway—even when your heart races, even when your hands shake, even when the path ahead is wrapped in uncertainty.

You, dear reader, are the very essence of strength. The fact that you made it here proves that you have the courage to keep moving forward, to rise after every fall, and to turn every scar into a story of triumph. The world may not always be gentle, and life may not always be fair, but you are unstoppable—just like the Phoenix this book was inspired by.

So, as you close this book, open your arms to life's next adventure. Don't wait for the perfect moment, the perfect plan, or the perfect version of yourself to show up. Just take the step. Trip if you must, twirl if you can, but whatever you do, don't stop dancing. The world is waiting. Your story is still being written. And I have a feeling… the best is yet to come.

Now tell me, are you ready to rise once more?

20 CONFESSIONS I HAVE TO MAKE AT 20

So, here I am, officially two decades old, and guess what? I still don't have life figured out. But I have learned a few things—some the easy way, most the hard way (because why make life simple, right?). So, here's a little **survival** guide straight from my 20-year-old brain—take what you love, ignore what you don't, and most importantly, live life your way!

1.   There is enough love in this world… you just have to find it at the right place at the right time!

Love is NOT like an iPhone charger that disappears when you need it the most. It's everywhere—you just need to stop looking for it in the wrong places (*ahem* toxic people). Trust me, the right love finds you when you're vibing at the right frequency.

2.   Humility is the key to survival—drop the ego before it drops you!

Ego is like an overinflated balloon—sooner or later, it's gonna pop and make a mess. Stay humble, respect everyone, and remember that no matter how high you fly, the ground is what holds you up.

3.   Spread love, be humble, and don't act like you invented oxygen.

Seriously, being kind costs zero rupees/dollars/whatever currency you believe in. Be that person who makes the world a little softer, a little warmer, and a lot more loving.

4.   Embrace every opportunity and be grateful for it!

Even if it looks like a disaster at first. Sometimes, opportunities come disguised as challenges, bad dates, or that weird internship your parents forced you into. Just say yes—you never know what doors might open!

5.   Opportunities are EVERYWHERE—you just need to work on yourself to attract them.

Nope, they don't come knocking on lazy, complaining people's doors. Be the kind of person who is so good, opportunities have no choice but to chase you.

6.   If you think there's a problem in your life, you're probably just using the wrong key.

Life isn't a locked door—it's a puzzle. And all the pieces (or keys) are right in front of you. You just need to stop panicking and pick the one that actually fits.

7.   Have a belief system of your own—or else, you'll be stuck borrowing someone else's.

Create your own philosophy, question things, and decide what you truly stand for. If you don't, the world will happily hand you a borrowed set of beliefs (and trust me, it's usually expired wisdom).

8.   Be respectful—no matter where the other person stands.

From CEOs to janitors, from professors to that waiter bringing your coffee—respect is a reflection of your character, not theirs.

9.   Trust the universe. Trust the timing.

Yes, it's frustrating. Yes, waiting sucks. But everything unfolds exactly when and how it's meant to. Stop rushing and start trusting.

10.   Life is beautiful. No, really—it is.

Look up from your phone, breathe, and just *see* it. Sunsets, laughter, music, the smell of coffee - beauty is hiding in the little things.

11.   The day you stop figuring out life is the day you actually start living it.

Spoiler alert: No one actually has life figured out. Not even that one friend who acts all put together. Just go with the flow.

12.   Forget the past, and shoot for the future.

Your past is a place of reference, not residence. Don't live there—pack up, move on, and aim for the stars.

13.   Make time for yourself to decode the meaning of life.

No, really. Sit alone, go for a walk, journal, stare at the sky—do whatever helps you understand yourself better. The world can wait.

14.   Keep the people who stood by you in your struggling days—they are diamonds.

People who clapped for you when no one else did? Protect them at all costs. They are rare, and they are your real ones.

15.   Keep your family close—and your parents even closer.

They might not understand your memes, but they understand YOU. Nothing in this world will ever replace their love.

16.   Worship your work if you want your work to worship you.

Give your work your 100%—whether it's a passion project or a boring assignment. If you respect your work, success will eventually respect you back.

17.   Do your work happily, because someone out there is praying for the opportunity you have.

That boring job? That tiring schedule? Someone out there is dreaming of being in your place. Be grateful.

18.   Whenever you feel like giving up, close your eyes and think of your parents.

Their sacrifices, their dreams for you, their endless love—it's all fuel. Keep going.

19.   Don't fear difficulties—make difficulties fear YOU.

You are stronger than your problems. They should be scared of YOU, not the other way around.

20.   There are no rules to life—live the way YOU want.

Society's rulebook? Throw it away. Your life, your choices, your journey—live it unapologetically.

And that's it - 20 lessons from a 20-year-old who's still figuring it all out!

Maybe in ten years, I'll look back and laugh at this list (*or maybe I'll write another one*).

But for now, this is me, raw and real, sharing what I've learned. Now go out there and live a life that's loud, messy, fearless, and full of love. Because it's yours and it'll go exactly the way YOU want it to.

ACKNOWLEDGMENT

First things first—biggest shout out to the OG boss of the universe: The Almighty. For real, without that cosmic energy, luck, and divine chaos working in my favor, I wouldn't be here. Whether it's the *perfectly timed* moments, the unexpected life lessons, or just the strength to keep pushing forward—thank you for always having my back, even when I didn't realize it.

Next up, my real-life superhero—Mom. From being my biggest critic to my biggest cheerleader, from waking me up with *daant* to tucking me in with silent care, you've been my rock. This journey wouldn't even exist without you.

To my family, friends, and those rare gems who believed in me— y'all are the reason I keep going. Whether it was hyping me up, offering a reality check (*sometimes painfully honest*), or just existing in my chaotic little world—I appreciate you more than words can say.

And finally, a little pat on my own back (*because why not?*). For sticking it out, pushing through, and making it this far. This is just the beginning!

COPYRIGHT
Copyright©2025 JasmeharKaur